Combatting Sexual Harassment in Higher Education

Editors
Bernice Lott and Mary Ellen Reilly
University of Rhode Island

AN NEA PROFESSIONAL LIBRARY PUBLICATION
National Education Association
Washington, D.C.

LC
212.862
C65
1996

ACKNOWLEDGMENTS

We want to thank Rachel Hendrickson whose idea it was to do this book and whose encouragement we needed to get the job done. We also want to acknowledge the able and cheerful assistance of Heather Bullock and Joan Bentley of the women's studies program at the University of Rhode Island and the wonderful cooperation of all the contributors. As always, Albert Lott and Barbara F. Luebke provided support and respected our efforts.

Bernice Lott, Ph. D.
Mary Ellen Reilly, Ph. D.

Printing History
First Printing: January 1996

Note

Unless explicitly otherwise noted, the opinions expressed in this publication should not be construed as representing the policy or position of the National Education Association. Materials published by the NEA Professional Library are intended to be discussion documents for educators who are concerned with specialized interests of the profession.

This book is printed on acid-free paper.   This book is printed with soy ink.

ACID FREE
∞

Library of Congress Cataloging-in-Publication Data
Combatting sexual harassment in higher education/editors, Bernice
    Lott and Mary Ellen Reilly
        p. cm.— (Excellence in the academy)
    Includes bibliographical references and index.
    ISBN 0-8106-2678-0
    1. Sexual harassment in universities and colleges—United States—
Prevention. I. Lott, Bernice E. II. Reilly, Mary Ellen.
III. Series.
LC212.862.C65 1995   95-33568

CONTENTS

4   Contents

CONTRIBUTORS

Marcia Bedard is a professor of women's studies at the California State University, Fresno. Her current research is on applications of hypermedia and other instructional technologies in the women's studies classroom. (Address: Women's Studies Program, Social Science Bldg., Room 226A, 5340 N. Campus Drive, California State University, Fresno, CA 93740-0078)

Lloyd D. Elgart was a professor of law and management and dean of the Andreas School of Business at Barry University in Miami Shores, Florida. His thesis at Oxford University (postgraduate Diploma in Law) compared equal employment practices of major corporations in the U.S. and U.K. (Dr. Elgart died in March 1994)

Louise F. Fitzgerald is a professor of psychology and women's studies at the University of Illinois at Urbana-Champaign. The winner of numerous scholarly awards, she has published widely, conducted research on sexual harassment in academia and the workplace, and is a member of the American Psychological Association's Taskforce on Male Violence Against Women. She was a consultant to Professor Anita Hill's legal team during the Clarence Thomas confirmation hearings, serves as a consultant to universities and organizations, testifies frequently as an expert witness, and does clinical work with victims. (Address: Department of Psychology, University of Illinois, Urbana, IL 61001)

Sherna Berger Gluck directs the oral history program and teaches women's studies at California State University, Long Beach. She has been active in faculty unionism since she joined the California State University in 1977 and has held several leadership positions in the California Faculty Association. (Address: Department of History, California State University, 1250 S. Bellflower Blvd., Long Beach, CA 90840)

Lynn P. Gordon is an associate professor of education and history, and an associate of the gender and society cluster at the University of Rochester. Her book, *Gender and Higher Education in the Progressive Era* appeared in 1990, and she is currently writing a biography of journalist Dorothy Thompson, (Address: Graduate School of Education and Human Development, 1339 Dewey Hall, University of Rochester, Rochester, NY 14627)

Beth Hartung is an associate professor of sociology at California State University, Fresno. She teaches popular culture, women's studies, stratification, and the family. She is currently studying adult children who have returned home to live with their parents. (Address: Sociology Department, Social Science Bldg., Room 223, 5340 North Campus Drive, California State University, Fresno, CA 93740-0107)

Rachel A. Hendrickson is a higher education specialist with the National Education Association. She is involved in industrial relations in the public sector, with a special emphasis on higher education issues in collective bargaining. She has a Ph.D. in English and an MS in industrial relations and is currently studying the impact of the Family and Medical Leave Act on collective bargaining contracts. (Address: NEA, 1201 16th St., NW, Washington, DC 20036)

Doric Little is a professor of speech at Honolulu Community College, currently on leave to the John A. Burns School of Medicine, University of Hawaii at Manoa serving as coordinator of student development. She writes and speaks frequently on the implications of sexual harassment law for sexual relations in academe, ethics in higher education, and credibility in speaking. (Address: Office of Medical Education, University of Hawaii at Manoa, 1960 East-West Road, Honolulu, HI 96822)

Bernice Lott is a professor of psychology and women's studies at the University of Rhode Island. She is past president of division 35 (The Psychology of Women) of the American Psychological Association, the winner of awards for scholarship and leadership, and author of empirical and theoretical works on gender issues and interpersonal attraction including *Women's Lives: Themes and Variations in Gender Learning*, now in its second edition and *The Social Psychology of Interpersonal Discrimination* (co-edited with Diane Maluso.) (Address: Department of Psychology, University of Rhode Island, Kingston, RI 02881)

Loralee MacPike is a professor of English at California State University, San Bernardino. She is the author of a book on Dickens and Dostoevsky and editor of an anthology of writings by gay and lesbian parents about "coming out" to their children. Her current work is on the construction of lesbian sexuality and iconography in the 1920s and 1930. She is also the editor of the *Lesbian Review of Books*. (Address: Department of English, California State University, 5500 University Parkway, San Bernadino, CA 92407-2397)

Michele A Paludi is the author/editor of seven textbooks, including *Ivory Power: Sexual Harassment on Campus*, co-author of *Academic and Workplace Sexual Harassment: A Resource Manual*, co-author (with Bernice Sandler) of *Educator's Guide to Controlling Sexual Harassment*, and editor of *Working 9 to 5: Women, Men, Sex, and Power*. She is director of Michele Paludi & Associates, Consultants in Sexual Harassment, and served on former NY Governor Mario Cuomo's Task Force on Sexual Harassment. (Address: 1606 Lenox Road, Schenectady, NY 12308)

Mary Ellen Reilly is a professor of sociology and women's studies at the University of Rhode Island. She has served as director of the Women's Studies Program since 1983. Her research and publications in the last decade have focused on sexual harassment and assault, lesbian issues, Irish society, and women's studies. She is co-author of *Women's Studies Graduates: The First Generation* about 89 graduates from 42 programs in the U.S. (Address: Women's Studies Program, 315 Roosevelt Hall, University of Rhode Island, Kingston, RI 93881)

Lillian Schanfield is a professor of English and coordinator of women's studies at Barry University in Miami Shores, Florida. She holds graduate degrees in English literature (Ph.D.), anthropology, and business administration, and serves on the board of a shelter for battered women. (Address: Barry University, 11300 Northeast Second Ave., Miami Shores, FL 33161)

Barbara G. Taylor is associate vice chancellor for human resources at the University of Arkansas. She has served on the executive board of the National Women's Studies Association and as a national and regional officer for the American Association for Affirmative Action. She holds graduate degrees in English, is Chair of the Arkansas Humanities Council, and consults on issues of mediation, alternative dispute resolution, affirmative action, sexual harassment, gender studies, and cultural diversity. (Address: Department of Human Resources, 222 Administration Building, University of Arkansas, Fayetteville, AR 72701)

John A. Thompson is a professor of educational administration at the University of Hawaii at Manoa. He has chaired the Higher Education Council of the National Education Association, and has served on the NEA Standing Committee on Higher Education. (Address: Dept. of Educational Administration, University of Hawaii at Manoa, Honolulu, HI 96720)

Ann T. Truax is assistant to the director, Office of Equal Opportunity and Affirmative Action, University of Minnesota, and formerly director of the Minnesota Women's Center. She investigates and resolves sexual harassment complaints and educates employees and students about the issue. She is a nationally known consultant and speaker on sexual harassment. She co-founded the Women's Studies Department and the Center for Advanced Feminist Studies at Minnesota and is a leader in its Commission on Women. (Address: Office of Equal Opportunity and Affirmative Action, 419 Morrill Hall, University of Minnesota, 100 Church St., SE., Minneapolis, MN 55455)

PART I

INTRODUCTION

1

ISSUES AND QUESTIONS

by Bernice Lott and Mary Ellen Reilly

An advertisement such as the one shown above would not have appeared in a small-town newspaper (or any other mass audience periodical) until recently. Only within the past two decades have the subjects dealt with in this volume begun to be openly discussed and investigated, become the formal concern of government, business, and education, and the target of active pressures for social change

THE RECENT HISTORICAL CONTEXT

As many of the contributors to this volume note, the most significant event associated with changing our familiarity with the term "sexual harassment" and encouraging open discussion of its meaning and reality in contemporary life was the televised Senate Judiciary Committee hearings in 1991 on the Supreme Court nomination of Judge Clarence Thomas. Most of us know that during these hearings, law professor

Anita Hill, who had formerly worked for Thomas in both the Department of Education and the federal Equal Employment Opportunities Commission publicly accused him of sexual harassment. Despite the fact that she was treated with disrespect and disbelief by many and that Judge Thomas was endorsed for the High Court, her testimony has had an enormous impact. When she spoke before the Civil Justice Foundation, which honored her with its Champion of Justice Award, a "crowd of 850 lawyers, students, and others responded with two standing ovations" (Walker, 1993, p. A7).

Susan Wooley (1992) has described the reactions of many Senate Committee members and others as "utterly incredible" in their exaggerated expression of "shock and disgust" at hearing the allegations against Thomas. Wooley argues that such reactions were intended to distance the listener from the harassing behaviors described, behaviors that could thus be labeled as aberrant or abnormal. If one believes that "no normal man could ever engage in such behavior" (p. 5), and Judge Thomas was clearly a "normal" man, it would follow that Anita Hill is the person to be criticized as (in Wooley's terms): a witch; a soiled woman; having unnatural ambitions (for a woman); or fantasizing men's sexual interest in her. Indeed, such responses were not uncommon. But there were also the nods of recognition by women and men who had observed sexual harassment in their social, work, and educational environments; in the behaviors of ordinary, "normal" persons; and who had tolerated it with confusion, anxiety, and forbearance.

A sizable literature has been generated by the Thomas hearings and reactions to it, including a collection of articles edited by Toni Morrison (1992) that address the intersections between race/ethnicity and gender that were spotlighted by these hearings. Not only was Anita Hill denigrated by many as a woman, but she was also considered by some to be a traitor to her people. So heated was the debate that hundreds of African American women placed an ad in the Sunday *New York Times* ("African American women," 1991) to support Professor Hill. Books and articles presenting opposing viewpoints continue to be published.

Although sexual harassment had been defined, discussed, researched, and recognized as illegal sex discrimination in the two decades preceding Anita Hill's testimony, there seems little question that, since then, women have come forward in greater numbers than before to speak of their mistreatment by employers, supervisors, professors, co-workers, or student peers. We have witnessed a United States senator, Brock Adams, withdraw from a re-election campaign in the State of Washington following allegations of sexual misconduct by women who had worked for him. As of this writing, another United States senator, Bob Packwood of Oregon, accused of sexual harassment by a number of women, is under investigation by the Senate Ethics Committee. We have seen negative sanctions applied in universities as in the case of Gerald Silverberg, who was removed from his administrative position as head of the department of neurosurgery at Stanford University Medical School after he was accused of sexist behavior by his colleague Dr. Frances Conley. Silverberg was asked to leave his post following the report of a university committee that had investigated the charges (Holden, 1992).

Most recently, the United States Supreme Court ruled unanimously, in an opinion written by the senior woman on the Court, Sandra Day O'Connor (*Harris v. Forklift Systems*, 1993), that federal law prohibits sexually harassing behaviors that produce a hostile work environment, regardless of whether the victim can demonstrate extreme psychological injury. The effect of this latest ruling by the Court is of great significance. As noted by Lynn Shafran of the NOW Legal Defense and Education Fund (cf. Greenhouse, 1993), it shifts the legal focus from the person bringing the complaint to "the behavior of the alleged harasser and how this behavior alters circumstances in the workplace." This outcome was supported by the American Psychological Association which argued, in a friend-of-the court brief, that requiring those who allege sexual harassment to prove psychological or job performance injury "focuses the court's inquiry on the victim's 'ability to withstand harassment' when it should properly be on the 'conduct of the harasser'" (DeAngelis 1993, p. 19).

The *Harris v. Forklift* Systems (1993) decision puts employers clearly on notice that they must be in compliance with Title VII of the 1964 Civil Rights Act and have policies and procedures in place for prevention and corrective action. There is no longer any doubt that sexual harassment is a serious violation of the law and that targets of harassment need not demonstrate that their job performance has been seriously affected or that they have suffered intense psychological damage. In separate opinions, Justices Antonin Scalia and Ruth Bader Ginsburg emphasized that the key factor in a legal determination of harassment is whether the behaviors in question "had the effect of altering the working conditions in a discriminatory way" (Greenhouse 1993). Workplace equality is violated, wrote Justice O'Connor,"when women or men are subjected to 'intimidation, ridicule and insult'...because of their gender" (Savage, 1993).

The law under which workplace sexual harassment cases are brought to the courts is Title VII of the Civil Rights Act of 1964 which prohibits discrimination on the basis of race, sex, religion, and national origin. Ironically, the word "sex" was added by amendment after the word "religion" as a joke by a group of southern members of the House of Representatives who were intent on finding ways to defeat the entire measure. Some supporters of the civil rights measure opposed the amendment, fearing that it would indeed kill the bill and even a strong advocate for women like Representative Edith Green "opposed the amendment, stating that it would 'clutter up the bill'" (Roth, 1993, p. 85). The amendment and the bill were both approved by the House and, four months later, the Civil Rights Act was passed by the Senate and signed into law by President Johnson. In 1980 the Equal Employment Opportunity Commission (EEOC) issued its first set of guidelines that interpreted Title VII's prohibition of sex discrimination as covering sexual harassment, but it was not until the Supreme Court ruling in *Meritor Savings Bank v. Vinson* (1986) that this interpretation was upheld by the High Court. In a unanimous opinion, the Court agreed that the creation of a hostile environment directed against a person or persons on the basis of their gender constituted a form of sex discrimination and that employers were responsible to take steps against it.

The view that working environments can become hostile or abusive by acts of sexual harassment has been logically extended to academic environments. It is now understood that such environments can be hostile for students as well as for workers. The EEOC guidelines of 1980 noted that sexual harassment is prohibited in schools receiving federal funds by virtue of the ban against sex discrimination contained in Title IX of the 1972 Education Amendments. Twenty years later, in *Franklin v. Gwinnett County School District* (1992), the Supreme Court clarified its position that sexual harassment in schools is indeed a form of discrimination and that victims are entitled to monetary damages.

Other implications of this decision for higher education seem clear. As pointed out by Lindgren and Taub (1993), "Although Franklin claimed to have been the victim of quid pro quo harassment at the hands of a teacher, this ruling implies that the hostile environment form of harassment, at the hands of fellow students, also violates Title IX. This opens the door to suits...against schools in which...[students] are subject to verbal and physical abuse because of their sex, what in the past was dismissed as 'teasing'" (p. 318). This decision as well as others also present challenges for higher education as many writers have recently noted ("The legal issues," 1993; Mangan, 1993; Riggs, Murrell, & Cutting 1993). Educational institutions are being challenged to devise and implement policies and procedures to eliminate harassment. Riggs, Murrell, & Cutting, urge that not only must colleges and universities be proactive in defining behavior that will not be tolerated, but that they must, by consensus, establish an organizational culture in which the beliefs and values that are shared will make harassment an unlikely event. In a pamphlet focused on deterrence, the American Council on Education (1992) has outlined the key components of a campus program that includes definitions of harassment, grievance procedures, and policies.

ABOUT THIS BOOK

How the decisions and interpretations about workplace sexual harassment impact schools, colleges, and universities is among the issues and questions raised and discussed by contributors to this volume. What sexual harassment means for students, professors, college staff members, administrators, and unions is the focus of the papers included in this book, most of which were published separately by NEA within the past four years. Rachel Hendrickson, of NEA's Office of Higher Education conceived the idea of bringing together in one book the individual papers on sexual harassment in higher education that had appeared in *Thought & Action* and in a monograph written for NEA by Louise Fitzgerald (1992). We agreed to take on the task of putting such a plan into action, of contacting contributors, suggesting revisions, soliciting postscripts and organizing the previously separate papers into a single collection.

We undertook this project because we believe that having these insightful and provocative papers on sexual harassment in one place will increase their value as resource materials and the probability that they will be shared with colleagues and students. The contributing authors come from a wide variety of academic disciplines spanning the humanities and the sciences, from colleges and universities of differing sizes and locations across the United States, and are engaged in a wide assortment of jobs within their institutions. The diversity in authorship is reflected by a diversity in perspective and in focus. The wide range of questions considered by the contributors should make this volume welcomed by all who are interested in expanding their knowledge about sexual harassment in higher education. We expect the book to be helpful to educators and scholars in their research and teaching, as well as to administratrors and staff members in developing workshops and educational interventions and in formulating policies.

Lynn Gordon's chapter situates the contemporary problems of sexual harassment on college campuses within the historical context of the opening up of higher education opportunites for women in the United States. Such a context helps us to understand that sexual harassment is not an isolated phenomenon but part of a pattern of gender inequality that characterizes our social institutions generally. As argued by

Schacht and Atchison (1993), for example, "Sexual harassment at college or work is an instrument by which males erode and control females' career aspirations" (p. 43).

Following the introductory chapters, a group of papers by Louise Fitzgerald, Anne Truax, and Marcia Bedard and Beth Hartung explore the varying definitions of sexual harassment and problems presented by these definitions, and the phenomenon of differing perceptions or interpretations of relevant behaviors. When presented with real or hypothetical incidents, people disagree about whether sexual harassment occurred, who was to blame, and what should be done. These authors also address the issue of who sexual harassers are likely to be, their status and power relationship to those they victimize, and the frequency with which such behavior is known to occur on our campuses. We learn that while women are the most likely targets of sexual harassment, some men, too, report such experiences, and that while sexual harassment is most often directed at persons who are vulnerable because of age or status, a student may harass a professor or another student, or a colleague may harass someone of equal professional status. A recent large scale study of the sexual harassment of women professors ('In' Box, 1994a) found that nearly one in seven at U.S. colleges had been harassed "at some time during her career at her current institution" (p. A17). Black women professors were found to be more likely than other women to report harassment.

The significance of legal developments and their impact on university policies and procedures are the focus of discussions in another section of the book that includes papers by Louise Fitzgerald, Doric Little, Little and John Thompson, and Lloyd Elgart and Lillian Schanfield. These authors consider questions dealing with faculty-student behavior and sexually harassing interactions between peers. Issues of due process and academic freedom have been raised by a number of recent cases (Leatherman, 1994b). One case which has drawn national attention is that of a tenured professor of Communications at the University of New Hampshire who was suspended "for a year without pay after two campus panels reviewed student complaints about his remarks and determined that they had created a hostile environment. As a condition of returning to work, he was to undergo psychotherapy" (Leatherman, 1994a, p. A18). The professor sued the university and a district court judge ordered the university to reinstate him. This decision "is thought to be the first to address the conflict between free speech and sexual harassment at a university" (Leatherman, 1994c, p A22). The university appealed and then chose to settle the case, reinstating the professor and agreeing to pay him $170,000 in legal fees and $60,000 in back pay. It also agreed to remove references to the sexual harassment allegations from his personnel file ('In' Box, 1994C). In the final section, Loralee MacPike, Sherna Gluck, Rachel Hendrickson, Michelle Paludi, Bernice Lott, and Barbara Taylor discuss the vast array of consequences of sexual harassment— for our educational institutions, for union policy, for society in general, and for individuals, both those who are the targets of harassment and those who are the harassers. Remedies are presented and evaluated. Readers are urged to do the same and to work toward creative solutions to the complex problems associated with sexual harassment.

ADDITIONAL QUESTIONS

While the present collection of papers explores a wide array of issues and problems, there remain still others for us to consider and reconsider. Among additional questions being asked are ones that seek to identify the underlying factors that produce the problem of sexual harassment so that solutions can take them into account and thereby increase the probability that efforts directed toward effecting change can be successful.

The need to answer some very basic, interlocking questions about the conditions under which sexual harassing behaviors are learned, their manifestation in children, and the contexts in which they appear was dramatically indicated by the results of a national study commissioned by the American Association of University Women (AAUW) of public school students in grades 8 through 11. This survey, conducted in 79 schools across the continental United States, documents the pervasiveness of sexual harassment in the lives of teenagers. Among the findings are that: "Four in 5 students (81%) say they have experienced some form of sexual harassment during their school lives: 85% of girls and 76% of boys"; "sexual comments, jokes, looks, and gestures—as well as touching, grabbing, and/or pinching in a sexual way—are commonplace in school"; "experiences of student-to-student harassment outnumber all others"; "notably higher numbers of girls than boys say they have suffered as a result of sexual harassment in school; African American girls have suffered the most" (*Hostile Hallways,* 1993, pp. 22-24). There are indications from news reports all over the country that the findings are, indeed, accurate (Gross, 1992).

It is clear from the findings of the AAUW study that children have learned to express hostility toward one another in sexual ways and that educational programs to prevent and eliminate sexual harassment must begin in elementary schools. These findings also highlight the urgency with which we must direct research to questions such as the following: (1) What is the relationship between the sexual harassment that appears to be endemic among today's children and similar behaviors on college campuses and adult workplaces? (2) Do children and adults learn that aggression expressed sexually is more likely to be tolerated and successful than aggression expressed in other ways? (3) What conditions are necessary for children and adults to learn to distinguish between sexual behavior that achieves power enhancement goals and sexual behavior that expresses sexual attraction?

Findings from other studies suggest the importance of another question: (4) Are girls and women "oversensitive" to sexual harassment and/or are boys and men "undersensitive"? As pointed out by Popovich et al. (1992), "One of the most consistent findings in the literature on sexual harassment has been sex differences in perceptions of such incidents...with females often perceiving certain behaviors as more likely to be sexual harassment than do males" (p. 610). The same behavior that a woman may see as an expression of power may be perceived by a man as an acceptable expression of sexual attraction. A recent poll by the Scripps Howard News Service of over 1,000 randomly selected adults found that men tended to agree with women that men often sexually harass women but, at the same time, 43% of men, as compared with 30% of women, said that "many sexual harassment claims come from overly sensitive women" who are "misreading the situation" (Hargrove & Stempel, 1993).

Another question suggested by discussions within this volume and the work of others is: (5) How do we recognize contrapower sexual harassment and what are the possible preventative steps and remedies? This term, first suggested by Benson (1984), refers to the harassment of faculty by students (or of apparently higher-status persons by those of lower status). A review of the survey research literature led Kathleen McKinney (1992) to conclude that "Anywhere from 6% to 50% [of college faculty] report such experiences. . . . Behaviors reported include sexist verbal comments, sexual comments written on course evaluations, obscene phone calls. . . , physical advances, uninvited sexual looks or body langauge, sexual bribery, and sexual assaults" (p. 629). Women faculty report more experiences of contrapower harassment, being more disturbed by it, and suffering more adverse effects than men faculty.

(6) Can we begin to predict the situations most likely (and least likely) to be associated with sexual harassment, and the characteristics of persons most and least likely to harass? Intriguing findings relevant to this question were reported from a study of ethical problems in academic research that involved surveying 2,000 doctoral candidates and 2,000 doctoral faculty sampled from 99 of the largest graduate departments in chemistry, civil engineering, microbiology, and sociology. The authors of this study (Swazey, Anderson, & Lewis 1993) were interested in a variety of ethical problems including that of sexual harassment. They found that, among all those surveyed, between 15% and 40% of faculty and between 5% and 35% of students reported knowledge of sexual harassment by faculty, and between nearly 10% and 25% of both faculty and students reported knowledge of sexual harassment by students. While this high level of illegal and

disruptive behavior on the part of leading scientists in this country is cause for alarm, the investigators found important differences in the frequency of harassing behaviors among the four areas surveyed. Sexual harassment was reported most often among sociologists, both faculty and students, least often among civil engineers, and at intermediate levels among chemists and microbiologists. In trying to account for these differences, the investigators note that "Although the low rates of this behavior among civil engineeers may reflect the preponderance of males in the field, microbiology has a female-to-male ratio not far below that of sociology" (p. 549). Some factors other than the presence of women, then, account for sexual harassment.

Other questions, though not exhaustive of those remaining to be answered, are the following: (7) How can we keep the definition of sexual harassment clearly distinct from other forms of sexist behavior? (8) Does same-gender sexual harassment tend to receive more swift and stringent reprisal from authoritative sanctioning bodies than heterosexual harassment?; (9) Should policies and procedures be tailored to the characteristics of particular campuses and student bodies, as suggested by Dziech (1993)? (10) Should the university represent students, faculty, or staff members who have complained of harassment and are then sued by the accused after the institution has taken disciplinary action against the alleged harasser?

(11) The American Council on Education (1992) suggests that institutions consider providing "Specific guidance discouraging romantic relationships between professors and students, professors and teacher assistants, teacher assistants and undergraduates, and faculty and support staff" (p. 12f.). How this can be done without infringing on individual freedom and how much responsibility should be taken by colleges and universities are questions addressed in this volume by Louise Fitzgerald and Barbara Taylor. In a letter to the editor of *The Chronicle of Higher Education*, a graduate student (Gilcher, 1994), recounts her own painful experience in a consensual relationship, and writes:

Although I like to think that the professor I dated was not completely aware of how intensely I felt the power he had over me, and although I was very flattered by the attention at the time, the relationship—unavoidably—placed me in an extraordinarily precarious and vulnerable position. Professors must become aware of the predicament in which they place students when they date them.

(12) How do stereotyped images of heterosexual relationships and sanctioned violence as a means of resolving conflicts so frequently portrayed in media images, professional sports, and popular music contribute to the prevalence of sexual harassment? And, finally,

(13) How should colleges and universities address severe forms of sexualized hostility believed to be occurring at an escalating rate such as the videotaping or audiotaping of intimate sexual acts by hidden observers, harassing phone calls, and leaving visible signs of masturbation in public places? While the killing of Jeanne Clery at Lehigh University influenced the passage of federal laws requiring the reporting of crimes and increased attention to security, the rampages at McGill University, the University of Iowa, and Simon's Rock College of Bard make chillingly clear that violence on campuses is not a rarity.

While we seem to be ending this introductory chapter on a somber note, readers should be heartened by the serious attention being given to the understanding of sexual harassment and to efforts to eliminate it through education, policy implementation, and negative sanctions. Examples of such efforts are discussed within this volume. The contributors have boldly faced the complex issues of definition, support for persons who complain of harassment, due process for those accused, differences in perception, legal remedies, and the challenges to institutions of higher education and to unions. While it is possible to become overwhelmed by the complexities involved in dealing with sexual harassment on our college campuses, we hope that readers will finish this volume more knowledgeable about the issues and more optimistic about solutions than when they started. As noted by Dziech (1993, p. A48), "The only way in which people can rescue themselves from the confusion and controversy over sexual harassment is to stop attacking one another and start talking...[and] the American campus should be the place where that dialogue begins."

REFERENCES

African American women in defense of ourselves. (1991, November 17). *New York Times, Campus Life,* p. 53.

American Council on Education. (1992). *Sexual harassment on campus.* ACE, One Dupont Circle, Washington, DC 20036.

Benson, Katherine A. (1984). Comment on Crocker's "An analysis of university definitions of sexual harassment." *Signs, 9,* 516-519.

Dank, Barry M. (1994, June 29). Campus romances and consenting adults. *The Chronicle of Higher Education,* p.B4.

DeAngelis, Tori (1993, August). APA files amicus brief in sex harassment case. *APA Monitor,* pp. 19-20.

DeLoughry, Thomas J. (1994, November 16). Carnegie Mellon eliminates 3 Bulletin Boards with sexual themes from its computer system. The *Chronicle of Higher Education* p. A22.

Dziech, B. W. (1993, December 8). The bedeviling issue of sexual harassment. *The Chronicle of Higher Education,* p. A48.

Franklin v. Gwinnett County School District, 112 S. Ct. 1028 (1992).

Gilcher, A. (1994, January 19). Letter to the editor. *The Chronicle of Higher Education,* p. B5.

Greenhouse, Linda (1993, November 10). Court, 9-0, makes sex harassment easier to prove. *New York Times,* p. A1f.

Gross, Jane (1992, March 11). Schools are newest arena for sex-harassment cases. *New York Times,* pp. A1, 8.

Hargrove, Thomas, & Stempel, Guido H. III. (1993, July 30). Poll finds sexes agree on harassment issues. *San Francisco Examiner,* p. A7.

Harris v. Forklift Systems, Inc. No. 92-1168 S. Ct. (1993). U.S. Lexis 7155.

Holden, Constance, (1992). Stanford responds to sexism charges. *Science,* 255 , 1208.

Hostile hallways: The AAUW survey on sexual harassment in America's schools. (1993, June). AAUW Educational Foundation, 1111 16th St. NW, Washington, DC 20036.

'In' box. (1994a. April 6). *The Chronicle of Higher Education*, p. A17.

'In' box. (1994b, May 25). *The Chronicle of Higher Education*, p. A14.

'In' box. (1994c, December 14). *The Chronicle of Higher Education*, p. A19.

Lindgren, J. Ralph, & Taub, Nadine. (1993). *The law of sex discrimination* (2nd ed.). Minneapolis/St. Paul: West Publishing.

Leatherman, Courtney. (1993/December 8). Dealing with sexual images in Iowa classrooms. *The Chronicle of Higher Education*, p. A22.

Leatherman, Courtney. (1994a, January 12). U. of New Hampshire wrestles with issue of sexual harassment in wake of professor's suspension. *The Chronicle of Higher Education*, p. A18.

Leatherman, Courtney. (1994b, March 16). Fighting back. *The Chronicle of Highr Education*, p. A17.

Leatherman, Courtney. (1994c, September 28). Free speech or harassment? *The Chronicle of Higher Education*, p.A22.

Leatherman, Courtney (1994, December 7). A tragic toll. *The Chronicle of Higher Education*, p. A 35.

Mangan, Katherine S. (1993, August 4). Thorny legal issues face colleges hit by sexual-harassment cases. *Chronicle of Higher Education*, p. A13.

McKinney, Kathleen (1992). Contrapower sexual harassment: The effects of student sex and type of behavior on faculty perceptions. *Sex Roles, 27,* 627-643.

Meritor Savings Bank FSB v. Vinson. 477 U.S. 57, 106 S. Ct. 2399 (1986).

Morrison, Toni (1992). (Ed.) *Race-ing justice, and gender-ing power: Essays on Anita Hill, Clarence Thomas, and the construction of social reality.* NY: Pantheon.

Painter, Nell I. (1994, March 23). It's time to acknowledge the damage inflicted by intolerance. *The Chronicle of Higher Education*, p. A64.

Popovich, Paula M. Gehlauf, DeeAnn N., Jolton, Jeffrey A., Somers, Jill M., & Godinho, Rhonda M. (1992). Perceptions of sexual harassment as a function of sex of rater and incident form and consequences. *Sex Roles, 27,* 609-625.

Riggs, Robert O., Murrell, Patricia H., & Cutting, JoAnne C. (1993). *Sexual harassment in higher education: From conflict to community.* ASHE-ERIC Higher Education Report 93-2. George Washington University, School of Education and Human Development, One Dupont Circle, Suite 630, Washington, DC 20036.·

Roth, Elizabeth (1993, March/April). The civil rights history of "sex": A sexist, racist congressional joke. *Ms.,* pp. 84-85.

Savage, David G. (1993, November 10). High Court bolsters harassment protection. *Providence Journal Bulletin,* p. A1.

Schacht, S. P., & Atchison, Patricia H. (1993). Heterosexual instrumentalism: Past and future directions. *Feminism & Psychology, 3,* 37-53.

Swazey, Judith P., Anderson, Melisa S., & Lewis, Karen S. (1993). Ethical problems in academic research. *American Scientist, 81,* 542-553.

The legal issues in sexual-harassment cases. (1993, September 15). *Chronicle of Higher Education,* p. B3.

Walker, Thaai (1993, August 5). Anita Hill tells of stress in sex harassment cases. *San Francisco Chronicle,* p. A7.

White, Lawrence. (1994, May 25). Hate-speech codes that will pass constitutional muster. *The Chronicle of Higher Education,* p. A 48

Wooley, Susan (1992). Anita HIll, Clarence Thomas and the enforcement of female silence. *Women & Therapy, 12* (4), 3-23.

2

WOMEN ON CAMPUS: HISTORY TO USE

by Lynn D. Gordon

By the late 1960s and early 1970s, white middle-class women had finally succeeded in achieving parity in higher education, or so most people thought. The Ivy League, as well as smaller, prestigious, liberal arts colleges, Catholic men's institutions, and even the military academies had begun admitting women. Catholic women's colleges and some of the "Seven Sisters" schools accepted men.

Though women students on formerly all-male campuses sometimes encountered hostility, even sociologists Janet Lever and Pepper Schwartz (1971), in their well-known *Women at Yale* felt that gender relations were rapidly stabilizing. Yet in the past ten years, sexual harassment, date rape, obscene graffiti, and threatening phone calls have become common features of campus life. The murder of women engineering students in Montreal in December, 1989 was a tragic and extreme example of a widespread and deeply rooted anger about women's changing aspirations and social roles.

Studies indicate that as many as 40% of undergraduate women have experienced some form of sexual harassment—minority women students seem particularly vulnerable to physical and verbal assaults. And these problems have surfaced not only in institutions that have recently begun admitting women, but in those that have been coeducational for a hundred years (Minorities, 1989; Symposium, 1989).

Few educators have asked just what is happening to women on contemporary college campuses and why it should be happening after two decades of progress, but the history of

An earlier version of this chapter appeared in *Thought and Action,* Spring 1990, *6* (1), 5-20.

women in higher education provides both perspective and, potentially, some resolution.

Only a small number of American women attended colleges and universities in the 1840s and 1850s. Their real movement into colleges and universities occurred after the Civil War, mostly in new institutions—the state universities created by the Morrill Act of 1862 and new private schools such as Cornell, Stanford, and Chicago.

In the East and South, the well-established men's colleges refused to consider coeducation. Instead, a number of philanthropists and educators established women's colleges, or women's coordinate colleges within universities. Later, with the real drive coming in the 1920s, Catholics founded a nationwide network of women's colleges as well.

Despite these colleges for women, most female students attended coeducational institutions almost from the beginning, and an ever-growing number accepted them as students. The number of women undergraduates rose quickly, constituting 20% of the student population by 1870, 47.3% by 1920. Of these, 41.1% attended coeducational colleges in 1870, 81.3% in 1920 (Newcomer, 1959).

Because many of the new institutions that admitted women were western, contemporary observers who favored the practice viewed it as a sign of frontier democracy, and the expanding benefits of American civilization. But the rhetoric of equality was notably absent from the speeches and writings of educators and legislators, even those who agreed that women should enter universities. In most cases, these educators and legislators had simply succumbed to pressure from taxpayers who wanted their daughters to be able to earn a living as teachers before they married—or longer, should they be so unfortunate as to remain unwed.

In a few cases, women's rights advocates successfully encouraged institutions to open their doors. More commonly, universities regarded such pressure as a reason to resist. And most parents and their daughters consciously and explicitly distanced themselves from the women's rights movements (Gordon, 1990).

Nineteenth-century proponents of coeducation, both male and female, used arguments derived from a 60-year tradition of the relationship between gender and education. Beginning after the American Revolution, proponents of women's education argued that the future of republican government rested in the homes of America and the hands of its mothers. Thus, the mothers themselves needed to be educated. Economic changes in the early and mid-19th century, particularly in the Northeast, enhanced the theory of "republican motherhood." Urbanization and the growth of industrial capitalism, drawing fathers and husbands out of the household and into the marketplace to earn a living, left women at home to educate children. And as young men found economic opportunities in the business world or the West, school systems grew to depend on young women as teachers (Hoffman, 1979; Kerber, 1980).

Early Victorians supported their socioeconomic and domestic relationships with an ideology of God-given "separate spheres" of activity for males and females. Later in the century, biologists and psychologists added the sanction of science to these social arrangements—as when Dr. Edward Clarke in 1873 told women that studying like men would dry up their ovaries, undermine their health, and keep them from bearing normal children. To women belonged the responsibilities and glories of hearth, home, and elementary school. Men claimed the public arena for their own.

Despite its limitations, the "separate-sphere" ideology actually improved the lives of at least middle-class white women. And activist women used this ideology to gain themselves a place in public life and discourse, arguing that their special qualities made their influence and presence in the public arena necessary. Who better to crusade for moral reform and temperance, for example, than women whose home lives had been deeply affected by prostitution and drunkenness (Smith-Rosenberg, 1985)?

In the post-Civil War era, then, proponents of coeducation sought admission to colleges for women by arguing that higher education would improve their performance as wives, mothers, and teachers. But the colleges and universities that admitted women did so less on the basis of ideology than of necessity. Admitting women became a financial imperative for many 19th-and early 20th-century colleges and universities that needed the revenue provided by a larger student body.

There may somewhere have been a male college president or trustee who spoke of women's rights, but I have, as yet, found none. Even Michigan's President James B. Angell, a supporter of women's higher education, argued simply that women would cause no moral degeneration of campus life. Instead, said Angell and others like him, women would improve the tone of campus life and provide male students with living examples of true womanhood. Coeducation, in other words, would be good for men (Angell, 1881, 1904).

Unfortunately, students in the Victorian Era did not write admissions essays on "why I want to go to college." Still, we have ample though impressionistic evidence that a good many young women had broader aims for their higher education than becoming better wives and mothers. Some longed for culture and knowledge, others had career goals other than teaching, still others wanted financial and personal independence (Gordon, 1990; Woody, 1929).

At first—in the 1870s and 1880s—it appeared that having women on campus would have little institutional impact. The exclusively male faculty grumbled about their new students, but did not refuse to teach them. Some were pleasantly surprised by women's intellectual competence.

Student life in the late nineteenth century consisted largely of drinking and organized brawling. In the 1870s and 1880s a "rush" was not a fraternity party but a pitched battle between freshmen and sophomores or juniors and seniors. Needless to say, such activities afforded little scope for female participation.

Parents and educators alike assumed that higher education would not alter established gender roles. But from the beginning, faculty and students of both sexes sensed its potential to do so and were uncomfortable in their campus relations. In Victorian America, no other institution associated adolescent young men and women so closely together and engaged them in the same activities. Men and women attended classes, received grades, wrote papers, took examinations, and competed for academic honors.

Despite a good deal of discussion about a separate, gender-based curriculum, none ever materialized. Women voted in college elections long before they could do so off campus. And after graduation, some women—probably a significant minority—did not go on to lives of quiet but enhanced domesticity, or as school teachers. Instead, they blazed the trails for women in the professions and politics. And they experimented with unconventional forms of family life—having few or no children, or living in communities or with other professional women.

From its beginnings, then, collegiate coeducation was a curious combination of conservatism and gender revolution. Student awareness of this tension often created difficulties on campus. One of the more interesting sources on the early years of coeducation is *An American Girl and Her Four Years in a Boys' College*, a novel written by a University of Michigan alumna (Anderson, 1878), class of 1875. The heroine, Wilhelmine Elliott, was portrayed with a stereotypic combination of men's and women's qualities—her masculine nickname, "Will," her love of athletics and exercise, her rational intellect, and her desire to be a doctor were contrasted with her beauty, warmth, and nurturing attributes. Her problem lay in finding acceptance—of classmates not knowing just how to treat or understand her. On the way to class, Will accidentally got caught in the middle of a "rush." The young men ignored her plight, and she got a bloody nose as a result.

Her analysis, given the women friends who rescued her, was acute: "There is not one of those boys, but if you find him out of college, would have run to a lady's assistance and begged a thousand pardons for having had any hand in such an accident; but, would you believe it, not one of those two hundred and fifty boys offered any help or sympathy simply because they feel that we are trespassing upon their domains."[1]

Despite the difficulties that coeducation posed for both sexes, the 1870s and 1880s were a relatively peaceful period for campus gender relations, since the number of women on campus was small. But in the 1890s, the situation on and off campus changed, and women challenged men's control of college life.

In the world beyond the ivy walls, the period from 1890 to the end of World War I represented a time of major public achievements for women. During this time, the first college-educated women entered the professions, established careers, and became active in politics and the reform movements of the Progressive Era. Women's organizations of all kinds did battle in the public arena for social justice legislation. The suffrage movement gained momentum, eventually resulting in ratification of the Nineteenth Amendment in 1920.

Women also articulated a vision of how their participation in public life could both benefit and change society. They had no intention of becoming like men, they said. Instead, they wanted to bring unique womanly virtues, modified somewhat by the experience of a male-oriented college education, to bear on the issues of the day. Instead of aggression, competition, and accumulation, they offered society compassion, empathy, and a passion for justice (Glazer & Slater, 1987; Gordon, 1990).

On college campuses, notions of women's public mission translated into an increased number of women students. By 1900, women numbered more than half of the undergraduates at several important institutions. Unlike their predecessors, these college women could call on the support of alumnae and of the women faculty and administrators whom universities began to hire in small numbers. These college women resolved the confusion of Will Elliott's day by finding a way to participate in student life as women. They established their own clubs and organizations, paralleling the men's. On some campuses they formed separate student government organizations and student unions. Almost everywhere there were women's dramatics clubs, glee clubs, honor societies, athletic organizations, and even newspapers.

This creation of a separate extracurricular life did not lead to gender equality on campuses. Battles over student funds and space in the campus newspapers, for instance, reveal that men continued to command the greater share of resources and faculty interest. Still, in the decades before

World War I, the women's communities at coeducational institutions challenged male preeminence. These communities gave young women leadership opportunities they had not had before and could have developed nowhere else in early 20th-century America.

Then, at the height of their success, college women confronted a campus backlash from male students and faculty and a nationwide reaction against collegiate coeducation. Many institutions discussed ending or limiting coeducation, and a number of private schools did so. Stanford put a quota on women students, as did Michigan. The University of Chicago set up separate classes for male and female freshmen and sophomores. Wesleyan ended coeducation in 1913. Tufts, Western Reserve, and Rochester established coordinate women's colleges with separate instruction. And at many other schools—California, Wisconsin, Illinois—administrators, faculty and students would clearly have liked to limit or end coeducation but lacked the funds to do so (Gordon, 1990; Woody, 1929).

There was a change in campus extracurricular life, too, as men created an image for women students that reflected their feelings and fears. At the University of California, they called women students "pelicans," and named the campus humor magazine, a frequent vehicle for satiric comment on gender relations, *The Pelican*. The human pelicans, as depicted by campus wags, were tall, thin, and bony, with knobby knees and long, ungainly arms. They had straight stringy hair, pulled back in buns, with pencils protruding from them, beaky noses, and, of course, wore glasses. Pelicans became, or already were, old maid schoolteachers, because no man wanted to marry them.

The campus yearbook, *The Blue and Gold*, warned that, however pretty a freshman woman, if she studied too hard she would make her "pretty little nose very red," her "rosy cheeks" jaundiced, and her hair thin (*The Blue and Gold*, 1893). In another yearbook, the editors depicted a pretty young girl ("when she comes") next to a sour-faced woman with glasses, surrounded by books ("when she leaves"). In contrast, the boy "when he enters" squinted at his books and dressed poorly, but left college a handsome, polished gentle-men. In the same yearbook's "Ye Rime of Ye Ancient Co-Ed," a "pelican" lamented: "I have tried for twenty years to change my name/But in spite of all my efforts 'tis the same/But a masculine degree/Such as B.L. or A.B./Turns an old maid to a bachelor of fame" (*The Blue and Gold, 1893*).

Student authors of short stories also made it clear that women would have to choose between coeducation and the normal course of events for a young girl—romance followed by marriage and motherhood. At California, student fiction included brother and sister stories that stressed how boys and girls could be raised similarly and participate in the same activities—up to a point. As they grew older, some dramatic event made it clear to the girl that she was not like her broth-er and should not try to behave like him (Riley, 1907; Thompson, 1903).

The men students also restricted women physically. They reserved certain benches, walkways, and restaurants for themselves, and women who dared to walk by these sacro-sanct places became the objects of leering, jeers, taunts, and sometimes pushing and shoving. The men called this practice "piping the flight," untroubled by the illogic of their wanting to observe the "pelicans" they claimed were so unattractive (*The Daily Californian*, 1918).

While the term "pelican" was unique to the California campus, the imagery, tone, and sentiments were not. At Wesleyan, where the term for women students was "quails," men formed a "PDQ Society" ("Put Down the Quails"), and wrote letters to incoming freshman women urging them not to attend Wesleyan. At Rochester, male students formed a physi-cal barrier surrounding classroom and building doors, forcing women to try to elbow their way through to get to class. At Chicago, men proposed barring women students from football games, or at least making them sit separately, arguing that their presence diverted men's attention from cheering and analyzing the finer points of the game (Gordon, 1990).

What was this all about? Why, after 10 to 30 years of vir-tually scandal-free coeducation and rising enrollments was there so much hostility and so many attempts to restrict access? As women moved into higher education and public life, their actions threatened, many believed, the foundations of family life and of civilization itself. Beginning in the 1890s, social critics complained about "race suicide." They maintained that the "best people" in America were not having children, abandoning the reproduction sweepstakes to Eastern and Southern European immigrants, mostly Roman Catholics and Jews, whose abundant offspring posed a threat to the Anglo-Saxon purity of American middle-class culture.

And who was to blame? Middle-class white women, particularly college-educated "New Women," whose low marriage and birth rates signaled their desire to abandon the proper duties of their sex and have careers like men (Hall, 1906; Smith-Rosenberg, 1985).

Similarly, on some campuses male faculty and students argued that coeducation would produce an "amalgamation" of the sexes and a "poor and feeble hybrid which is as unsatisfactory to the one side as to the other." Familiarity, said one student,

> breeds contempt.... Woman, man's ideal, is immeasurably more powerful than woman, man's equal. We don't want the unlikeness destroyed. When woman becomes man in character, man must necessarily cease to be man (Keane, 1905)

Faculty in particular were concerned about the numbers of women—and decreasing numbers of men—coming to colleges and about the prevalence of women in humanities classes. They complained that their presence interfered with the intellectual quality of student life. Women students got better grades, they said, not because they were brighter or better students, but because they were diligent note-takers and memorizers.

At some institutions, women found themselves excluded from prize competitions, Phi Beta Kappa keys, or other honors on the grounds that if women won too many prizes it would look as though the university could not attract good male students. Some faculty complained that, with women in class, they could not tell their best jokes or discuss the bawdier passages in Chaucer and Shakespeare. Others talked of the "effeminization" of the university, comparing it to the "effeminization" of other areas of American life, such as religion and culture.

Like male students, faculty could not separate an idealized vision of womanhood from the reality. At Chicago, instructors "found it impossible to use sufficient severity with girls in class to produce the best results." Girls monopolized the corridors, stairs, and grounds, they charged, "making the halls crowded and leading to too much physical contact." Chicago's president, William Rainey Harper, noted that "thoughtful men and women are not unanimous that the type of comradeship which coeducation has promoted between men and women is altogether an improvement" (Gordon, 1990).

Despite, or perhaps because of all this, by the 1910s many women in coeducational institutions were explicitly feminist. They joined suffrage organizations, demanded career conferences, and challenged the men for control of the campuses. Instead of docility and a distancing from political movements, the reaction to coeducation produced the opposite of what was intended: women became activists. The diminishing number of men during World War I also gave women new opportunities to serve as campus leaders. And with the male presence not quite as overpowering, women sometimes overturned old customs about where they might walk, sit, and eat.

The outcry against coeducation and effeminization gradually died down. By 1920, it was unusual to find a journal article on the subject or to hear university presidents making pronouncements on the place of women at their institutions. No major institutions adopted new restrictions on women's admission after World War I. Unfortunately, this lack of protest did not indicate campus acceptance for college women or gender equality at coeducation institutions. In the end, protests over coeducation and the pernicious effects of educating women ended because society generally and colleges in particular contained and deflected the threat of "effeminization." College women themselves aided this process. The ideology of "separate spheres" and the accompanying development of women's campus communities gradually disappeared, as the rhetoric of equality captured feminists' imaginations, especially after the achievement of woman suffrage (Cott, 1987).

At the same time college women were no longer content to be "pelicans." Not wishing to emulate the unmarried women who were their teachers and mentors, the younger generation was interested in men. This is not to say, as some historians of college students maintain, that these young women weren't concerned about anything else. Organizational, political, social reform, and suffrage activities continued to characterize their campus lives. But they were very troubled about choosing between domesticity and career.

Student fiction reveals anxieties about this conflict. In the stories written by women at coeducational institutions, marriage usually won the day, while in those published by students at women's colleges, the career often triumphed—though not without great anguish.[2] These stories manifest the growing unrest among college women and their determination to reach out to men. The 1913 "tango crisis" exemplified their new concerns. When students discovered and began to practice dancing styles requiring close bodily contact, their explicitly sexual nature created a furor. But while most campuses instituted regulations against the tango, most students did not observe them.

As women students were changing their attitudes toward romance, marriage, and "separate spheres," the political climate became more conservative, especially after World War I. The split in the feminist movement over the Equal Rights Amendment in the mid-1920s, the defeat of other constitutional amendments and social welfare measures, and the elections of Harding and Coolidge decreased campus interest in liberal progressivism and women's rights. Women's campus communities were not replaced by integrated egalitarian student organizations.

Gradually, college men hailed the disappearance of the "pelican" and the advent of the "chicken"—a pretty, cheerful, easy-going, not very serious "coed" of doubtful virtue, whose chief aim in going to college was to attract the right kind of male attention (Gordon, 1990). The chicken was much easier to live with than the pelican. Chickens did not threaten male prerogatives. Instead, they were simply an updated version of the proper white, middle-class American girl out to spend her time in a reasonably useful way as she surveyed her marriage prospects. Around 1910, the marriage rate of women college students began to rise, until by the mid-1930s the demographic profile of educated women could not be distinguished from that of other middle-class women (Cookingham, 1984a, 1984b).

But to say that women college students themselves decided that they were no longer interested in careers or politics and freely chose love, marriage, and domesticity would be an oversimplification. The objectification of women students as pelicans, chickens, flappers, or coeds made it difficult for them to make choices at all, because the alternatives were so starkly and unattractively portrayed. When college women were interested in having careers and being socially or politically active, their male peers dubbed them "pelicans," making it clear that ambitious women could expect not to be loved. When they evidenced an interest in marriage, and in freer styles of courting and sexual behavior, they were viewed as "chickens," incapable of sustained achievement and destined for a purely domestic future.

The American system of gender relations contained no prototypes for women who wanted both work and a traditional family. And this impoverishment of the imagination infected both sexes. As well as men, few educated women believed they could, as the modern saying goes, "have it all."

American higher education thus successfully contained the "woman peril" that threatened the nation's campuses between 1890-1920. And, as far as gender relations were concerned, the mid-20th century American campus was relatively peaceful—incidents of violence against women did not form a pattern of harassment.

But this history may help us understand the violence and harassment that is happening now. Women of the 1960s, 1970s, and 1980s have made great strides toward gender equality, as had those in the 19th century. Not only have many previously all-male institutions opened their doors to women, but graduate and professional schools have become more welcoming.

Such things as the modern feminist movement, government affirmative action requirements, and families' increased need for two incomes have made it possible and even desirable for women to have professional careers and not preclude marriage and children by doing so. Today, women constitute a majority of undergraduates. The young undergraduate woman attends college for the same reason as the young man, to prepare to earn a living and to make social contacts among classmates of both sexes. Like the earliest women college students (1870-1890), most contemporary young women take their opportunities as a matter of course and only vaguely identify with feminist ideologies (Komarovsky, 1985).

But, as in the 19th century, the new opportunity in women's higher education stems from a consideration of the interests of men. The public rhetoric at places like Princeton and Bowdoin argued that the institutions could no longer afford to lose the top male students who preferred coeducational colleges. Coeducation would help keep the colleges' intellectual standing high. Admitting women would improve the social tone of the campus.

An official at a prestigious liberal arts college even stated that male students were bringing women from the local junior college onto campus for long, drunken, and debauched weekends—and that, after all, these were not the kind of girls their parents would want them to marry. It would be much better, this official maintained, for the school to have its own women, with the proper class standing, available for the social needs of the men (Gordon, 1977).

It is as hard in the 20th century as in the 19th to find administrators, trustees, and faculty who advocate the admission of women in terms of their own needs or their right to the best education the country has to offer.

As in the 19th century, such attitudes affect women's campus experiences. Today's college men prefer attending schools where there are women, but they are uncomfortable with gender equality. We are seeing violence against women on campus 20 years after affirmative action began because once again gender roles are in flux, and many feel threatened.

Current research on college students suggests that

men accept and even like aspiring "career women." They expect college women to be committed to their work and would be bored, so they say, by women who wanted to be traditional homemakers. And yet, when the questions get more subtle, the answers reveal ambivalence, hostility, and aggression toward the "career women" who inhabit today's campuses. Male students want their girlfriends and future wives to have demanding careers, but to put those jobs aside at short notice to serve the needs of boyfriends, husbands, and eventually, children. They cannot imagine being married to someone who might put her professional needs ahead of theirs, or who might expect her husband to share domestic work and child-rearing. Recent research indicates that college women change career goals to please the men in their lives (Holland & Eisenhart, 1990).

This ambiguity spills over into the peer and courting relationships between college students—into decisions about who pays for what on a date, decisions or nondecisions about sexual activity, about how the couple spends time together, and whose work takes precedence (Komarovsky, 1976). And it spills over into the darker side of college life today—into the date rapes, the assaults, the pornographic graffiti, the verbal attacks, the harassing phone calls, the denigration of women studies' courses, and the obsessive fears of feminist or gay-rights groups.

History gives us a way of putting this into perspective. The last time there was an appreciable amount of violence and harassment of women students occurred during another era when gender roles were in transition, and the needs of men and women appeared then, as today, to be opposed. Such changes are very threatening and strike at the core of people's expectations—particularly young people, who are still experimenting with their cultural identities.

The mass murder in Montreal represents the murderer's belief that women threaten men's access to professional education and success—a belief common among young men today.

What can be done? As educators, we can fashion a curriculum in which gender relations are widely and intelligently discussed. We can encourage young women to develop a sense of community with each other and a commitment to feminism, strategies that proved successful in the early 20th century. And we can work to ensure that colleges and universities exemplify principles of equality and respect and do not fear social change.

NOTES

1. In 1885, a University of California newspaper published what was meant to be a humorous skit about a meeting of the Glee Club, which shows similar confusion and tension. Club members were planning the annual concert and party, when "Miss N" remarked: "The young ladies must have escorts. Last term several of the young ladies were left unasked, and others were asked so late that they did not have time to make their cakes nor even to fix up pretty." Her trivial remark raised a complex issue. How should men treat female club members? As equals, with a common interest in music? As such, they surely had the right to attend the club's parties. And yet, they were "young ladies" who needed escorts and who baked cakes for the parties.

Miss N and a male club member made up a list of the women members and assigned an escort to each. Unaccustomed to having their objects of romantic attention selected for them, most of the men balked at taking their appointed partner to the party. The women were equally uncertain. Wanting to attend the party, but unwilling to be humiliated, they discussed holding a separate event. Lack of unity prevented the women from holding their own party, because those invited by men wanted to go with them. In the end, the arranged solution failed, and women club members without escorts missed the party again. ("The Old Story," The Occident, 15 May 1985, 135-7).

2. One of the most interesting stories comes not from campus archives at all, but from the pages of *The Ladies Home Journal*, the first American magazine to sell more than a million copies.

"When Men Come In" deals with the lives of two women professionals at a large private midwestern university noted for its emphasis on intellectual achievement. The narrator is a professional. She and her housemate, a doctor, have taken on the job of mentoring Estelle, a young and beautiful graduate student. Estelle has fallen in love and is torn between following the older women's example and pursuing a career or marrying her young man.

The narrator and the doctor want Estelle to follow in their footsteps. Yet they are beginning to regret the choices they made and to yearn for more traditional roles. At this point, the narrator's old love, whose proposal she rejected ten years ago to enter academic life, reappears on the scene—it is his younger brother who is involved with Estelle.

Ultimately, everyone finds the idea of women having careers absurd and ridiculous, and everyone gets married. In one of the final scenes, the narrator tells her fiance that she regrets having wasted ten years of her life doing something so foolish as earning a doctorate and teaching.

This extraordinary story came from the pen of Maude Radford, an 1896 graduate of the University of Chicago, whose student career was openly feminist, and whose mentors included some of the most prominent women academics in the country. (Maude L. Radford, "When Men Come In," *The Ladies' Home Journal,* March, April, May 1908.)

REFERENCES

Anderson, Olive San Louis. (1878). *An American girl and her four years in a boys' college.* New York: D. Appleton.

Angell, James B. (1881). Coeducation at Michigan University. *Pennsylvania School Journal, 29,* 281.

Angell, James B. (1904). Coeducation in relation to other types of college Education for women, *Proceedings of the National Education Association ,* 548-549. *The Blue and Gold.* (1893, 1900, 1905). University of California.

The Blue and Gold. (1893, 1900, 1905) University of California.

Clarke, Edward M. (1873). *Sex in education or a fair chance for the girls,* Boston: J. R. Osgood.

Cookingham, Mary E. (1984a). Combining marriage, motherhood, and jobs before World War II: Women college graduates, Classes of 1905-1935. *Journal of Family History, 9* (Summer), 349-364.

Cookingham, Mary E. (1984b). "Working after childbearing in modern America." *Journal of Interdisciplinary History, 14* (Spring), 773-792.
Cott, Nancy F. (1987). *The grounding of modern feminism.* New Haven: Yale University Press.

The Daily Californian. (1918, February 8).

Glazer, Penina Migdal, Slater & Miriam, (1987). *Unequal colleagues: The entrance of women into the professions, 1890-1940.* New Brunswick: Rutgers University Press.

Gordon, Lynn D. (1977) Interview with Bowdoin College official (1977). Brunswick, Maine.

Gordon, Lynn D. (1990). *Gender and higher education in the progressive era.* New Haven: Yale University Press.

Hall, G. Stanley. (1906). The question of co-education. *Munsey's Magazine, 34* (February), 588-592.

Hoffman, Nancy. (Ed.). (1979). *Woman's true profession: Voices from the history of teaching.* New York: The Feminist Press.

Holland, Dorothy C., & Eisenhart, Margaret A. (1990). *Educated in romance: Women, achievement, and college culture.* Chicago: University of Chicago Press.

Kerber, Linda K. (1980). *Women of the republic: Intellect and ideology in revolutionary America,.* Chapel Hill: University of North Carolina Press.

Komarovsky, Mirra. (1976). *Dilemmas of masculinity,.* New York: Norton.

Komarovsky, Mirra. (1985). *Women in college: Shaping new feminine identities.* New York: Basic Books.

Lever, Janet, & Schwartz, Pepper. (1971). *Women at Yale: Liberating a college campus.* Indianapolis: Bobbs-Merrill.

Minorities and higher education. (1989). *Thought and Action, 5* (Fall); 5-47.

Newcomer, Mabel. (1959). *A century of higher education for American women.* New York: Harper Brothers.

Riley, Zoe. (1907, February). The way of a sister. *The Occident,* 52.

Smith-Rosenberg, Carroll. (1985). *Disorderly conduct: Visions of gender in Victorian America,.* New York: Alfred Knopf.

Symposium on Sexual Harassment. (1989). *Thought and Action, 5* (Spring); 17-52.

Thompson, Kathleen. (1903) The parting paths. (12 May). *The Occident,* 44.

Woody, Thomas. (1929). *A history of women's education in the United States* (2 vols.). New York: Science Press.

PART II

WHAT IS SEXUAL HARASSMENT AND HOW FREQUENTLY DOES IT OCCUR?

3

DEFINITIONS OF SEXUAL HARASSMENT

by Louise F. Fitzgerald

The unnamed should not be taken for the nonexistent.
—MacKinnon, 1979

One of the most persistent problems in the sexual harassment literature has been the absence of a widely agreed-upon definition of the concept, a definition broad enough to comprehend the variety of experiences to which the term refers, and yet specific enough to be of practical use. As MacKinnon (1979) notes, "It is not surprising. . . that women would not complain of an experience for which there (was) no name. Until 1976, lacking a term to express it, sexual harassment was literally unspeakable, which made a generalized, shared and social definition of it inaccessible" (p. 27). She notes that Working Women United Institute appears to have been the first to use the term, in connection with the case of Carmita Wood. Wood, in 1975, was one of the first women to seek unemployment compensation after leaving a job due to the sexual advances of her superior (*In re Carmita Wood*, 1975). It was also advanced at about the same time by the 1976 Cambridge-based Alliance Against Sexual Coercion and by Brodsky (1976).

The Project on the Status and Education of Women (1978) was among the first to apply the concept to higher education. Referring to sexual harassment as a "hidden issue", it produced a list of various categories of behavior that women students and employees had found objectionable. Till (1980) derived five categories of harassment from a content analysis of incidents described by students who responded to

An earlier version of this chapter appeared in *Sexual Harassment in Higher Education: Concepts and Issues* (pp. 9-15). Washington, DC: NEA.

his national survey, and Phyllis Franklin and her colleagues (Franklin, Moglin, Zatlin-Boring, & Angress, 1981) published the first, and still one of the best, scholarly discussions of sexual harassment in the academy.

Despite the explosion of interest, research, and litigation that has marked the decade since these discussions first appeared, MacKinnon's "generalized, shared and social definition" remains beyond our reach. This chapter analyzes legal and institutional definitions of sexual harassment in higher education, and examines research bearing on factors that inhibit consensus in this area.

LEGAL DEFINITIONS

The legal theory of sexual harassment was first articulated in 1979 by Catherine MacKinnon in her influential work, *Sexual Harassment of Working Women*. MacKinnon argued that sexual harassment is a version of sex discrimination (i.e., it is overwhelmingly aimed at women, who would not be at risk if it were not for their sex) and thus is prohibited under Title VII of the Civil Rights Act, which prohibits discrimination in employment.

In 1980, the Equal Employment Opportunity Commission (EEOC) issued its Interim Interpretive Guidelines on Sex Discrimination, which offered the first formal legal definition of sexual harassment. According to EEOC, "Unwelcome sexual advances, requests for sexual favors, and other verbal or physical conduct of a sexual nature constitute sexual harassment when:

1. submission to such conduct is made either explicitly or implicitly a term or condition of an individual's employment;

2. submission to or rejection of such conduct by an individual is used as the basis for employment decisions affecting such individual; or

3. such conduct has the purpose or effect of substantially interfering with an individual's work performance or creating an intimidating, hostile or offensive working environment" (EEOC, 1980).

The EEOC Guidelines suggest, then, that sexual harassment is of two general types: (1) *quid pro quo*, which occurs when an attempt is made to coerce an individual into sexual cooperation by promises of rewards or threats of punishment; and (2) the creation of a *hostile environment*, one which is pervaded by offensive, degrading or intimidating behavior, but where explicit benefits are not conditioned on sexual cooperation. This distinction was first articulated by MacKinnon, who referred to the second type as *conditions of work.*

These definitions and guidelines arose in the employment context and, although defining and prohibiting the harassment of women who work in the academic environment, did not speak directly to the situation of students. Contemporaneously with these developments, however, there arose a similar interpretation of Title IX of the Education Amendments of 1972. Although it has not yet published its own definition, the Office for Civil Rights (OCR), the primary enforcement agency for Title IX, has acknowledged that "Sexual harassment of students is a real and increasingly visible problem of serious consequences in higher education....Academic institutions must address the problem in order to ensure all students a just and equal learning opportunity" (OCR, 1984). In practice, educational institutions have generally adopted the EEOC Guidelines and extended them to include the situation of students.

INSTITUTIONAL DEFINITIONS

In the decade or so since the legal definition of sexual harassment was first advanced, and particularly since sexual harassment was recognized by the courts as a cause of action under Title IX (*Alexander v. Yale*, 1980), the majority of colleges and universities have developed institutional definitions to guide their policy in this area. In addition, professional and regulatory bodies have issued guidelines for institutions to consider when making decisions about what constitutes sexual harassment in a university setting. Thus, the National Advisory Council on Women's Educational Programs prohibits "the use of authority to emphasize the sexuality or sexual identity of a student in a manner which prevents or impairs that student's full enjoyment of educational benefits, climate or opportunities" (in Till, 1980). The Project on the Status and Education of Women (1978) of the Association of American Colleges and Universities identified the following set of behaviors as objectionable:

- verbal harassment or abuse
- subtle pressure for sexual activity
- sexist remarks about a woman's clothing, body, or sexual activities
- unnecessary touching, patting or pinching
- leering or ogling at a woman's body
- demanding sexual favors accompanied by implied or overt threats concerning one's job, grades, letters of recommendation, etc.
- physical assault

Reflecting on this list of behaviors, Franklin et al. (1981) articulated an important distinction often ignored in discussions of harassment. They noted: "For many the most difficult kind of behavior included as a form of sexual harassment (is) verbal harassment or abuse, by which students often mean pejorative (sexist or stereotyped) assumptions made about women as a group in classrooms or other learning environments by persons in positions of authority. Such behavior seems qualitatively different from (other forms of harassment). It is this kind of behavior that we are designating *gender harassment*. We believe that such a distinction is helpful because it clarifies the dual nature of the problem and so can simplify the development of a code and grievance procedure."

This distinction is an important one. Many institutions limit their definitions to the clearly *sexual,* which obscures the fact that most harassment has little to do with erotic concerns and is not designed to elicit sexual cooperation but to insult, deride, and degrade women. Similar to racial harassment in its purpose and practice, gender harassment has been part of academic life for women since they first won reluctant admittance to the university. Anderson and Zinsser (1988) recount the experiences of the first women medical students at the University of Edinbugh in 1870. Seeking to enter the required course in anatomy "(they) found their way blocked by male students, who barricaded the doors to the hall, threw mud at the women, and shouted obscenities. When the women made their way into the hall, they found their male classmates had placed a sheep in the room, explaining that they understood that now 'inferior animals' were no longer to be excluded from the classroom" (p. 189). Over a century later, in 1980, a woman geographer recalls her graduate school experiences: "Sexual harassment was a way of life. Field trips—a tradition for geographers—were abandoned because women were considered contaminants. One memorable instructor (whose course was required of all graduate students) regularly informed each new generation of graduate students that women are not good for much of anything but sexual exercises. He enjoyed going into graphic description of the trials and tribulations of a journey taken with a group of students during which one female experienced the onset of menstruation. 'Blood all over the damn place,' our professor told the class, 'had to hike miles out of the canyon to find wadding to stuff in her crotch'" (Till, 1980, p. 9). Although the majority of gender harassment is somewhat less dramatic, these examples make clear the nature of the hostility that women often experience even now in their pursuit of higher education. Thus, it is important that institutional definitions be written in a way that does not ignore this very widespread form of harassment.

Two very influential professional statements on sexual harassment are those of the National Education Association (NEA) and the American Association of University Professors (AAUP). The National Education Association (1991) has issued a strong condemnation of sexual harassment in higher education (NEA, 1991). In addition, NEA encourages its affiliates and institutions of higher education to include in their harassment definitions a statement to the effect that sexual relationships between a faculty member and a student for whom he [1] has any teaching or supervisory responsibility are unprofessional. The AAUP also cautions faculty members against entering into romantic or sexual relationships with their students.

The AAUP recently revised its guidelines on this issue, and offered this model definition, "Sexual advances, requests for sexual favors, and other conduct of a sexual nature constitute sexual harassment when:

1. Any such proposals are made under circumstances implying that one's response might affect such academic or personnel decisions as are subject to the influence of the person making such proposals; or

2. Such conduct is repeated or is so offensive that it substantially contributes to an unprofessional academic or work environment or interferes with required tasks, career opportunities, or learning; or

3. Such conduct is abusive of others and creates or implies a discriminatory hostility toward their personal or professional interests because of their sex." (AAUP, 1990, p. 42)

When examining definitions and policies developed by educational institutions around the country, one is struck by their variability. Although the legal definitions of harassment, as stated by EEOC and further articulated by case law, prohibit each of the three forms of harassment—*quid pro quo*, as well as both forms of hostile environment, i.e., *gender harassment* and *unwanted sexual approaches*—institutional definitions vary in scope from campus to campus. Although the model definition parallels the EEOC Guidelines, some colleges restrict their definitions to *quid pro quo* harassment, and are less likely to prohibit hostile environment forms. A small but growing number follow the lead of NEA and AAUP and extend prohibitions against harassment to include so-called consensual romantic relations between faculty and students, and a similarly small number—usually private colleges, especially those with religious affiliations—have no specific definition or policy at all. The following section examines some of the factors that inhibit consensus in this area.

FACTORS AFFECTING DEFINITIONS

Research in the behavioral sciences documents extensive variability in individual perceptions and definitions of harassment. Fitzgerald and Ormerod (1991) found that, although faculty and students agreed in their evaluation of harassing behaviors, considerable differences in such evaluations existed between men and women. Both sexes agreed that *quid pro quo* behaviors constituted harassment. However, the men were significantly less likely to evaluate hostile environment behaviors (e.g., sexist or degrading comments, sexual jokes, "come on's ") as harassing. Other studies confirm that women are consistently more likely than men to view such behavior as harassment (Kenig & Ryan, 1986), as offensive (Padgitt & Padgitt, 1986), or both.

A second factor that has been shown to affect perceptions of harassment is initiator status. In studies of the workplace, individuals are much more likely to define an incident as harassing if the harasser has formal, supervisory authority and is thus presumably able to back up his demands with some form of action. Students, of course, always have less power than their professors. Still, echoes of this attributional process can be found in arguments defending sexual relationships between faculty members and students they do not directly supervise, or with graduate students who are older and thus presumably more able to "know what they are doing" (see Fitzgerald, Gold, Ormerod, & Weitzman, 1988, for data on this point).

Although *quid pro quo* behaviors are almost universally accepted as sexual harassment, even these can be moderated by "seductive" behavior on the part of the female student (Reilly, Carpenter, Dull, & Bartlett, 1982). Similarly, individuals are much less likely to consider a behavior harassing if those involved had been dating or formerly had a romantic relationship. Although experience and common sense both suggest that it is in just such situations (e.g., the aftermath of a romantic breakup) that harassment can be most destructive, the cultural norm that female sexual consent—once given—cannot be withdrawn operates to cloud both individual and institutional judgment in this area.

In short, the variation in institutional definitions of sexual harassment parallels the vagaries of individual perceptions—perceptions that are powerfully influenced by cultural stereotypes about appropriate behavior between the sexes, the nature of romantic relationships, women, and sexuality. Like individuals, most institutions define *quid pro quo* behaviors as sexually harassing, but are often careful to specify that the behavior must be *unwanted*, suggesting that some sexual threats and coercion *are* wanted or desired by their recipients. Similarly, although women as a group agree that gender harassment is offensive and degrading, most institutional definitions state that such behavior must "substantially" interfere with performance or the environment. This suggests that there may be an "acceptable" level of interference (see also the EEOC Interpretive Guidelines). Finally, the general omission of consensual sexual relationships from university definitions and policies reflects academic discomfort and reluctance to interfere in this supposedly private arena. The result is a patchwork of differing definitions and policies reflective mostly of the idiosyncratic history and consciousness of each institution.

SUMMARY

In recent years, definitions of sexual harassment have been articulated under the law and in the policy and procedures of most American colleges and universities. Of the two major forms of sexual harassment, sexual coercion (*quid pro quo*) is widely prohibited by academic institutions. The behaviors that constitute hostile environment harassment are somewhat less widely proscribed. Complicating these definitions—and their acceptance by the academic community—are gender differences in perceptions and definitions, a narrow construction of the professor's zone of influence and power, and historical and cultural mythology concerning women's responsibility for male sexual behavior.

As Crocker (1983) has noted, "Definitions...are important because they can educate the community and promote discussion and conscientious evaluation of behavior and

experience. Students learn that certain experiences are official-
ly recognized as wrong and punishable; professors are put on
notice about behaviors that constitute sexual harassment; and
administrators shape their understanding of the problem in a
way that directs their actions on students' inquiries and complaints" (p. 697). She notes that a good definition contains
four elements: the labeling of sexual harassment as sex discrimination; inclusion in the definition of the full range of
harassing behaviors; acknowledgment that harassment pollutes the nature of the academic exchange; and an understanding that sexual harassment reflects the imposition of
unwanted behavior by a person with the power to do so. "By
bearing in mind these four areas, we can devise and incorporate into the fabric of academic life definitions that better
serve the entire community" (Crocker, 1983, p. 707).

POSTSCRIPT

Since this chapter first appeared in 1992, we have
experienced a virtual revolution in our understanding of sexual harassment. Nowhere has this change been more apparent
than in our legal and institutional definitions of this issue and
our knowledge of the factors that influence them. Recent
work by Gelfand, Fitzgerald, and Drasgow (under review)
confirms Fitzgerald and Shullman's (1985) early speculation
that Till's (1980) original five categories can be accounted for
more parsimoniously by only three distinct but related factors:
gender harassment, unwanted sexual attention (both verbal
and physical), and *sexual coercion* (the extortion of sexual
cooperation through bribery or threat, whether subtle or
explicit). Working with three large data sets and confirmatory
factor analytic procedures, this three-factor structure has been
demonstrated to be identical across both setting and target
populations (i.e., employed women and students), as well as
across at least two cultures (the United States and Brazil). As
the investigators note, "It is striking evidence for the stability
and generalizability of the (three factor) model that (it held)
even in a culture whose language (Portuguese) possessed no

words for the concept, at least at the time the study was conducted." They argue that their model provides a definitive answer to the question "What is sexual harassment?", at least from a behavioral perspective.

Gelfand et al. also note the importance of disentangling the behavioral construct of sexual harassment from the legal standard. As Fitzgerald, Swan, and Fisher (in press) have argued, whether a particular behavioral exchange is psychologically harassing (i.e., stressful, noxious) is related to but distinct from the question of whether it constitutes illegal sex discrimination. Gelfand et al. (under review) articulate the relationship of their three-factor behavioral model to current legal formulations, noting that the behavioral construct of sexual coercion is isomorphic with the legal concept of *quid pro quo*, wheras gender harassment and unwanted sexual attention constitute the two ways in which a hostile environment can be manifested. These relationships are shown in Figure 3.1 on the next page.

Finally, it is important to note that the EEOC has recently issued a statement underscoring that *gender harassment*, often considered a less serious form of the problem, is explicitly prohibited in the workplace. EEOC defines this concept as "verbal or physical conduct that denigrates or shows hostility or aversion" (Equal Employment Opportunity Commission, 1993, p. 51269); examples include epithets, slurs, taunts, and gestures, the display or distribution of obscene or pornographic materials; gender-based hazing; and threatening, intimidating or hostile acts. It is unclear at this point how these guidelines will affect the educational context, given the current debate concerning academic freedom and First Amendment concerns and their relationship to issues of gender (and other) equity (Dessayer & Burke, 1991; *Doe v. University of Michigan*, 1989; Hartman, 1993).

NOTE

1 Throughout this chapter, the victim is referred to as she and the harasser as he, both for purposes of simplicity and to reflect the reality that the overwhelming majority of harassment victims are women. This is not to deny that men can be, and occasionally are, harassed, by other men.

Figure 3.1
Behavioral Model

The relationship between a three-factor behavioral model of sexual harassment and legal formulations.

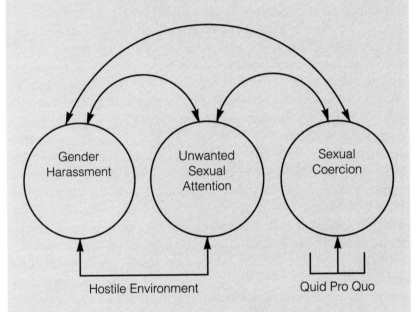

REFERENCES

Alexander v. Yale University, 631 F.2d 178 (2d Cir. 1980).

American Association of University Professors. (1990). Sexual harassment: Suggested policy and procedures for handling complaints. *Academe*, September-October, 42-43.

Anderson, B. S. & Zinsser, J. P. (1988). *A history of their own: Women in Europe from prehistory to the present*. (Vol. 2). New York: Harper & Row.

Brodsky, C. M. (1976). *The harassed worker*. Lexington, MA: Lexington Books.

Crocker, P. L. (1983). An analysis of university definitions of sexual harassment. *Signs,. 8*, 696-707.

Dessayer, R. M., & Burke, A. J. (1991). Leaving them speechless: A critique of speech restrictions on campus. *Harvard Journal of Law and Public Policy, 14*.

Doe v. University of Michigan:, 721 F.Supp. 352,854 (E.D. Michi. 1989).

Equal Employment Opportunity Commission. (1980). Guidelines on discrimination because of sex. *Federal Register, 45*, 74676-74677.

Equal Employment Opportunity Commission. (1993). Proposed harassment guidelines. *Federal Register, 58*, 51266.

Fitzgerald, L. F., Gold, Y., Ormerod, A. J., & Weitzman, L. (1988). Academic harassment: Sex and denial in scholarly garb. *Psychology of Women Quarterly, 12*, 329-340.

Fitzgerald, L. F., & Ormerod, A. J. (1991) . Perceptions of sexual harassment: The effect of gender and context, *Psychology of Women Quarterly, 14*, 281-294.

Fitzgerald, L. F., & Shullman, S. L. (1993) Sexual Harassment: A research analysis and agenda for the 1990s, *Journal of Vocational Behavior, 42*, 5-27.

Fitzgerald, L. F., & Shullman, S. L. (1985). *The development and validation of an objective measure of sexual harassment*. Paper read at meeting of the American Psychological Association, Los Angeles, CA.

Fitzgerald, L. F., Swan, S., & Fisher, K. (in press). Why didn't she just report him?: The psychological and legal implications of women's responses to sexual harassment. *Journal of Social Issues*.

Franklin, P., Moglin, H., Zatling-Boring, P., Moglin, H., Zatling-Boring, P., & Angress, R. (1981). *Sexual and gender harassment in the academy*. New York: Modern Language Association.

Gelfand, J., Fitzgerald, L. F., & Drasgow, F. *The structure of sexual harassment: A confirmatory analysis across cultures and settings* (under review).

Hartman, R. G. (1993),. Hateful expression and first amendment & values. Toward a theory of constitutional constraint on hate speech at colleges and universities after R.A.U. v. St. Paul. *Journal of College and University Law, 19*, 343-371.

Kenig, S., & Ryan, J. (1986). Sex differences in levels of tolerance and attribution of blame for sexual harassment on a university campus. *Sex Roles, 14*, 535-549.

MacKinnon, C.A. (1979), *Sexual harassment of working women.* New Haven, CT: Yale. University Press.

Matsude, N. J, (1989). Public response to racist speech: Considering the victim's story. *Michigan Law Review, 87*, 2320.

National Education Association. (1991). NEA resolution on sexual harassment in higher education. *NEA Higher Education Almanac.* Washington, DC: NEA.

Office for Civil Rights. (1984). *Sexual harassment: It's not academic.* Washington, DC: U.S. Department of Education.

Padgitt, S. C., & Padgitt, J.S. (1986). Cognitive structure of sexual harassment. *Sex Roles, 14*, 9-19.

Project on the Status and Education of Women. (1978). *Sexual harassment: A hidden issue.* Washington, DC: Association of American Colleges and Universities.

Reilly, T., Carpenter, S., Dull, V., & Bartlett, K. (1982). The factorial survey: An approach to defining sexual harassment on campus. *Journal of Social Issues, 38*, 99-109.

Till, F. J. (1980). *Sexual harassment: A report on the sexual harassment of students.* Washington, D.C.: National Advisory Council on Women's Educational Programs.

4

THE PREVALENCE OF SEXUAL HARASSMENT

by Louise F. Fitzgerald

On occasion, in certain forms, it appeared as romance: the naive student swept into bed by her brilliant professor. . . . Charlotte Bronte wrote about it more than a hundred years ago; in the popular confessions magazines, authors write about it still. In functional form, it remains the stuff that fantasies are made of, fantasies that reflect and reinforce the tendency of our society to limit the definition of women to the sexual and domestic spheres and to soften. . . the linking of sexual dominance with the powerful and of sexual submission with the powerless. —Franklin et al., 1981

How widespread is sexual harassment in the university? A considerable amount of research has attempted to examine this issue, addressing such questions as: How extensive is the problem? What types of harassment are experienced most frequently? Who is most likely to be harassed, and so forth. Despite the numerous studies conducted over the last decade, there are still no good answers to these questions. The most commonly cited figure is 30% (Dziech & Weiner, 1990; Rubin & Borgers, 1990). But, reported frequencies vary depending upon how the questions are framed, the nature of the student sample—graduate or undergraduate—and whether the researcher actually uses the term *sexual harassment* to label the behaviors being studied.

SEXUAL HARASSMENT OF STUDENTS

In the first published survey of the sexual harassment of students, Benson and Thomson (1982) studied the experi-

An earlier version of this chapter appeared in *Sexual Harassment in Higher Education: Concepts and Issues* (pp. 16-23). Washington, DC: NEA, 1992.

ences of 269 randomly selected seniors at the University of California, Berkeley. They reported that nearly one in three had experienced some form of harassment from professors over the course of their college careers. In a finding that was to be replicated many times, these investigators reported that sexual bribery and coercion (the *quid pro quo* form of harassment) were relatively infrequent. Rather, unwanted seductive behavior was much more common.

In the wake of this initial study followed a series of conceptually similar, though methodologically diverse, investigations. Wilson and Kraus (1983) reported that 33% of the female students in their survey of East Carolina University reported being sexually harassed by male teachers. Once again, the *quid pro quo* behaviors were experienced less frequently than the other forms. Maihoff and Forrest (1983) found that 25% of the female students in their Michigan State survey reported at least one incident of sexual harassment. Other studies reported similar (Cammaert, 1985), as well as lower (Metha & Nigg, 1982; Allen & Okawa, 1987) and higher (Schneider, 1987) frequencies.

Thus, although many institutions have undertaken self-studies, as well as attempted to determine how various constituencies (e.g., students, professors) define harassment, the differing definitions and methodologies have made it difficult to compare results across studies and achieve some clarity concerning base rate frequencies. In the first edition of their book, Dziech and Weiner (1984) called for the development of a standardized survey instrument that individual campuses could use to measure frequency so that a national profile could be drawn. Although such national data are still unavailable, a standardized instrument was developed recently and made available for general use (Fitzgerald et al., 1988), along with the results of a large-scale study involving two major universities and over 2,000 students.

The Sexual Experiences Questionnaire (SEQ) is a 28-item inventory based on the five types of harassment identified by Till (1980) from his qualitative survey of colleges and universities around the country. The SEQ contains multiple questions addressing Till's five general areas. All questions are written in behavioral terms, and the words *sexual harassment* do not appear until the end of the questionnaire. It thus avoids the necessity for the respondent to make a subjective judgment as to whether or not she has been harassed before she can respond (an important consideration given the lack of agreement concerning exactly what the term sexual harassment encompasses). The instrument was piloted on a sample of over 400 students, and subjected to various analyses to determine its reliability and validity; a full report of this research is available in Fitzgerald et al. (1988). It was then used in a large-scale study of two major universities, one in the midwest and the other on the west coast. Data were collected on both male and female participants as well as on undergraduate and graduate students. In all, over 2,000 students participated in the study, making it the largest and most representative investigation of academic harassment conducted to date.

The results of this investigation indicate that harassment is much more widespread than had been previously thought. Approximately 50% of the women at one university, and nearly 76% of the women at the other, answered at least one of the questions in the affirmative direction, indicating that they had experienced some form of harassing behavior during their college careers. As might be expected, the most frequently reported situations were those involving gender harassment or seductive behavior. Of the 10 most frequently reported, all were of this variety. However, on average, approximately nine percent (or nearly one in 10) of the women had been directly propositioned by a professor or instructor, and five percent of the total sample had been subtly bribed for sexual cooperation. With respect to physical advances, nearly nine percent had experienced unwanted attempts to touch or fondle them, and a large percentage of these experiences were described as forceful in nature. At one university, nearly 30% of the graduate student respondents had received unwanted sexual attention from professors, and almost 15% had been directly propositioned. Despite these dramatic numbers, less than eight percent of the total female sample indicated—in answer to a separate question—that they had been sexually harassed, a result testifying to the importance of using neutral behavioral terminology when attempting to collect data on this problem. There were no clear patterns of institutional differences, nor of differences due to graduate or undergraduate status. This suggests that although there are clear and reliable differences in the base rates of different types of harassment—gender harassment is by far the most common, unwanted seductive behavior, touching or fondling being second, and *quid pro quo* the least frequent—institutions will need to conduct self-studies to determine where their most serious problems lie (for example, graduate or undergraduate students, disciplinary or departmental differences, and so forth).

Our data, and that of other researchers, make very clear that harassment has a "real world" impact on women's educational careers. On a separate section of the questionnaire, five percent of our female respondents indicated that they had dropped a course to avoid such situations. And, nearly 20% noted that they had avoided taking a course for this reason. Despite this interference with their academic endeavors, very few of the women (3%) attempted to report the harassing situation. Many of the students who had been harassed indicated that they felt that they would not be believed, or that they had not wanted to cause trouble and/or be labeled as troublemakers. A few noted that they had dealt with the situation themselves, or had not felt it was serious enough to report. Fitzgerald, Gold, and Brock (1991) discuss this tendency for students to avoid engaging the institution on this issue, or even to simply respond assertively. Interestingly, our data demonstrated that women undergraduates are much more likely to recommend and endorse assertive responses *for other women* than they are to actually make such responses themselves. Ormerod (1991) offers further experimental data linking this reluctance to a fear of negative consequences from the institution. The need for institutions to design their grievance procedures in such a way that victims are encouraged to come forward has been underscored by recent legal decisions (e.g., *Meritor Savings Bank, FSB v. Vinson,* 1986).

Summary

Although national data are still unavailable, the best information currently suggests that the frequently cited 30% incidence rate may be a serious underestimate of the number of women who are harassed during their college or university careers. In particular, the widespread nature of gender harassment and intrusive sexual attention that is not explicitly coercive in nature is typically underestimated and trivialized despite its very real and damaging effects on women's lives (Koss, 1990). Although exceptions may exist, there is no reason to believe *a priori* that any particular institution, type of institution, or academic discipline is exempt from the problem. Informal observation, some theory, and folklore all suggest that women may be most at risk in the traditionally male disciplines where their presence is still somewhat of a rarity. Reliable data are sparse on this point but the hypothesis is logical, and what information does currently exist supports it. Institutions are strongly encouraged to undertake their own self-studies to determine the nature and extent of the problem, as well as to examine student awareness and the perceived effectiveness of the sexual harassment policies and procedures on their campuses. It is only then that any institution can begin to develop a realistic assessment of its unique problems and weaknesses in this area.

EXPERIENCES OF FEMALE FACULTY

Long before sexual harassment was identified as a problem for students in higher education, it had been discussed by social scientists (Gutek, 1985) and legal scholars (MacKinnon, 1979) as a serious problem for women in the workplace. In what is clearly the largest and probably the most well-known study conducted so far, the U.S. Merit Systems Protection Board (1981) investigated harassment in the federal workplace and found that 42% of all female employees reported being sexually harassed. Merit Systems noted that many incidents occurred repeatedly, were of long duration, and had a sizable practical impact, costing the government an estimated minimum of $189 million over the two-year period covered by the study. When explicit behaviors were examined, 33% of the women reported receiving unwanted sexual remarks, 28% reported suggestive looks, and 26% reported being deliberately touched. These behaviors were classified as less severe forms of harassment. When more severe incidents were examined, 15% of the women reported experiencing pressure for dates, 9% reported being directly pressured for sexual favors, and 9% had received unwanted letters and telephone calls. One percent of the sample had experienced actual or attempted rape or assault. Merit Systems repeated their study in 1987 and reported essentially identical results (U.S. Merit Systems Protection Board, 1987).

The most extensive study of the civilian workplace was conducted by Gutek (1985). Based on telephone interviews generated through random digit dialing procedures, Gutek reported that 53% of her women subjects had experienced at least one incident that they considered harassing during their working lives, including insulting comments (19.8 %); insulting looks and gestures (15.4 %); sexual touching (24.2 %); socializing expected as part of the job (10.9 %); and expected sexual activity (7.6 %). The actual incidence rates for these behaviors were considerably higher, as this discussion utilizes figures only for those behaviors that the women considered to be harassing. Although the differences between the Gutek and Merit Systems methodology make comparisons difficult, their overall estimates are fairly comparable, i.e., approximately half the female workforce has been sexually harassed.

Despite these figures, it is only recently that any attention has been given to the academic workplace and the ways that harassment affects the women faculty who work there. In one of the few studies of this kind, our research group (Fitzgerald et al., 1988) examined the experiences of 300 women faculty, administrators, and staff who were employed at a medium-sized public university in the midwest. Using an adaptation of the SEQ described above, we found that large numbers of these women reported patterns of experiences that met the legal definition of sexual harassment.

Over half the 61 women faculty and 75% of the 61 female administrators in our sample had experienced some form of gender harassment in the academic workplace. Specific behaviors they reported included the telling of suggestive stories and offensive jokes, crude sexual remarks, seductive comments, nonverbal harassment such as staring, leering or ogling, the use or distribution of sexist material or pornography, a pattern of sexist remarks about women, and—most frequently—simply being treated less well because they were women.

In addition, over 20% of the women professors—one in five—and nearly one in three of the administrators reported being the object of unwanted sexual advances, including persistent requests for dates, repeated attempts to establish a sexual relationship, unwanted discussion of personal or sexual matters, and unwanted sexual attention. Over 25% of the administrators reported receiving outright sexual propositions. Approximately half of these women reported being physically touched or handled at work in ways that made them uncomfortable, and a substantial minority of these incidents were persistent or forceful in nature. Finally, although only a small number of women professors reported *quid pro quo* harassment, over 13% of the women administrators reported being subtly or directly bribed to be sexually cooperative. Nearly 10% noted that they had received subtle threats. And eight percent had experienced actual negative consequences for refusing to cooperate sexually.

Although these data may be the most detailed currently available, subsequent research has demonstrated that they are in no way unique. In a study of academic and nonacademic employees at Central Michigan University, Goodwin, Roscoe, Rose, and Repp (1989) reported that 39% of the women reported experiencing some form of sexually harassing behavior that made them uncomfortable. The most frequent experiences were sexist behaviors, sexual comments and body language, although 18% of the women also reported physical advances. Bandy (1989) studied faculty, staff and academic professional women at Southern Illinois University and reported that approximately one-third of each group had experienced sexual harassment during the two-year period covered by the study. Although rates did not differ substantially among the three groups, women working in nontraditional areas were considerably more likely to have been harassed.

WHO HARASSES WOMEN FACULTY?

Studies of harassment generally note that it has to do with the abuse of power, and either assume or assert that harassers are individuals with more power than their victims, although studies of the general workplace indicate that much harassment can be traced to peers or colleagues. In an important paper, Katherine Benson (1984) argued that it is also possible for the harasser to have less formal (achieved) power than his victim, a situation she refers to as contrapower harassment. She notes that although professors have more formal power than students, men in American society have considerably more power than women simply by virtue of being men. This is a situation that can equalize if not reverse the power differential between female professors and male students. Such an argument suggests that female academics may be at risk of harassment not only from institutional superiors and colleagues, but also from their male students. A small but important body of research demonstrates that this is indeed the case (see, for example, Chapter 7 of this volume).

In 1989, Elizabeth Grauerholz studied the women faculty at Purdue University and found that nearly half of her sample reported having been sexually harassed by one or more of their male students. These incidents ranged from the merely annoying (sexist or sexual comments) to the outrageous (e.g., sexual propositions, bribery). Seventeen percent of these women professors had received obscene phone calls from male students, and one respondent had been raped. In addition, open-ended questions elicited a wide range of other, sometimes bizarre and frightening, experiences "such as defacing the professor's office door or spray-painting obscenities on the instructor's automobile. . . students shouting obscenities and insults at the professor while she was walking, or in one case, while in her office working. One woman described being chased physically in her office and then to her car by a student" (pp. 789-794). McKinney (1990) provides additional evidence of faculty members harassed by students.

CAN MEN BE SEXUALLY HARASSED?

Although sexual harassment is generally perceived as a problem for women, some have suggested that it may also be an issue for men as well. The available research base suggests that this is unlikely to be so. Metha and Nigg (1983) report that only five percent of male respondents at their university reported being sexually harassed. Reilly, Lott and Gallogly (1986) found the percentages of men reporting harassment at the University of Rhode Island to be quite low. Similarly, in the Fitzgerald et al. (1988) study, harassing behavior directed at men was virtually nonexistent. The one exception to this was in the area of gender harassment, and it was unclear from the data whether the men experienced situations such as suggestive stories or jokes as inappropriate or harassing.

Although it is clearly possible for male students to be harassed [see, for example, *Korf v. Ball State University* (1984), where a male professor was discharged for sexually exploiting several male students], it is also clear that this is generally unlikely to happen and that harassment is overwhelmingly a female problem. University affirmative action officers note an increase in male complaints in the past year or so (Cowan, 1991); however, such complaints still represent only a tiny fraction of those received by university offices. A complicating factor here is the stigma often associated with homosexuality, which may serve to inhibit men from coming forward. (As in the more general case of female victims, harassers of male students are almost universally men as well.) Although it is critical for institutions to ensure that all students are protected from sexual exploitation, it is clear by now that harassment is not an equal opportunity phenomenon. This fact has important implications for institutional programming in this area.

It is instructive here to keep in mind Mills's (1959) distinction between private troubles and public issues. Hoffman

(1986) reminds us of this when she writes: "Private troubles occur when isolated events cause personal difficulties for individuals—they are the vicissitudes of individual biographies, related peripherally at best to the location of the individual in the social structure. Public issues, on the other hand, are structurally induced problems affecting large numbers of individuals in particular social locations. Since they are the consequences on individual lives of the institutional arrangements within which individuals live, they are not amenable to individual solution. . . . The sexual harassment of men by women is a private trouble, that of women by men a public issue" (p. 110).

Summary

For women, the academy is rarely an ivory tower; rather, it is a frequently hostile and sometimes violent environment. Reskin (1990) has noted that Western universities were founded by European men to further their intellectual endeavors and those of their (male) students; women, to this day, are outsiders to some degree. It should go without saying that this state of affairs is not generally intentional, but rather the historical outcome of a system that has expanded to include the presence of women without many of the normative, psychological or structural changes that would allow their full integration. The exploitation of and hostility towards women that are documented here and elsewhere are the most dramatic forms of a marginality that is still, too often, rationalized or ignored.

POSTSCRIPT

Although the explosion of interest in sexual harassment in the last few years has led to several important theoretical advances (see, e.g., Tinsley & Stockdale, 1993, and Fitzgerald, in press, for reviews), little in the way of new or more definitive prevalence data has so far appeared. Several methodological advances have been reported, however, and the first formal outcome data have recently appeared (Kilpatrick, 1992; Saunders, 1992).

With respect to methodology, the *Sexual Experiences Questionnaire (SEQ)* has recently been revised (Fitzgerald, Drasgow & Gelfand, 1993; see also Fitzgerald, Hulin, & Drasgow, in press, and Fitzgerald & Shullman, 1993) to reflect the three-factor structure of sexual harassment proposed by Gelfand, Fitzgerald, and Drasgow (under review). Revisions include the substitution of a 5-point Likert formant for the former dichotomous response scale, thus improving the psychometric characteristics of the scale and allowing for the calculation of subscale scores. It is now possible to assign continuous scale scores to *individuals* with respect to the three types of harassment, where as before it was only possible to assess the incidence of harassment in *environments* or, at most, the lifetime prevalence of harassment of individuals, measured as a dichotomous variable. This rescaling greatly improves the SEQ's sensitivity of measurement and should allow for a much finer-grained examination of the relationship between the experience of sexual harassment and its antecedents and consequences.

With respect to outcome date, Kilpatrick (1992) has recently reported the first formal data concerning the relationship between sexual harassment and psychological injury. In a nationally representative sample of 3,020 women surveyed through a telephone interview procedure, he found that women suffering from PTSD and depression were more likely to have been sexually harassed than women without such symptoms. Although Gutek and Koss (1993) have noted that these results are still preliminary in nature, they emphasize that if the initial patterns of results hold, they implicate sexual harassment in a variety of psychological and health-related problems encountered by women. These results are particularly important as they are the first to be collected on samples other than self-identified victims. As with nost current research, however, these results apply to employed women and their applicability to undergraduate and graduate students in the university environment remain to be demonstrated. Large-scale prevalence and outcome studies in nationally representative samples of students continue to be badly needed.

REFERENCES

Allen, D., & Okawa, J. B. (1987). A counseling center looks at sexual harassment. *Journal of the National Association for Women Deans, Administrators, and Counselors, 51*, 9-16.

Bandy, N. (1989). *Relationships between male and female employees at Southern Illinois University.* Unpublished doctoral dissertation, Southern Illinois University, Carbondale, IL.

Benson, K. (1984). Comment on Crocker's "An analysis of university definitions of sexual harassment." *Signs, 9*, 516-579.

Benson, K. J., & Thomson, G. E. (1982). Sexual harassment on a university campus: The confluence of authority relations, sexual interest and gender stratification. *Social Problems, 29*, 236-251.

Cammaert, L. P. (1985). How widespread is sexual harassment on campus? *International Journal of Women's Studies, 8*, 388-397.

Cowan, L. (1991). Personal communication. Nonacademic Affirmative Action Office, University of Illinois, Champaign, IL.

Dziech, B. W., & Weiner, L. (1984). *The lecherous professor: Sexual harassment on campus.* Boston: Beacon Press.

Dziech, B. W., & Weiner, L. (1990). *The lecherous professor: Sexual harassment on campus* (2nd ed.). Urbana, IL: University of Illinois Press.

Fitzgerald, L. F. (1994). No safe haven: Violence against women in the workplace. In APA Task force on Male Violence Against Women (Eds.), *No safe haven: Violence against women at home, at work and in the community.* Washington, DC: American Psychological Association.

Fitzgerald, L. F., Drasgow, F., & Gelfand, M. (1993). *Sexual Experiences Questionnaire-Revised.* Unpublished research scale, Department of Psychology, University of Illinois at Urbana-Champaign.

Fitzgerald, L. F., Hulin, C. S., & Drasgow, F. (in press). The antecedents and consequences of sexual harassment in organizations: An integrated model. In G. Keita & S. Sauter (Eds.)., *Job stress 2000: Emergent issues.* Washington, DC: American Psychological Association.

Fitzgerald, L. F., & Shullman, S. L. (1993). Sexual harassment: A research analysis and agenda for the 1900s. *Journal of Vocational Behavior, 42*, 5-27.

Fitzgerald, L. F. Shullman, S. L., Bailey, N., Richards, M., Swecker, J., Gold Y., Ormerod, A. J., & Weitzman, L. (1988). The incidence and dimensions of sexual harassment in academia and the workplace. *Journal of Vocational Behavior. 32*, 152-175.

Franklin P., Moglin H., Zatling-Boring, P., & Angress, R. (1981). *Sexual and* gender harassment in the academy. New York: Modern Language Association

Gelfand, M., Fitzgerald, L. F. & Drasgow, F. (under review). The structureof sexual harassment: A confirmatory analysis across cultures and settings.

Gutek, B., & Koss, M. P. (1993). Changed women and changed organizations: Consequences of coping with sexual harassment. Journal of Vocational Behavior, 42, 28-48.

Grauerholz, E. (1989). Sexual harassment of women professors by students: Exploring the dynamics of power, authority and gender in a university setting. Sex Roles, 21, 789-801.

Gutek, B. A. (1985). Sex and the workplace. San Francisco: Jossey-Bass.

Hoffman, F. L. (1986). Sexual harassment in academia: Feminist theory and institutional practice. Harvard Educational Review, 56, 105-121.

Kilpatrick, D. G. (1992, June 30), Treatment and counseling needs of women veterans who were raped, otherwise sexually assaulted or sexually harassed during military service. Testimony before the Senate Committee on Veterans Affairs.

Korf v. Ball State University, 726 F.2d 122 (7th Cir. 1984).

Koss, M. P. (1990). Changed lives: The psychological impact of sexual harassment. In M. A. Paludi (Ed.), Ivory power: Sexual harassment on campus. Albany, NY: SUNY Press.

MacKinnon, C. A. (1979). Sexual harassment of working women. New Haven,: Yale university Press.

Maihoff, N., & Forrest, L. (1983). Sexual harassment in higher education: An assessment study. Journal of the National Association for Women Deans, Administrators, and Counselors, 46, 3-8.

McKinney, K. (1990). Sexual harassment of university faculty by colleagues and students. Sex Roles, 23, 421-438.

Meritor Savings Bank, FSB v. Vinson, 477 U.S. 57, 106 S. Ct. 2399 (1986).

Metha, A., & Nigg, J. (1983). Sexual harassment on campus: An institutional response. Journal of the National Association for Women Deans, Administrators, and Counselors, 46, 9-15.

Mills, C. W. (1959). *The sociological imagination.* New York: Grove Press.

Omerod, A. J. (1991). *The effect of self-efficacy and outcome expectations on responses to sexual harassment.* Unpublished master's thesis, Department of Educational Psychology, University of Illinois, Champaign, IL.

Reilly, M. E., Lott, B., & Gallogly, S. M. (1986). Sexual harassment of university students. *Sex Roles, 14*, 333-358.

Reskin, B. (1990). *Outsiders in academe: Playing the game by other people's rules.* Paper presented at the Allerton Conference on Cultural Values and Ethics, University of Illinois, Monticello, IL.

Rubin, L. J., & Borgers, S. B. (1990). Sexual harassment in universities during the 1980's. *Sex Roles, 23*, 397-411.

Saunders, B. E. (1992, October 23). *Sexual harassment of women in the workplace: Results from the National Women's Study.* Paper presented at the Eighth Annual North Carolina/South Carolina Labor Law Seminar, Asheville, NC.

Schneider, B. E. (1987). Graduate women, sexual harassment and university policy. *Journal of Higher Education, 58*, 46-65.

Till, F. J. (1980). *Sexual harassment: A report on the sexual harassment of students.* Washington, DC: National Advisory Council on Women's Educational Programs.

Tinsley, H. E. A., & Stockdale, M. S. (1993). Special issue on sexual harassment in the workplace. *Journal of Vocational Behavior, 42*, Whole No.1.

U.S. Merit Systems Protection. Board. (1981). *Sexual harassment in the federal government: Is it a problem?* Washington, DC: U.S. Government Printing Office.

U.S. Merit Systems Protection Board,. (1987). *Sexual harassment in the federal government: An update.* Washington, DC: U.S. Government Printing Office.

Wilson, K. R., & Kraus, L. A. (1983). *Sexual harassment in the university. Journal of College Student Personnel, 24*, 219-224.

5

SEXUAL HARASSMENT IN HIGHER EDUCATION: WHAT WE'VE LEARNED

by Anne T. Truax

Our attitudes about relations between the sexes are in transition. But we have not come as far as our rhetoric suggests. The many years I've spent at the Minnesota Women's Center observing and addressing the problem of sexual harassment have convinced me that the position of women in American society has not changed as much as I once thought. Few men will verbalize their belief that women are subordinate, but many still operate on that basis. We as a society continue to think of women primarily in their sex roles as wife, mother, and daughter, rather than as colleagues and fellow professionals.

At my campus, the University of Minnesota's Twin Cities site, the Faculty Senate adopted a sexual harassment policy in 1981. The policy included a sunset provision that required a review after three years. After the 1984 review, the policy was made permanent and strengthened considerably.

Most people on campus now believe that our large university community—about 60,000 students and 16,000 employees—needs a sexual harassment policy. The current policy covers everyone at the university—students, faculty, and support employees, regardless of their jobs or activities. Students on internships and post-docs are covered, as are teaching assistants.

Nationally, about 95% of all sexual harassment reports involve men harassing females. About 3% of these cases involve males who harass other males. There are also cases of females harassing females, male students harassing female faculty, and students harassing students. But the primary problem remains: males harassing females.

An earlier version of this chapter appeared in *Thought and Action*, Spring 1989, 5 (1), 25-38.

Harassment affects about 35 to 40% of the women on a typical college campus. No matter where surveys are done, this ratio holds true. Of those harassed, not more than one in 10 actually report the harassment. As a result, we must base our understanding of harassment on a small number of cases. We assume that those complaints that are filed represent a random sample that reflects the overall harassment problem. But we don't know for sure.

We do know that a real, immediate problem exists. Not only have women decided to do something about sexual harassment, so have the courts. We are building a sizable body of law based on state and federal decisions. Academic institutions now have no choice but to begin to respond to harassment complainants, and if necessary, the courts.

The perceptions of most men and of most women about what constitutes sexual harassment are extremely different. There are few cases in which the parties disagree about what happened. Here's a typical scenario. First, the victim's story:

> Professor X came to my apartment uninvited on a Sunday morning. He said he wanted to teach me a folk song from the country that we're working on right now and asked if he could come in. I said yes. He came in, kissed me, and said, "Why don't we go to bed?"

The accused professor, asked his version of the incident, replied:

> I went to her apartment uninvited on a Sunday morning and I said I was going to teach her about a folk song and I kissed her and said "Why don't we go to bed?"

The student in this case thought that she had been harassed. She felt intimidated and worried. She did not know how to handle the relationship. The professor thought he was being friendly, comforting, and building a relationship where one did not exist. The problem is not the veracity of the accounts, but the conflicting interpretations of these events.

Today, men can no longer afford to harass, because women will no longer stand for it. Harassers need to understand that their behavior is intolerable—and might even lead to dismissal and legal penalties. The faculty member described in the case above was, in fact, sued in a private suit and forced to pay damages.

Educating the campus community about sexual harassment policies is now our primary job at Minnesota. This education is a considerable challenge. Our campus, for instance, has about 500 post-docs who conduct research for a year or two. These post-docs are transients. Reaching them is one of the worst problems that we face. Graduate students encounter greater problems than undergraduates because they are subject to greater leverage. We have had graduate students who complain that their graduate advisor sleeps with all his female advisees. Sometimes, when one student protests, the other advisees complain that she has spoiled their situation. It isn't easy to deal with these situations. Before Minnesota implemented its sexual harassment policy, we experimented with removing the right of a faculty member to advise graduate students. But this remedy is tantamount to saying that students could no longer be educated in the professor's academic specialty area. We now use a variety of thoughtful and creative sanctions in order to maintain our academic offerings.

We have gained some knowledge of the kinds of people who harass. Sometimes, the problem has cross-cultural roots. Men who come from countries where women's status is not very high think they can apply their ideas to American women. They are often caught up short. Some American males believe that women of certain cultural backgrounds will be less likely to resist their advances. An international specialist, for instance, figured that all Asians were passive. He felt safe picking on Asian women. Many harassers are arrogant men who seek control over their total environment. That dominance includes controlling the women around them. Many harassers are repeaters with a *modus operandi*. They use the same words. They proposition the students they advise in the same way at the same time in their graduate careers. These harassers are predictable. Institutions need to actively intervene against all such patterns of behavior.

Higher education is particularly prone to harassment problems because the campus organizational culture is less linear and direct than a corporation. A university cannot "just fire somebody" who has seriously misbehaved. University dismissal processes are long and complex. In addition, we in academe are both traditional and avant garde at the same time, both moralistic and libertarian. Faculty members have a great deal of autonomy. Sexual harassment has been depicted as an eccentricity that higher education often rewards. Women will no longer let it be so depicted. The experiences of women who are sexually harassed are similar to the experiences of women who have been battered and sexually assaulted.

These individuals, who are all victims, are more likely to be victimized again. A fair percentage—about 35% in my experience—of the women with harassment complaints are previous victims of incest or assault. Victimization does indeed breed victimization. It is uncanny how a victim can identify herself as harassable to the person who wants to harass. A dynamic is at work that we do not understand.

Some women victims may indeed be mentally ill. I will never forget the first time that I encountered such a case. I had a student who was hallucinating while she sat in my office. But her story about harassment turned out to be absolutely true. Counselors must be extremely careful to make sure that a story stands on its own merit. The story is not necessarily related to the illness. Worse, it may be a cause of that mental illness.

But even the victim who does not suffer from mental illness ordinarily feels guilty and responsible—that she has invited or encouraged the harassment. She thinks that nothing will be done to help her. She fears retaliation. Whether or not she files a complaint, the victim often drops out of school, changes her major, or otherwise gets herself out of that situation.

Only rarely will a victim do more than make a verbal report. The most frequent comment I hear: "I want to talk about this situation, but I don't want to do anything about it. I just wanted to let you know that it's happening and see if you can help me feel more comfortable about it." As educators, we must work with victims to change this pattern. Sometimes, we can convince victims to file a written complaint. But this is not always possible, especially in some of the worst cases.

Even when the victim complains, she may well pay the price for the harassment. If a department head harasses a clerical staff member, for instance, the university will never force that department head to start anew in another building, with a new staff, and a new discipline. The university will usually instead say to the harassed clerical member: "We feel very sorry for you. We will continue to employ you. We may give you a little raise or some other kind of help. But you're going to have to move to a new job. You're going to work in new quarters with new people."

Still, the decision by a victim to complain appears to be a good decision. Filing a complaint appears to resemble a decision to go into therapy. The victim decides that she will no longer participate in the exploitive behavior and will make some changes in her personal dynamic. We must encourage such decisions. Saying to yourself that you will no longer be a victim is a very important step.

At Minnesota we try to educate everyone about sexual harassment. We explain that an individual is obligated to report sexual harassment if she experiences it herself or sees it happen to someone else. Everyone is also responsible for educating their colleagues about the importance of creating a campus climate that will not revert to the status quo ante.

Sexual harassment occurs in employment settings. In an employment setting, there are appropriate patterns of behavior. Campuses are not singles bars or locker rooms. This would seem self-evident, yet the concept of appropriateness discomforts many people on campus. In speaking on sexual harassment to faculty, I have sometimes found enormous hostility and antagonism.

Some in the campus community consider sexual harassment a joking matter. At Minnesota the student book-store was forced to stop selling a mug that read: "Sexual harassment is not a problem around here; it's one of the ben-efits." The student newspaper asked: "Why be so fussy?" The answer is that if you aren't fussy, there are some people who will not know what is appropriate. These people must be dealt with clearly and strictly.

Most institutions respond to both informal and formal complaints. We encourage victims to speak to anyone they trust. Most victims are referred (or go directly) to a women's center or a counseling center. Both formal complaints and informal reports must be addressed promptly. We must immediately decide upon a possible sanction against the harasser. That might mean moving that person to another building or directing that an offensive poster be taken off a wall. It could mean tealling an instructor not to use particularly offensive jokes in his classroom any more.

In the cases we address, we first attempt to rectify the situation. We let the complainant tell us what she needs. Victims usually request far less than what we would ask. The victim almost always only wants the harassment to stop. She wants peace and the ability to heal. She may want to drop a class without it showing on her record. She may want a tuition refund. She may want to change her major without losing any credit. We try to help victims in many ways. But we must always be timely. The courts take timeliness into account in deciding institutional liability.

We can only take action from the standpoint of the victim. The law does not care that the perpetrator intended to be paternal. The law only looks at what happened to that victim. A college or university must look at sexual harassment from the same standpoint. Harassment can be visual as well as verbal. In one case at Minnesota, for instance, an advisor had a poster of a nude on his wall. Of his 15 women advisees, one student said the poster made her uncomfortable. She told us that she became sick every time she entered his office. The advisor took down the poster, but was furious. He said that the student was an adult and ought to have known better.

The individual who decides on sanctions faces genuinely difficult problems. Is your sanction enough to make the harasser stop? At what point do you hurt the institution by sanctioning an offender? The balance is very delicate. Some of the steps that we tried at first, we no longer take. We no longer require anyone to go into therapy. Therapists complained that the people who went into therapy did no work. But we have suspended people, removed pay, taken travel money and awards away from harassers. We moved them physically from one building to another. We have fired people or put them on probation.

We report to our faculty Senate every year. The report details the status of the offender and the victim, the situation, and the sanction. The report itself is a sanction. Its annual appearance probably deters some potential harassers—and proves to victims that something can be done. Few universities, unfortunately, publish similar documents.

The law that covers sexual harassment has emerged from Title VII of the Civil Rights Act of 1964. The EEOC 1980 guidelines are based on this act. These guidelines are the basis for sexual harassment policies in the majority of universities and colleges. One important clause prohibits a hostile or intimidating atmosphere. This clause covers the visual harassment case discussed above. Title IX of the Education Amendments also prohibits sexual harassment. Although the Reagan Administration did little to enforce Title IX, the Civil Rights Restoration Act may provide another legal recourse.

An educational institution without a sexual harassment policy is now asking for problems. Few students actually go to court, but they have the right to do so. In one creative case, a graduate student collected money under the professor's home insurance policy. The few litigated cases come under tort law, where the victim claims personal injury. Victims raise issues of emotional distress, assault, battery, intentional interference with a contract (a contract is implied every time you teach somebody), wrongful discharge or dismissal, and negligent supervision.

The university itself may also be liable in such cases. Every time a college communicates with a potential or current student or signs an agreement, it enters into a contract. If the university doesn't fulfill the terms of that contract, the student or the employee can sue. If we promise that our campus is a place of great beauty, peace, and learning, and if the student finds that a professor is not greatly interested in learning, she can sue on the grounds that the institution failed to fulfill its contract. A supervisor, campus employee, a faculty member, or another student may create a "hostile environment." In *Meritor Savings Bank v. Vinson* (1986), the U.S. Supreme Court ruled that an institution without a policy that clearly prohibits sexual harassment can be sued even if the employee suffers no tangible loss.

Many colleges and universities have addressed the issue of relations between consenting adults. The original policy at Minnesota made no mention of consent. But when a committee that included anti-policy members reviewed the sexual harassment policy, it called for a strong consent clause. The clause stated that in a relationship that turns bad, a subordinate's apparent consent cannot be used as a defense against harassment charges.

I look forward to the day when behavior is no longer based on gender stereotypes, when male perceptions of what constitutes harassment will be very similar to female perceptions, and when men will no longer feel they must control women. The victimization of women based on that conrol will be eliminated. At that point our society will move beyond the time when punishment must be used to enforce changing concepts of appropriate behavior.

New forms of relationships can be possible only as the socialization of boys and girls changes to allow them to consider one another as peers in all aspects of their lives. As these people grow and move into the worlds of education and work, they will continue to build more equal relationships, and sexual harassment will vanish.

APPENDIX: FACTS ON SEXUAL HARASSMENT

This summary of information on sexual harassment is handed out after presentations on sexual harassment at the University of Minnesota and elsewhere.

1. Sexual harassment is the misuse of power that involves two people of perceived unequal authority and status, in a situation which has sexual overtones.

2. Men as well as women are sexually harassed.

3. Sexual harassment occurs in all combinations: male-male, female-female, female-male and male-female.

4. Sexual harassment is primarily a problem for women. More than 95% of reported cases occur when a male of greater power harasses a female of lesser power. Exact statistics are not available. About 3 to 4% are cases of men harassing other men.

5. Sexual harassment affects women of all kinds: all races, ages, occupations, and classes.

6. Surveys show that 33 to 42% of all college women report some form of sexual harassment. Recent studies indicate the frequency may be over 60%. Within this group, 5 to 8% report serious harassment.

7. Sexual harassment is at least as severe for women faculty members and support staff as it is for students.

8. These problems raised by sexual harassment are often exacerbated by miscommunication based on stereotypes about race or culture.

9. Men and women perceive sexual harassment very differently. Women often see it as threatening, offensive, humiliating or inappropriate. Many men believe the same conduct to be flattering or friendly.

10. Reports of sexual harassment are almost never false, or made out of a desire to harm or embarass someone. In a majority of cases the harasser verifies the victim's account. Failure to report sexual harassment is a much greater problem that complicates institutional efforts to end harassment.

11. As women's status improves, women are much less willing to accept discriminatory behavior or sexual harassment. Such refusal is related to similar protests about rape, assault, incest or other forms of violent behavior.

12. Sexual harassment is a form of sexual assault. Federal Bureau of Investigation statistics show that one out of four women will be sexually assaulted during their lifetimes. Women between the ages of 18-25 are the most vulnerable age group, but all ages are affected. These reports do not include sexual harassment figures.

13. A victim of sexual assault is likely to become a victim of further assaults. Psychological and emotional pressures on the individual increase with every incident.

14. The person with physical, emotional, psychological, or economic power must assume the responsibility for maintaining relationships that are free of harassment or intimidation.

15. Sexual harassment is legally a form of discrimination. Title VII of the 1964 Civil Rights Act and Title IX of the Education Amendments of 1972 prohibit sexual harassment. Through case law, state and federal courts continue to define sexual harassment; the responsibilities of perpetrators, employers and supervisors; and the remedies available to victims.

16. Harassers often repeat the same pattern of behavior. They use the same approach and words with successive victims. Understanding and interrupting these patterns can deflect potentially embarassing, even dangerous, situations.

17. Serious cases can lead to severe psychological, physical and emotional damage to the individuals affected. These cases also lead to expensive administrative and legal problems for the institution.

ANNOTATED BIBLIOGRAPHY

Adams, Aileen, and Gail Abarbanel, *Sexual Assault on Campus: What Colleges Can Do* (Santa Monica, CA: 1988). Obtain from: Rape Treatment Center, Santa Monica Hospital Medical Center, 1225 Fifteenth Street, Santa Monica, CA, 90404.

A good introduction to the issue that reviews the problems and offers recommendations for establishing sexual assault policy, procedures, and programs. Contains a bibliography.

American Council on Education, *Sexual Harassment on Campus: Suggestions for Reviewing Campus Policy and Educational Programs* (Washington, DC: American Council on Education, 1986).

This short pamphlet was written in response to the 1986 Supreme Court ruling *Meritor Savings Bank, FSB v. Vinson*. The pamphlet stresses the importance of having policies and procedures against sexual harassment. It offers guidelines for developing, implementing, and publicizing such policies, and for training supervisors.

Benson, Donna, and Gregg Thomson, "Sexual Harassment on a University Campus: The Confluence of Authority Relations, Sexual Interest and Gender Stratification," *Social Problems 29*: 236-251.

This excellent article shows how male faculty use their power position to further their sexual interests in women students. Other authors assert that sexual harassment is about power, but not about sex. Benson and Thomson argue that sexual harassment is about both: "Sexual harassment occurs as the confluence of authority relations and sexual interest in a society stratified by gender. To understand the phenomenon, adequate attention must be paid to each of the three components."

Cnudde, Charles F., and Betty A. Nesvold, "Administrative Risk and Sexual Harassment: Responsibilities on Campus," *PS* (Fall, 1985): 780-789.

This article informs department chairs of their legal responsibilities in handling sexual harassment situations. It reviews and interprets federal law, EEOC guidelines, and court rulings. The article treats sexual harassment complaints as bothersome liabilities, but the authors recommend that departmental chairs respond to complaints in a legally prescribed manner.

Cole, Elsa Kircher, "Recent Legal Developments in Sexual Harassment," in *Sexual Harassment on Campus: A Legal Compendium* (National Association of College and University Attorneys Publications, 1988), 3-20.

This publication reviews recent court decisions on sexual harassment and explains how previous cases have (or have not) been used as precedent.

Dovan, Judi, Marc Grossman, Joni Kindermann, Brenda Lehrer, Susan Matula, Donna Mulcahy, Julie Ostwald, Michele Paludi, Carole Anne Scott (Hunter College Women's Career Development Research Collective), "Sexual and Gender Harassment in the Academy: Introduction to Ivory Power," in M.A. Paludi, ed., *Ivory Power: Sexual and Gender Harassment in the Academy* (Albany, NY: State University of New York Press, 1990).

This essay comprehensively reviews current research and theories.

Dziech, Billie Wright, and Linda Weiner, *The Lecherous Professor: Sexual Harassment on Campus* (Boston: Beacon Press, 1984).

This list is excerpted from *Academic Sexual Harassment: An Annotated Bibliography* (1988), available from the Minnesota Women's Center, University of Minnesota, Minneapolis, MN 55455.

This book is a popular study by two academic women.

Ellis, Kathryn, and Lynne Carroll, "Shippensburg University: Sexual Harassment Faculty Attitude Survey," presented at the "Women as Catalyst" National Association of Women Deans and Counselors Conference, Pittsburgh. March 18, 1988).

This presentation surveys faculty attitudes and experiences with sexual harassment and harassing.

Fitzgerald, Louise, Lauren M. Weitzman, Yael Gold, and Mimi Ormered, "Academic Harassment: Sex and Denial in Scholarly Garb," *Psychology of Women Quarterly 12* (1988): 320-340.

This is a survey of 235 male faculty members at a "prestigious, research-oriented university." Twenty-six percent of the respondents report sexual involvement with women students. The authors examine three types of behavior between faculty and students: mentoring, sexual interaction, and sexual exploitation.

Franklin, Phyllis, Helene Moglen, Phyllis Zatlin-Boring, and Ruth Angress, *Sexual and Gender Harrassment in the Academy: A Guide for Faculty, Students, and Administrators* (New York: Commission on the Status of Women in the Profession, The Modern Language Association of America, 1981).

The authors discuss professional ethics and the inappropriateness of sexual relationships between professors and students. Their discussions of "institutional integrity," "a healthy learning environment," and consent in graduate student-professor relationships are excellent. Some material here is now dated.

Gagliano, Christine L., "Surviving Sexual Harassment: Strategies for Victims and Advocates," a paper presented at the Women in Higher Education Conference, Orlando, Florida, 1987.

This thoughtful paper explains the role of advocate, and includes suggestions on how best to empower the victim of sexual harassment to make her own choices and validate her perceptions.

Glaser, Robert D., and Joseph S. Thorpe, "Unethical Intimacy: A Survey of Sexual Contact and Advances Between Psychology Educators and Female Graduate Students," *American Psychologist 41* (1) (1986), 43-51.

This is an anonymous survey of female members of Division 12 of the American Psychological Association. It examines the women's graduate experiences of sexual intimacy with and sexual advances from psychology educators, as well as their past and current perceptions and evaluations of these experiences. Many women now perceive the contacts as extremely exploitative and harmful, with 31 perent of those surveyed reporting sexual advances. The respondents to this survey were all professional psychologists. Women who changed career plans because of harassment were thus not included.

Haber, B., "Why Not the Best and the Brightest? Equal Opportunity vs. Academic Freedom," *Forum* (January, 1981, 20-25).

This article examines the ways academic freedom has been used as a cover for discrimination.

Keller, Elisabeth A., "Consensual Amorous Relationships Between Faculty and Students: Policy Implications and the Constitutional Right to Privacy," in *Sexual Harassment on Campus: A Legal Compendium* (Washington, DC: National Association of College and University Attorneys Publications, 1988), 67-98.

This essay addressed the conflict between the right to privacy and the right to freedom from sexual harassment. It suggests the application of a "bright-line test": that consensual relationships outside the instructional or employment context be protected from interference, while relationships within those contexts be subject to sexual harassment implications.

Merton, Andrew, "Return to Brotherhood," *Ms.* 14 (3) (1985), 60-65, 121-122.

This article suggests that fraternities are an ideal refuge for those young men who are unwilling or unable to deal with women as equals. As feminism influences more campuses, conflicts between fraternities and others on campus become more frequent. The author compares the situation in the 1950s and 1980s, and suggests that Greek men feel less in control of their lives than non-Greeks.

Northwest Women's Law Center, *Sexual Harassment in the Schools: A Project for Secondary and Vocational Schools*, revised edition. (Northwest Women's Law Center, 119 South Main Street, #330, Seattle, WA 98104, 1986).

This report contains nine sections: societal norms and sexual harassment, what is sexual harassment, studies on sexual harassment in employment and education, victims effects and costs, what students can do, what employees can do (including sections on union grievances and unemployment compensation), legal remedies, legal liabilities, and strategies for administators and teachers (including a checklist and guidelines for conducting internal investigations). The resource section of the report is especially useful.

Padgitt, Steven C., and Janet S. Padgitt, "Cognitive Structure of Sexual Harassment: Implications for University Policy," *Journal of College Student Personnel* (January, 1986), 34-39.

This article examines male and female attitudes about specific behaviors. Eight behaviors were tested, of which three items were particularly problematic: sexist comments, body language, and invitations in which sexual behavior might be expected but was not made explicit.

Pryor, John B., "Sexual Harassment Proclivities in Men," *Sex Roles* 17 (5/6) (1987).

Pryor conducted three studies in an attempt to establish a "Likelihood to Sexually Harass" (LSH) index. The first study indicated that adversarial sex beliefs and rape myth acceptance affect LSH, as do non- or anti-feminist beliefs. The second study indicated that those with a high LSH hold more negative views of sex and sexuality. Pryor concluded from a third, problematic study that high LSH men describe themselves and women stereotypically and have a tendency to behave in sexually exploitative ways when their motives can be disguised by situational excuses.

Rowe, Mary P., "Dealing with Sexual Harassment," *Harvard Business Review* 59(3) (1981), 42-46.

This is a classic article by a university administrator with many years of experience in working with sexual harassment. The article includes sound suggestions for working with gross problems quietly.

Sandler, Bernice R., and Jean O'Gorman Hughes, *Peer Harassment: Hassles for Women on Campus* (Project on the Status and Education of Women, Association of American Colleges, 1818 R St., NW, Washington, DC 20009, 202-387-1300, September, 1988).

This article demonstrates that sexual harassment is business-as-usual for a large number of college males. At least three of every four women have experienced some form of sexual harassment from their male peers. The authors examine the many forms of sexual harassment. Topics include: women colluding; the role of alcohol, drugs, and pornography; legal considerations, and the role of the institution in establishing nonsexist and non-racist environments. A list of education and policy/procedure suggestions is included.

Schneider, Beth E., "Graduate Women, Sexual Harassment, and University Policy," *Journal of Higher Education* 58 (1) (1987), 47-65.

This survey of the sexual harassment experiences of women graduate students was conducted at an east coast public university in 1978. The author discusses the effects of harassment of women and considers the appropriateness of university sexual harassment policies in light of her findings.

Stokes, Jean, "Effective Training Programs: One Institutional Response to Sexual Harassment," *Journal of the National Association of Women Deans and Counselors* 46 (2) (1983), 34-38.

This is an excellent resource piece for anyone planning sexual harassment training on campus.

Sullivan, Mary, and Deborah I. Bybee, "Female Students and Sexual Harassment: What Factors Predict Reporting Behavior?" *Journal of the National Association of Women Deans and Counselors* (Winter, 1987), 11-18.

This study examined perceptions and responses to sexual harassment. The subjects were undergraduate women, primarily white (88 percent) and young (58 percent were 18 or 19 years old) at Michigan State University.

REFERENCES

Equal Employment Opportunity Commission (1980). Guidelines on discrimination because of sex, *Federal Register,* 45, 74676-74677.

Meritor Savings Bank v. Vinson, 106 S. Ct. 2399 (1986).

6

SEXUAL HARASSMENT ON CAMPUS: A CONTINUING CONTROVERSY

by Barbara G. Taylor

For a decade and a half, college and university administrators, attorneys, affirmative action officers, women's advocacy groups, student judicial advisors, counselors, and interested students, faculty, and staff have discussed the issue of sexual harassment on campus, developed and revised policies, conducted prevention programs, and compared notes with other institutions. They have been encouraged and guided in this process by the position statements, publications, and conference sessions of their professional associations. Resources such as electronic discussion lists, brochures, videotapes, policy guidelines, training materials, and bibliographies have proliferated. The courts, compliance agencies, and Congress have helped refine the definition of sexual harassment, addressed responsibility for its prevention, and affirmed individual and institutional liability for compensatory and punitive damages. Media coverage and public awareness of sexual harassment have increased dramatically, and the visibility of the issue has given new impetus to campus education and prevention programs.

While some of these developments have provided answers, increasingly complex questions arise about policy, procedural, and legal issues surrounding sexual harassment in higher education. Many colleges and universities are revising their policies and procedures for the third or fourth time and are coming to understand that there will be a continuing need to update them in the foreseeable future. Policies are being criticized by some feminists who want them made stronger

This chapter is a very extensive revision of an earlier article that appeared in *Thought and Action*, Spring 1989, 5 (1), 39-44 ("Who is responsible for sexual harassment?").

and by political conservatives who believe they have gone too far. Sexual harassment on campus is discussed more and is more controversial than ever before.

Although a few colleges and universities adopted sexual harassment policies and mechanisms for implementing them in the late 1970s,[1] most developed their first policies soon after the Equal Employment Opportunity Commission (EEOC) issued its 1980 guidelines interpreting sexual harassment as a form of sex discrimination prohibited under Title VII of the Civil Rights Act of 1964. Typically, those first policies were reviewed and revised after the U.S. Supreme Court decision in *Meritor Savings Bank v. Vinson* (1986). In December 1986, the American Council on Education (ACE) published guidelines for reviewing campus sexual harassment policies and grievance procedures in light of *Meritor,* and later reiterated its strong recommendation to member institutions that they adopt sexual harassment policies (American Council on Education, 1992).

A number of significant developments followed. In 1990 the EEOC issued two "policy guidance" documents addressing sexual harassment. One dealt broadly with the definition of both *quid pro quo* and hostile environment sexual harassment and with issues of employer liability. It reviewed the implications of the *Meritor* decision and of other subsequent court decisions, and provided guidance on determining whether sexual conduct is unwelcome, evaluating evidence of harassment, responding to sex-based harassment that does not involve sexual activity or language, and employer liability for harassment by supervisors (Equal Employment Opportunity Commission, 1990a). The second policy guidance document dealt with sexual favoritism as a form of sexual harassment and with the ways that sexual favoritism in the workplace may discriminate against third parties (Equal Employment Opportunity Commission, 1990b). In the same year, the Office of Civil Rights of the U.S. Department of Education (1990) published a brochure that dealt with the prohibition of sexual harassment of students and others in the academic setting under Title IX of the Education Amendments of 1972.

The year 1991 was an important one for legislative

and judicial developments and for the awakening of public interest in the issue of sexual harassment. The court hearing the Florida case, *Robinson v. Jacksonville Shipyards* (1991), found a sexually hostile environment violating Title VII in a workplace where women were a small minority of the workforce and crude language, sexual graffiti, and pornography were pervasive. The 9th Circuit in *Ellison v. Brady* (1991) used the standard of the "reasonable woman," as opposed to a "reasonable person," finding that male and female sensibilities differ, and that what might appear inoffensive to the average man might be so offensive to the average woman as to create a hostile work environment.

The 1991 event that brought the greatest public attention to the issue of sexual harassment was, of course, the series of Senate Judiciary Committee hearings on the nomination of Clarence Thomas to the U.S. Supreme Court. Women who had never used the term sexual harassment identified with Anita Hill, and a number of men reexamined their own behavior after hearing her accusations. The public debate over the nature and scope of sexual harassment, its impact, its prevention, and its remedies became widespread with the Hill-Thomas confrontation, and awareness of sexual harassment made it more difficult to ignore. One result was that in the next two years, the number of sexual harassment claims filed with the EEOC doubled.[2]

Less dramatic, but equally effective in its impact on employers, including colleges and universities, was the Civil Rights Act of 1991, which was passed with an amendment providing for jury trials and for increased compensatory and punitive damages for sex discrimination and sexual harassment. The prospect of a $300,000 per case potential liability for sexual harassment commanded attention. The dollar issue was raised again when the Supreme Court, in *Franklin v. Gwinnett County Public Schools* (1992), confirmed that students and other victims of intentional gender discrimination, specifically sexual harassment, are entitled to monetary damages under Title IX.

In the wake of these changes, the American Council on Education (ACE) issued further guidelines for institutions of higher education in a publication entitled *Sexual Harassment on Campus: A Policy and Program of Deterrence* (1992). The introductory section suggested that colleges and universities review their sexual harassment policies and educational programs once again, repeating the EEOC advice that prevention is the best tool for the elimination of sexual harassment. The National Association of College and University Business Officers (NACUBO), concerned about higher education institutions minimizing their potential liability for sexual harassment, reprinted the ACE model program in the *NACUBO Business Officer.*[3] A more recent report providing policy guidance to colleges and universities is *Sexual Harassment in Higher Education: From Conflict to Community* (1993) by the Association for the Study of Higher Education (ASHE).

While the ASHE publication was in press, the U.S. Supreme Court heard another landmark case, *Harris v. Forklift Systems* (1993). The *Harris* decision established that employees do not have to experience severe psychological injury before they can bring hostile atmosphere sexual harassment charges, nor does the harassment have to interfere with their job performance. In *Harris,* the Supreme Court also affirmed the appropriateness of the tests and definitions of hostile environment sexual harassment set forth in *Meritor.* The newest Associate Justice, Ruth Bader Ginsburg, asked attorneys arguing the case "why sexual harassment should not be defined simply as conduct that on the basis of an employee's sex makes it more difficult for one person than another to perform the job." She also suggested that sexual harassment could be found if "one sex has to put up with something the other sex doesn't have to put up with."[4]

Despite Justice Ginsburg's clear statement of the essential nature of sexual harassment, the debate about sexual harassment on campus has become more heated, and higher education continues to encounter questions and to contend with problems that businesses, industries, and other organizations seldom face. Many of academe's unique issues relate to the sexual harassment of students and the obligation to protect them, as well as employees, from sexual coercion and exploitation. Other complications stem from the traditions of academic freedom, faculty tenure, and the forms of mentoring that take place in colleges and universities.

It may be impossible for colleges and universities to meet their obligation to respond strongly, clearly, and responsibly to the threat posed by sexual harassment and yet satisfy the academic community that they are not imposing unnecessary restrictions or compromising traditional academic values. Even when institutional legal obligations are obvious, the complexity of the issues means that there are few or no easy answers, and the best policies, procedures, and educational programs to prevent sexual harassment leave institutions in a continual balancing act.

Among the difficult issues are those relating to confidentiality. Complainants often ask that they not be identified. They are afraid that their employment or educational status will be jeopardized, that they will be perceived as troublemakers, that the institution will not be able to protect them from subtle forms of retaliation. Some would rather not pursue a complaint than have their identity revealed. But the obligation to stop sexual harassment and the liability for not doing so require that every incident of which the institution is aware, or should have been aware, be investigated. The institution's interest in protecting the identity of the accuser must always be balanced against the need to stop the harassment and against the rights of the accused. Colleges and universities cannot always guarantee confidentiality.

Although the parties to a sexual harassment complaint usually want confidentiality, and sound investigative procedures include cautioning them not to talk about the case and limiting the number of people aware of the complaint, a number of factors can interfere with confidentiality. The due process rights of the person accused may require disclosure of the identity of the accuser. The investigation may involve interviewing witnesses, who will at least infer that a problem exists. If disciplinary action is taken, department heads, deans, and others need to be informed.

There are related questions about the confidentiality of records of sexual harassment investigations. While most student records are protected from disclosure under the Family Education and Privacy Act, and employee personnel records are usually protected, some state freedom of information laws allow disclosure of investigation records if an employee is suspended or terminated as a result of a sexual harassment charge.[5] Campus crime-reporting requirements may threaten the confidentiality of complaints handled through a student judicial system, although this concern may be more pertinent to cases of sexual assault than sexual harassment.

Some colleges and universities have attempted to create an "institutional memory," recording complaints that the alleged victim refused to pursue or that were not substantiated, in order to identify chronic harassers. But there are problems with keeping secret files. There are questions about whether unsubstantiated accusations can be raised during later investigations. If the main purpose of an investigation is to stop the offensive behavior, the harasser needs to be confronted with it. Furthermore, alleged harassers have a right to know that records of complaints against them are being maintained. They need to be informed about every accusation, whether it is substantiated or not, and should be reminded each time of the policy prohibiting harassment and potential consequences for violating it.

Sexual harassment charges are very serious. They can damage reputations and destroy careers. Some argue that to be accused of sexual harassment is to be considered guilty until proven innocent. Defamation of character, slander, and libel suits have been filed by alleged harassers against their accusers. Although it is unlikely that people will use sexual harassment charges to damage someone they are angry with for other reasons, policies prohibiting sexual harassment should also prohibit willfully making false charges. But because sexual harassment typically takes place in private, with no witnesses or other corroborating evidence, it is often not possible to determine whether harassment actually occurred, and it is similarly difficult to determine that a charge is false. An unsubstantiated charge of sexual harassment is not necessarily a false charge. And, in our concern about the potentially damaging effects of false reports, we must not forget that sexual harassment is extremely damaging to its victims, and that it, too, can destroy careers.

Charges made by third parties also create quandaries. If a witness reports sexual harassment, the obvious first step is to interview the person who was allegedly harassed. If the alleged victim confirms that there was sexual harassment but refuses to press charges, the institution's obligation to address the problem remains. If the third party claims to have been damaged indirectly by the harassment (when, for example, the person who submits to harassment receives favored treatment), the institution has an obligation to take action, even though the person being harassed insists that the behavior is welcome.

Some claims of third-party harassment may stem from consensual relationships. Sexual harassment charges may also be filed by a person in a consensual relationship who later decided that the power differential between the people involved made the relationship less than fully consensual. Some colleges and universities prohibit all consensual sexual relationships between students and faculty and between employees and supervisors. Others, concerned about infringing on constitutional rights, warn against such relationships, but do not forbid them. The issue is complicated by the prevalence of faculty-student marriages and other long-term relationships. There is general agreement that institutions should address the conflict of interest created by such relationships; whether they should go beyond that, is hotly debated. If the conflict of interest can be addressed, by assuring that a faculty member will have no influence on a student's academic status or evaluation, or by making certain that the supervisor does not evaluate or otherwise affect the employee's working conditions, most of the fair treatment issues fade, although other ethical concerns remain. Sometimes the easiest way to address conflicts of interest arising from consensual relationships appears to be to move the less powerful person to another position or another program of study. Such a solution should be considered very cautiously, as it may be unfair to the person who is moved and therefore may create further institutional liability.

There are many situations in higher education that pose a special risk for sexual harassment, but that are of such potential value that changing them may be counterproductive. For example, the process of intellectual collaboration and mentoring that traditionally occurs between faculty and students, and particularly graduate students, creates a closeness that may easily be abused if its boundaries are misunderstood. Does that mean that faculty and students should never work closely? Should a faculty member never be alone with one student, but work only with two or more? Should faculty advisors always keep their doors open when they meet with advisees? In some psychology, counseling, social work, and other programs, faculty are required to provide students with one-on-one supervision, which must be done in private because of clients' rights to confidentiality. Some faculty argue that they should not be required to report sexual harassment which they have been told about in confidence, by a student. Can the institution be held liable for not stopping sexual harassment that a faculty member chooses not to disclose? Is there a protected relationship between all faculty and the students whom they teach or advise?

Another much-debated issue is whether sexual harassment policies threaten free speech or infringe upon academic freedom. Colleges and universities often tread a fine line when they attempt to prevent hostile atmosphere sexual harassment by addressing the question of appropriate course materials and classroom techniques. Faculty and students have expressed concern about whether performances and works of art and literature that have sexual or erotic content can be construed as creating a sexually hostile atmosphere. And questions have been raised about cartoons, drawings, and other materials with sexual content that faculty display on their office doors or students put on their doors in a residence hall. Do postings like these create a hostile and offensive atmosphere? Or are they so easily ignored and avoided that they can be defended as a legitimate exercise of free speech?

Another complex issue for colleges and universities is peer harassment. Sexual harassment of faculty by other faculty and particularly of students by other students is notoriously difficult to prevent. Yet sexual harassment may take place when there is no formal power differential between the harasser and the person harassed. Sexual harassment between peers is probably as much an exercise of power as is *quid pro quo* harassment, but the damage to the victim is less obvious and its prohibition is therefore more difficult to defend. When the harasser has the power to damage the victim, we can see the potential damage to a student's grade in a course, progress toward a degree, work on a thesis or dissertation, recommendations for jobs or graduate school, or reputation in a department. The threat to an employee's promotions, salary increases, working conditions, or continued employment is also obvious. But the right to work or study in an atmosphere that is free from sexual hostility and intimidation is not always so clear, although it is certainly as important.

Many of the issues for colleges and universities are related to their complaint and investigation procedures. Departments often insist on dealing with problems internally. As a result, some institutions have designated individuals in every department or college who will receive sexual harassment complaints. Others have found that a single, easily identifiable office is more effective. Officials who are responsible for investigating all sexual harassment complaints on campus still have to work with department chairs, deans, and other administrators, but they can more easily ensure that complaints are investigated according to a standard procedure and that the institutions' response to each complaint is documented. But students, faculty, and staff may prefer to discuss problems with someone they already know or with a peer advocate. Under either structure, there is a possibility that some reports will not go to the right person and may not be handled appropriately. A few will never be reported, either because the victim does not understand what sexual harassment is and how to report it or because the victim reports it to a person with whom they have a legally protected confidential relationship, such as a therapist, or a religious advisor.

Related to the interest in addressing sexual harassment as locally as possible, is an interest in resolving complaints informally. Informal resolutions, whether through direct action on the part of the victim, intervention by the person who receives the complaint, or through mediation and other forms of alternative dispute resolution, are usually quicker than formal complaint or grievance procedures. They also tend to focus on stopping the offensive behavior and preventing future occurrences, and are therefore more forward-looking than formal procedures that look at past actions in order to determine guilt and impose punishment. But whatever the advantages of informal resolution processes may be for the institution, the victim, and the harasser, anyone who brings a sexual harassment complaint has the right to know about all of the options, including direct action, informal resolution, formal grievance procedures, and legal recourse.

When the person accused of sexual harassment is a tenured faculty member, there are special considerations. While there is no question that a tenured faculty member can be disciplined and even terminated for sexual harassment, the process is complicated and procedural errors can be disastrous. If the institution has not afforded the faculty member due process or not followed its own procedures for revocation of tenure, it could be forced to reinstate someone who has a history of harassing and could be liable for sizable compensatory and punitive damages. Tenure provides protection from arbitrary dismissal; but can it also be misused to protect unacceptable behavior?

Both faculty and students have been concerned about the statute of limitations for making sexual harassment complaints. The EEOC sets a 180-day limit. Policies ought to emphasize that the campus can respond to sexual harassment most effectively and will have a better opportunity to stop it when it is reported promptly. However, there are circumstances that seem to present a compelling case for an extended complaint period. A student who is being harassed by a faculty member may want to finish a course, complete a thesis or dissertation, or fulfill other degree requirements before pursuing a complaint. Students often express fear of jeopardizing a grade, their academic standing, or their reputation in a department, and such concerns are not always unfounded. It could be argued that a faculty member who has harassed a student deserves to live in perpetual fear that the past will come back to haunt him or her. But in reality, it is often impossible to investigate harassment that took place years ago. Some colleges and universities set no statute of limitations on filing sexual harassment complaints, some simply follow the EEOC guidelines, and others try to find a middle ground that allows for exceptions.

There is no end in sight to the controversy in the academic community over these and other issues related to sexual harassment. The debate may be tedious at times and many arguments will be silly, inflammatory, destructive, or otherwise counterproductive. But controversy is a very effective way of raising awareness and of educating, and education about sexual harassment remains the best tool for preventing it. Colleges and universities need to assume the responsibility of leadership during a time when our entire society is learning to deal with sexual harassment. They must begin by educating their own communities, even if doing so increases controversy in the short run, and by setting an example through policies and procedures that are progressive and well-thought-out. Students educated in an environment where sexual harassment is both prohibited and discussed are far less likely to harass or to tolerate harassment once they leave the academic community. They will know what harassment is and they will have much better ideas about how to stop it.

NOTES

1 The University of Washington was one of the first intitutions to develop and implement a policy. Some of the history of that process is recounted in a group of papers edited by Lois Price Spratlen, dated May 9, 1989, and distributed in photocopy form under the title *Prevention of Sexual Harassment in Academe* by the University of Washington, Seattle, WA 98915.

2 U.S. Equal Employment Opportunity Commission, 1993.

3 March, 1993, pp. 32-35.

4 *The New York Times,* October 13, 1993, p. 1.

5 The Arkansas Freedom of Information Act (Ark. Code Ann. SS 25-19-101 et seq.) has such a provision. See Opinion No. 88-162; Ark. Code Ann. SS 25-29-2105 (c) (2) (Cum. Supp. 1991).

REFERENCES

American Council on Education. (1992). *Sexual Harassment on Campus: A Policy and Program of Deterrence.* Washington, DC: ACE, One Dupont Circle.

Ellison v. Brady. 924 F. 2d 872, 54 FEP Cases 1346 (M.D. Fla., 1991).

Equal Employment Opportunity Commission. (1990a, January 12). *Policy guidance on employer liability under Title VII for sexual favoritism.* No. N-915-048.

Equal Employment Opportunity Commission. (1990b, March 19). *Policy guidance on sexual harassment issues.* No. N-915-050.

Franklin v. Gwinnett County Public Schools. 112 S. Ct. 1028, 60 U.S.L.W. 4167 (1992).

Harris v. Forklift Systems. S. Ct. No. 92-1168 (1993).

Meritor Savings Bank v. Vinson. 477 U.S. 57, 106 S. Ct. 2399 (1986).

Robinson v. Jacksonville Shipyards. 740 F. Supp. 1486, 57 FEP Cases 971 (M.D. Fla, 1991).

Sexual harassment in higher education: From conflict to community. (1993). (ASHE-ERIC Higher Education Reports). Washington, DC: ASHE-ERIC, One Dupont Circle, Suite 630.

U.S. Department of Education, Office of Civil Rights. (1990). *Sexual harassment: It's not academic.* Washington, DC: U.S. Government Printing Office.

7

BLACKBOARD JUNGLE REVISITED

by Marcia Bedard and Beth Hartung

In the 1955 movie *Blackboard Jungle,* an idealistic English teacher (Glenn Ford) is hired to teach the tough boys in an inner city VoTech high school. The students are genuine juvenile delinquents, not misunderstood teens, and they destroy the beloved jazz record collection of one teacher and sexually assault another. Nonetheless, Ford rejects the advice of the mean-spirited history teacher who refers to his students as "animals" and who tells him, "You've got to be a disciplinarian, and that means obedience. Never turn your back on a class" (Biskind, 1983). Only after Ford is physically attacked and refuses to identify his student assailants, does he begin to win over the students.

College classrooms are rarely featured in these kinds of pedagogical melodramas. College professors work with adults, and expect to avoid the kind of disciplinary problems that teachers of younger adolescents face, even in those required courses students don't want to take. Our situation is an unusual one. We teach women's studies on a campus where a noble experiment has been underway for the last few years. All of our students must take one class in women's studies or in ethnic studies as part of their general education requirement.[1] All good intentions aside, such a requirement provides a medium for adversarial relationships, for a *Blackboard Jungle* revisited.

In this essay we examine the women's studies class as a specific site of harassment, a particular irony given the history and intent of women's studies and feminist studies. We suggest that certain disruptive classroom behaviors should be understood in the larger context of campus violence against

An earlier version of this chapter appeared in *Thought and Action,* Spring 1991, 7 (1), 7-20.

women. Finally, we discuss the implications of this kind of behavior for teaching in general and teaching women's studies in particular.

THE FEMINIST TEACHER IN THE WOMEN'S STUDIES CLASSROOM

In this volume, Gordon offers a historical perspective on campus violence against women. Gordon draws parallels between the current backlash against women on campus and the campus climate for women in the late nineteenth and early twentieth centuries. In both earlier periods, gender roles were in transition and women were making significant gains in education. In both periods, male students expressed their ambivalence in hostile actions that ranged from mockery to assaults against female students.[2]

Today, misogyny on campus may take different forms. Throughout the 1980s, the Association of American Colleges Project on the Status and Education of Women cites episodes of harassment—often with racial or religious overtones—taking place on college campuses (Hall and Sandler, 1982; Hughes and Sandler, 1988a, 1988b). Collison (1988) documents similar occurrences. Hughes and Sandler (1988b) cite specific instances that show who female students are verbally harassed, publicly "rated" for physical attractiveness as they walk across campus, and physically assaulted at fraternity parties.

There is no way of determining whether the number of acts of sexual intimidation have actually increased or if women faculty and students are reporting more incidents. Even less research is available on in-class harassment, especially directed at faculty. What is known is that students of both sexes may try to disrupt a women's studies class because these classes involve exchanging difficult and controversial ideas.

Women's studies teachers attempt to maintain as democratic a classroom forum as possible, but this does not include letting bigotry or attack go unchallenged. When students are required to take women's studies courses, the classroom is palpably transformed. The balance of students shifts from those interested in and sympathetic to studying women toward students who are initially reluctant to take women's studies classes. Some of these students will remain passively resistant. That is their right as students, though it undercuts their chance to learn. Others are more actively hostile, and their resistance can transform the class into a battleground.

In a preliminary report, Hartung (1990) showed that male and female students evaluating their women's studies teacher—compared to teachers of other courses—were more likely to make negative and even cruel assessments, even in retrospect. Men however, gave a stronger and more negative assessment of women's studies instructors than did women students.

Other studies and commentaries suggest the gender difference in evaluation and response to material is not isolated to one campus or even one culture. Ghadially (1988) found resistance to her gender roles class from male engineering students in India. When she injected feminism into a mixed tutorial group in Great Britain, Mahony (1986) met with such outright anger from male students that her competence as a teacher was brought into question. Closer to home, in 1988 a senior in business at the University of Washington was asked to leave his course in women's studies after haarassing the instructors.[3] In that case, even the university failed to support its women's studies faculty.

Why are students so upset by Women's Studies? Rothenberg (1989) suggests that if students are not getting upset, we are failing to do our job:

Teaching this material provokes considerable resistance on the part of students. . . . I am convinced that the quantity and quality of the resistance I provoke from my students early in the course is the way to measure my success as a teacher. If things go too well too quickly, if I am not overcome periodically by a sense of despair and futility. . . then maybe I'm leaving out what students need to hear most.

Traditional-aged students—the 18- to 24-year-old crowd—may resist material presented in women's studies for a variety of biographical reasons: they are the children of early second-wave feminists who feel they were sacrificed to their mother's desires to be more than mothers (Kolodny, 1989); they honestly believe that women no longer suffer inequities (Turkel, 1986), and they reject information to the contrary, or they are furious to find that it's not so (Hearn, 1987); they find feminism threatening and feminists "shrill" (Mahony, 1986); and finally they are young adults who came of age with Ronald Reagan's rugged and cruel individualism.

Beyond their personal biographies, women's studies may enrage students by asking hard questions: Why do we try to dominate each other? Why do men dominate women? How can we end the sexual division of labor (Stimpson, 1989)? Confronted by these questions, students sometimes strike out at other students or at the instructor. We devote the rest of this discussion to identifying the form student hostility can take in the women's studies classroom, and how instructors can defuse it

HOW MEN DISRUPT THE CLASSROOM

As noted earlier, antifeminist harassment in women's studies classes can be instigated by any student, and directed at men or women students or the feminist teacher. Nonetheless, the literature reviewed above and our own experience indicates most incidents of harassment and disruption are directed at female students and faculty by male students.

We focus here on the problem of antifeminist male students harassing their female peers and instructors and disrupting women's studies classes generally. Many of these behaviors are discussed in the publication, "Overcoming masculine oppression in mixed groups" (Moyers and Tuttle, 1983). Forms of harassment may include the following:

- claiming male victim status or challenging facts with particularistic anecdotes to undermine the credibility of feminist reading materials and instructors.
- dominating class discussions (talking too much and too long so that no one else has a chance to express their views or speaking so loudly and aggressively that other students are silenced and the instructor is irritated).

- aggressively pointing out minor flaws in statements of other students or the instructor, stating the exception to every generalization, and finding something wrong with everything from quizzes to books.
- changing the topic abruptly in the middle of a class discussion, often to claim male victim status or shift discussion to a less threatening topic.
- formulating a challenge after the first few sentences of an instructor's lecture, not listening to anything from that point on, and leaping in to argue at the first pause.
- taking intransigent and dogmatic stands on even minor positions and insisting that the instructor recognize the validity of the rigid positions.

Only one or two hostile male students can have a deleterious effect on an entire class. Moreover, in a climate of misogyny, any women's studies classroom disruption can reach crisis proportions and set off a wave of antifeminist hostility throughout the campus and community. Even when these disruptions do not reach crisis proportions, they constrain the class environment throughout the semester.

Warnings to hostile students to stop are only minimally effective. They often bring an end to the most overtly hostile and aggressive comments, but negative body language like smirks, eye-rolling, and snide comments may continue throughout the course. Overall, a bad class is an emotionally draining and intellectually disappointing experience for instructors and for many of the students, especially those with high expectations for women's studies. Danforth (1990), for example, discusses the impatience of advanced feminist students in an introductory feminist class.

In our experience, when a class becomes a battleground, many women students drop out of class during the first few weeks or effectively drop by attending class infrequently. The result is a skewed gender ratio since, predictably, hostile male students rarely miss a class. To them, it becomes a game of "us guys versus the teacher." They get a lot of pleasure from verbal and nonverbal intimidation.

Bizarre and rude classroom behavior may seem unusual in a university setting, and may call into question the instructor's ability to manage the class effectively. But women's studies classes do provoke "considerable resistance" in a way other classes do not. Women's studies professors who have experienced these sorts of hostility in their classroom may earn high teaching evaluations from most of their students. Sometimes, instructors teach for several years without incident, only to have a few students ruin one class. Indeed, all women's studies instructors deal with resistance whether they are competent or not, which negates the argument that disruptions only happen to incompetent women professors. But if an instructor's teaching ability is not the critical factor in creating classroom disruptions, then what is?

COMMONALITIES AND DIFFERENCES IN CLASSROOM DISRUPTIONS

Women's studies classes disrupted by men share many common denominators, as well as some notable differences. The age of the students appears to make a big difference in how women students react to hostile and aggressive male peers. In one of our classes, women students and some of the men were extremely passive and intimidated by a few vocal men in the class throughout the semester. The instructor's attempts to model assertive feminist behavior did not change the student passivity, although in their private journals submitted periodically throughout the course, these students supported the instructor.

Why were the students so passive? In most lower division introductory women's studies courses, large numbers of students are fresh from high school. This affects the social ecology of the classroom in two important ways. First, these students are still very influenced by peer pressure. As they gain maturity, they will gain confidence in their own thinking and their own values. The pressure to achieve popularity by going along with the dominant peer group is intense in late adolescence—the last thing a student wants to do at this stage of development is be seen as different in any way.

Second, younger students lack the work and relationship experiences that validate points made in class about gender and power relations in our society. Because women's power in patriarchy is equated with youth and beauty, and men's power with their earnings and prestige, many young college women are at the peak of their power while their male counterparts may be at an all-time low. Further, students 18- to 24-years-old earn relatively equal salaries because both men and women work at similar minimum wage jobs while in school. Rix (1988, Table 2) reports that young women between the ages of 16 and 24 earn 89% of men's earnings. But after age 24 the wage gap steadily widens until age 65.

In their immediate experience, young men do *not* make more money than women. In fact, some women who waitress may be making more because of their tips. Thus, we might expect that the more very young students in a women's studies class, the more likely are students to reject the idea that sexism is still a problem in society, and the greater the potential for one or more hostile male students to try to disrupt the learning process without any resistance from their peers.

The importance of the age composition of a class is illustrated by one course disruption on our campus that resulted in several threatened lawsuits. At the end of a class period in an upper division women's studies class, a male student interrogated a female student about her experiences as a battered wife until she, and others in the class, were in tears. The student was prohibited from returning to class until he met with the instructor and the appropriate administrators to discuss what had happened. This discussion was not fruitful and the student was unrepentant. He insisted on returning to class, and threatened legal action against the instructor and the university if he was not allowed to do so. In this case, both the student and the instructor retained attorneys, but no lawsuits were filed.

Almost all the students in the class were seniors, and many were older adults in their 30s and 40s. When the class was disrupted, a group of older students staged a protest, petitioned the administration, and talked to the press. These older students were somewhat intimidated at first by the aggressive tactics of the student, his lawyer, and his friends (most of whom were very young), but they stood their ground. In other words, they were both willing and able to stand up for their own rights. The older students were outraged that a male student intimidated a female classmate, and they did not expect the instructor to handle the disruptive student by herself. They behaved as mature and responsible adults would behave because that is what they were.

One of the strategies for reducing the number of antifeminist classroom disruptions might be to require that students have at least sophomore standing before taking an introductory women's studies class. This would eliminate classes full of very young students just out of high school, as well as those who lack the ability or motivation to succeed in college.

Another critical factor in analyzing antifeminist disruptions of the women's studies classroom is the number of students, especially male students, who are members of hypermasculine campus subcultures. We find more initially resistant students are associated with one or more of the following campus programs: fraternities, organized ahtletics, and military (ROTC, AFROTC) and police sciences. Hughes and Sandler (1988b) indict athletic dorms and fraternities as places that reinforce masculinist culture and devalue women. Warshaw (1988) and Martin and Hummer (1989) document the high percentage of date rape that occurs in dormitories and fraternities.

No feminist teacher, regardless of her skill and experience, can maintain order when her classroom is peopled by a dozen men and supportive women from the same athletic team or fraternity house. Unfortunately, she may be unaware of the situation until it is too late. Block enrollment—when several students from one organization enroll in a single class—is something that schools should avoid at all costs.

IMPLICATIONS: IN AND OUT OF THE CLASSROOM

What are the implications of antifeminist harassment in and out of the classroom? We discuss four here: pedagogy, classroom control, legal problems, and career consequences. We intend to raise some questions for further research rather than present a fully developed analysis of the kinds of harassment we've described.

Pedagogy. Increased antifeminist harassment of women's studies faculty can water down the curriculum as instructors tend to avoid more volatile issues like racism, poverty, incest and rape, battering, lesbianism, and reproductive freedom. Some women's studies professors have already taken this step to protect themselves from further harassment. Untenured professors may engage in more self-censorship than those with tenure, but no one wants to set herself and her students up for a painful experience.

On the other hand, all students suffer when the more volatile issues central to feminist analysis are dropped from a women's studies course. No feminist teacher can forget that women of color, poor women, victims of male violence, lesbians, and students who have had abortions do not constitute "special interest" groups. Together, they constitute the majority of women students.

Our students, women and men alike, must not be deprived of important information if we are ever to bring about the social changes that enable dignity and equity.

Classroom control. Antifeminist harassment in the classroom involves issues of control. Whose voice will prevail in the class? A women's studies class deals openly with the domination of women by men. It is one of the few forums in the academy to do so. The issues raised in women's studies classes may provoke defensive anger in men, despite their best intentions and disclaimers that they are "not sexist, but . . ."

Hostile male students, when threatened, often attempt to control the situation they are in, to regain a state of emotional comfort. Women and men who are less assertive, or who do not feel comfortable participating in a competitive debate, are silenced by this dominating behavior.

Class discussions that have become struggles for control between the instructor and hostile male students cease to be learning environments. These discussions become charged with hostility, tension, and anger.

Legal Ramifications. These dynamics also raise important legal questions about student expression and professorial responsibility. Hostile male students usually cite First Amendment rights guaranteeing freedom of speech to justify verbal harassment of women peers or instructors. Instructors and students seeking classrooms free from intimidation and harassment cite the Fourteenth Amendment, which guarantees equal protection under the law.

In an effort to balance these countervailing rights, many colleges and universities are struggling to develop policies on classroom conduct that will pass constitutional muster if challenged in the courts. Most of these policies aim at limiting racial slurs, but many schools address sexist and homophobic slurs as well (Tatel, 1990; Wiener, 1990).

Free speech versus responsible speech is an issue that undoubtedly will be fought out in the courts during this decade. Until then, there is no firm legal ground on which to stand. This makes teaching women's studies increasingly stressful because the threat of a lawsuit is ever present and because serious classroom disruptions will occasionally occur.

Career consequences. All of the issues identified above have career consequences. Most college teachers do not enter the academy to be disciplinarians. Finding that certain topics turn the maturity clock back to junior high school in students who are biologically adult is amusing at first, and later, maddening.

For the sake of remaining fresh and engaged, women's studies teachers need to vary the courses they teach. The entry-level survey course is the most difficult and draining of all women's studies classes. Upper-division classes draw more interested students. Cross-listed classes draw students who can cling to a traditional discipline, like the sociology of gender roles.

Administrators and faculty from other departments who evaluate women's studies faculty for tenure, promotion, and retention should know that women's studies teachers may not win popularity contests. Indeed, ironically we are the faculty most likely to be accused of practicing "reverse sexism" and "reverse racism" because we document those injustices.

The movement of women's studies into the general education curriculum is an attempt—aided by feminist teachers—to integrate important scholarship into the mainstream of knowledge. But the contempt with which we are sometimes met suggests our colleagues in mainstream disciplines are not doing their part.

As long as feminist scholarship is ghettoized, students receive a clear message: Academic integrity is incompatible with activism, therefore faculty in women's studies are no more than ideologues. These messages legitimate and perpetuate classroom harassment.

Turning the other cheek to student harassment, as did a green Glenn Ford in *Blackboard Jungle*, is not a solution today. It is a retreat back to the passivity and silence of an earlier era when women were seen but not heard on campus and when the abuse of women in academe was not even regarded as such.

NOTES

1 Women's studies programs across the United States have grown from 17 classes in 1969-1970 to thousands of classes offered through the 503 women's studies programs in universities and colleges. Feminist scholarship continues to challenge and revitalize traditional disciplines including history, modern language, literature, and sociology. For a short history of women's studies see the report for Committee W., AAUP. (1989) Valuing and devaluing women's studies. *Academe,* 35-40.

2 Prior to the widespread admission of women to higher education, campus violence and violence between town and gown was common. Several historical accounts describe male students harassing male professors, who were often very young men themselves. See Kett, J. (1977). *Rites of passage: Adolescence in America 1790 to the present.* New York: Basic Books.

3 See for example, Musil, C. M. and Combs, C. (1988). A cautionary tale: Women's studies programs under attack.

NWSAction, 3, 1-2; and Musil, C. M. (1988). Can one male voice silence us? *NWSAction, 3,* 1. The episode was reported by Timothy Egan. Challenge in women's course roils U. of Washington campus. (1988, April 6). *New York Times.*

REFERENCES

American Association of University Professors. (1989). Valuing and devaluing women's studies. *Academe,* July-August, 35-40.

Biskind, P. (1983). *Seeing is believing: How Hollywood taught us to stop worrying and love the fifties.* New York: Pantheon.

Collison, M. (1988, December 14). No more boys will be boys. *Chronicle of Higher Education,* p. A25-26.

Danforth, A.D. (1990). *A View from the other side of the women's studies classroom.* Unpublished manuscript, Southern Illinois Unviersity at Carbondale, Department of Speech Communications.

Egan, T. (1988, April 6). Challenge in women's course roils U. of Washington campus. New York Times.

Ghadially, R. (1988). Teaching the psychology of sex roles to engineers in India. *Women's Studies Quarterly, 3/4,* 86-90.

Gordon, L. D. (1994). Women on campus. History to use. This volume.

Hall, R., & Sandler, B. (1982) *The classroom climate: A chilly one for women?* (Report from the Project on the Status of Women). Washington, DC: Association of American Colleges.

Hartung, B. (1990). Selective rejection: How students perceive women's studies teachers. *NWSA Journal, 2,* 255-264.

Hearn, P. (1987). Things you were never told about teaching women's studies. *Women's Studies, 13,* 373-379.

Hughes, J. O., & Sandler, B. (1988a). Harassing women a college sport. *New Directions for Women, 18,* 22.

Hughes, J. O., & Sandler, B. (1988b). *Peer harassment: Hassles for women on campus* (Report from the Project on the Status of Women). Washington, DC: Association of American Colleges and university.

Kett, J. (1977). *Rites of passage: Adolescence in America 1790 to the present.* New York: Basic Books.

Kolodny, A. (1989). Dancing between left and right: Feminism and the academic minefield in the 1980s. *Feminist Studies, 3,* 453-466.

Mahony, P. (1986). Boys will be boys: Teaching women's studies in mixed sex groups. *Women's Studies International Forum, 3*, 331-334.

Martin, P. Y., & Hummer, R. A. (1989). Fraternities and rape on campus. *Gender and Society, 3*, 457-473.

Moyers, B., & Tuttle, A. (1983). Overcoming masculine oppression in mixed groups. In *Off their backs...and on our own two feet* (pp. 25-31). Philadelphia, PA: New Society Publishers.

Musil, C. M., & Combs, C. (1988). A cautionary tale: Women's studies programs under attack. *NWSAction, 3*, 1-2.

Musil, C. M. (1988). Can one male voice silence us? NWSAction, *3*, 1.

Rix, S. E. (1988). *The American Woman: 1988-89*. New York: W.W. Norton.

Rothenberg, P. (1989). The hand that pushes the rock. *The Women's Review of Books, 5*, 18-19.

Stimpson, C. R. (1989). Setting agendas, defining challenges. *The Women's Review of Books, 5*, 14.

Tatel, D. S. (1990, February 7). Clear, narrow policies on offensive speech may not run afoul of the First Amendment. *Chronicle of Higher Education,* pp. B1-3.

Turkel, K. (1986). Teaching about women to male-identified students. *Teaching Sociology, 3*, 188-190.

Warshaw, R. (1988). *I never called it rape*. New York: Harper and Row.

Wiener, J. (1990, February 26). Words that wound: Free speech for campus bigots? *The Nation,* pp. 272-276.

AUTHOR NOTES

An earlier version of this chapter was presented at the annual meeting of the Western Social Science Association in Portland, Oregon. Both authors contributed equally to this chapter.

We want to thank Bryce Johnson and a panel of anonymous reviewers for their comments.

PART III

THE LAW AND UNIVERSITY POLICIES AND PROCEDURES

8

THE LEGAL CONTEXT OF SEXUAL HARASSMENT

by Louise F. Fitzgerald

> The attraction of males to females and females to males is a natural sex phenomenon and it is probable that this attraction plays at least a subtle part in most personnel decisions.
> —*Miller v. Bank of America*, 1979

> Surely a requirement that a man or woman run a gauntlet of sexual abuse in return for the privilege of working and making a living can be as demeaning and insulting as the harshest of racial epithets.
> —*Henson v. City of Dundee*, 1981

> Sometimes, even the law does something for the first time.
> —MacKinnon, 1987

There is no longer any question that sexual harassment is a form of sex discrimination prohibited by both Title VII of the Civil Rights Act of 1964 and Title IX of the Education Amendments of 1972. Initially reluctant to recognize harassment as a cognizable offense, courts have become increasingly hospitable to such cases. Although the law is less well-developed with respect to harassment of students, that which does exist suggests that courts take an even more serious view of this offense within academia. This chapter summarizes the current legal situation with particular emphasis on the university community. The discussion is divided into three sections: the employee as a victim of sexual harassment, the student as a victim, and the employee charged with sexual harassment and the consequences thereof.

An earlier version of this chapter appeared in *Sexual Harasment in Higher Education: Concepts and Issues* (pp. 9-15). Washington, DC: NEA, 1992.

UNIVERSITY EMPLOYEES

The harassment of employees, including those who work in a university setting—faculty, staff, student workers—is illegal under the terms of Title VII of the Civil Rights Act, and depending upon the state, may be illegal under relevant state statutes as well. Employees may also be covered under Title IX. Although courts were originally reluctant to interpret Title VII as providing protection from unwanted or abusive sexual approaches [see, for example, *Corne v. Bausch and Lomb, Inc.* (1977) and *Miller v. Bank of America* (1979) where the courts appeared to fear the possibility of an avalanche of frivolous suits], this reluctance has increasingly given way to decisions supporting the theory that such behavior is actionable under this statute [see *Barnes v. Costle*, (1977); *Tomkins v. Public Service Electric & Gas Co.*, (1977), and other early cases; more generally, see Cole (1990) for a review of recent legal developments in sexual harassment and R. Schneider (1987) as well as Connolly and Marshall (1989) for detailed analyses of sexual harassment decisions as they pertain to higher education].

QUID PRO QUO HARASSMENT

Most well-developed at this point is the series of decisions indicating that *quid pro quo* harassment is a clear violation of Title VII. Indeed, so severely do the courts view this form of abuse that even a single incident is generally sufficient to sustain a case against an employer [Equal Employent Opportunity Commission (EEOC,) 1990; R. Schneider, 1987.] Additionally, in cases where the harasser has supervisory responsibility (a common situation in *quid pro quo* cases), the organization is generally held directly liable even though it had no knowledge of his behavior. Such liability historically was limited to the actual economic damage suffered by the victim, such as back pay. Punitive damages were not an available remedy under Title VII. The Civil Rights Act of 1991 amends Title VII to permit an award of limited punitive damages against private employers, but the prohibition of such damages against public employers remains. Compensatory damages are now available against public employers.

HOSTILE ENVIRONMENT HARASSMENT

Far more frequent than *quid pro quo* situations are those in which victims lose no tangible benefits of employment; rather, in the words of the EEOC, the harassing behavior "has the purpose or effect of unreasonably interfering with an individual's work performance or creating an intimidating, hostile or offensive working environment" (EEOC, 1980). Most complaints of sexual harassment are of this sort and cover situations where no job-related decision is conditioned on sexual cooperation. Rather, the victim is placed in an untenable situation either through persistent and unwanted sexual attention, or the creation of an offensive and degrading environment by a pattern of sexual remarks, conversation, suggestions, insults and the like.

Courts were originally slower to support the offensive environment theory of sexual harassment, first legally articulated in 1981 (see *Bundy v. Jackson,* 1981). However, a growing body of case law in the 1980s began to support the viability of this theory, culminating in the first harassment case to reach the Supreme Court, *Meritor Savings Bank, FSB v. Vinson* (1986). Mechelle Vinson was hired as a bank teller by Sidney Taylor, branch manager for a bank that eventually became Meritor Federal Savings. Shortly after the completion of Vinson's probationary period, Taylor allegedly invited her to dinner and during the course of the meal suggested that they go to a motel to have sexual relations. Vinson testified that she at first refused but, out of fear of losing her job, eventually agreed. Taylor thereafter made repeated sexual demands on her, usually at the branch office both during and after business hours. As a result of his demands, Vinson estimated that she had sexual intercourse with Taylor 40 or 50 times over the course of her employment at the bank. In addition, Taylor fondled her in front of other employees, followed her into the women's restroom when she went there alone, exposed himself to her, and even forcibly raped her on several occasions. Because she was afraid of him and of losing her job, Vinson never reported Taylor to his supervisors. The bank's complaint procedures required Vinson to report her complaint to her supervisor, in this case, the harasser. Four years after she was hired, she took sick leave for an indefinite period, and two months later the bank discharged her for abusing that leave. Vinson filed a Title VII discrimination suit against Taylor and the bank, alleging that he had sexually harassed her during the entire course of her employment.

In the original decision, the district court declined to entertain Vinson's claim, noting that any sexual relationship with Taylor was "voluntary" in nature, that Vinson had suffered no tangible harm due to this relationship which was thus not a violation of Title VII. The appellate court disagreed, ruling that the district court had not considered the merit of Vinson's claim under a hostile environment theory. The case eventually reached the Supreme Court, which ruled that a claim of hostile environment sexual harassment is indeed a form of sex discrimination that is actionable under Title VII, and that the language of Title VII is not limited to threat of economic or tangible job loss, although the plaintiff still must demonstrate that the harassment affected the terms or conditions of employment.

The importance and viability of hostile environment claims were recently emphasized by a Florida decision (*Robinson v. Jacksonville Shipyards, Inc.,* 1991) in which the District Court determined that posting pictures of nude and partially nude women is a form of sexual harassment. Previous cases had determined that pornographic pictures may contribute to an atmosphere of sexual harassment. *Robinson* is thought to be the first decision affirming that such pictures themselves can constitute harassment. The judge in the case, Howell Melton, reasoned that the resulting sexualized atmosphere was a significant impediment to women in the workplace and declared "a pre-existing atmosphere that deters women from entering or continuing in a profession or job is no less destructive to and offensive to workplace equality than a sign declaring 'men only'."

FEDERAL GUIDELINES

In addition to its original guidelines on sexual harassment (EEOC, 1980), the agency published an important document providing guidance for defining sexual harassment and establishing employer liability in light of *Meritor* (EEOC, 1990). EEOC notes that *Meritor* affirmed both its original EEOC definition of harassment and the basic principles of the 1980 Guidelines on Sexual Harassment. The agency then offers an extensive discussion of how to determine whether a work environment is hostile and ways to evaluate evidence of sexual harassment. The discussion proposes three important elements for determining whether sexual harassment has occurred: the *unwelcomeness* of the behavior, the *pattern* of behavior, and the *evaluation* of the behavior.

With respect to unwelcomeness, the Supreme Court noted in *Meritor* that the *sine qua non* of a sexual harassment claim is that the alleged advances are "unwelcome." Thus, Title VII does not prohibit all sexual behavior among employees in the workplace, but only that which is unwelcome and offensive to the recipient. Arguing that the distinctions between invited, welcome, tolerated, and rejected behavior are not always easy to determine from the available evidence, EEOC underscores that such distinctions are nonetheless crucial "as sexual conduct becomes unlawful only when it is unwelcome" (EEOC, 1990). It suggests that, in addition to confronting the harasser, telling him to stop, etc., the victim's claim will be considerably strengthened if she contemporaneously makes a protest or files a complaint. It should be pointed out, however, that *Meritor* established that a victim does not automatically lose her right to Title VII relief simply because she chooses not to file a complaint. In Vinson's case, the complaint procedure established by the company did not address issues of sexual harassment and required her to complain first to her supervisor, the person responsible for the harassment. Had the complaint procedure contained alternatives, the employer might have made a stronger case for nonliability because of Vinson's failure to invoke the available procedure.

EEOC (1990) emphasizes that hostile environment claims must generally establish a pattern of offensive behavior, unlike *quid pro quo* claims, which can be triggered by a single event. For example, *Neville v. Taft Broadcasting Co.* (1987), demonstrated that one sexual advance is generally not sufficient to create a hostile environment. EEOC cautions, however, that "a single, unusually severe incident of harassment may be sufficient to constitute a (hostile environment) Title VII violation; the more severe the harassment, the less need to show a repetitive series of incidents. This is particularly true when the harassment is physical" (p. 17).

Finally, the agency advocates the use of a "reasonable person" standard for determining whether a work environment is hostile. In this regard, it should be pointed out that the U. S. Court of Appeals for the Ninth Circuit recently ruled that the appropriate standard is conduct that a "reasonable woman" would consider sufficiently severe or pervasive to "alter the conditions of employment and create an abusive working environment" (*Ellison v. Brady*, 1991). The court declared that a sex-blind "reasonable person" test would tend to be male-biased and ignore the perspective of women, thus arguing that a "reasonable woman" standard was the correct benchmark. This ruling is in accord with the great preponderance of evidence showing that: (1) victims of harassment are, overwhelmingly, female; and (2) men consistently demonstrate a much narrower conception of sexual harassment than women and reliably consider fewer behaviors and situations to be harassing (Fitzgerald & Ormerod, 1991; and others).

LIABILITY

Unlike *quid pro quo* harassment, hostile environment cases are generally thought to trigger employer liability only when the organization knew or should have known of the sexual misconduct. The EEOC argued in its *Vinson* brief that complaints to management or the EEOC, pervasive harassment, or lack of a harassment policy or grievance procedure all contribute to establishing direct or constructive knowledge on the part of an employer. The Supreme Court declined to make a definitive ruling on the issue of employer liability in hostile environment cases, although it quoted the EEOC brief at length.

There is currently disagreement not only over the nature of employer liability, but also over the effectiveness and, therefore, desirability of various forms of liability for inhibiting harassment. Although the law is somewhat unsettled in this area, it seems clear that the most potent protection for an employer is to have a strong anti-harassment policy and clear grievance procedures for implementing it. Additionally, the policy should be one that is "calculated to encourage victims of harassment to come forward" (*Meritor*, 1986, p.2409).

Summary

The sexual harassment of any university employee, be that person faculty, staff or student worker, is a violation of Title VII of the Civil Rights Act and places the university at risk for liability for the harasser's actions. In addition, such behavior may violate relevant state statutes. In cases of *quid pro quo* harassment, even one incident may be sufficient to support a charge against the university, which then may be held responsible even if it had no knowledge of the sexual misconduct.

Charges of hostile environment harassment generally, but not always, require a pattern of unwelcome behavior that a "reasonable woman" would find offensive. Although the extent of employer liability for offensive environment charges is currently unclear, universities can best protect themselves by instituting: (1) strong policies against sexual harassment that are designed to encourage victims to come forward; and (2) clear grievance procedures for implementing such policies.

STUDENTS

Despite the considerable body of formal literature documenting the extent of sexual harassment of college and university students, as well as the wealth of informal, anecdotal and media reports, it is only recently that institutions of higher learning have found themselves the targets of litigation concerning this matter. Title IX of the Education Amendments of 1972 is the relevant federal statute prohibiting sexual discrimination against students in educational institutions that receive federal funding. As noted above, students who are also employed by the university as teaching and research assistants may also claim a cause of action under Title VII, and relevant state statutes may apply as well.

Franklin v. Gwinnet County Public School District (1992)

This case was decided by the Supreme Court in February 1992. At issue was whether a student could sue a school district under Title IX for compensatory damages. In 1988 Franklin alleged that, as a student, she had been subject to a pattern of sexual harassment by one of her teachers. Following what she believed to be an unsatisfactory investigation by the school district and pressure on her to drop her complaint, Franklin filed a Title IX complaint with the Office of Civil Rights of the United States Department of Education. O.C.R. found that the school district had violated Title IX by subjecting Franklin to physical and verbal sexual harassment and by interfering with her right to complain about it. Franklin filed a federal suit in 1988 requesting compensatory damages, basing her case on the theory that the courts can expand remedies in cases of intentional discrimination and that the express desire of Congress to eliminate discrimination on the basis of sex would be thwarted without an adequate remedy for the victims. The court found that compensatory damages are available under Title IX through the filing of private lawsuits. The monetary ramifications of this decision for educational institutions are enormous. Title IX also covers employees and may afford remedies beyond Title VII because there are no caps on punitive damages.

In the federal courts, three additional sexual harassment suits under Title IX further clarify the issue: *Alexander v. Yale* (1980), *Moire v. Temple University School of Medicine*

(1986), *Lipsett v. University of Puerto Rico* (1988). Although the student complainants did not prevail in any of these three cases, the decisions established that sexual harassment charges do lie within the purview of Title IX. The cases also outlined the grounds for further litigation in this area. Because Title IX imposes a requirement that institutions establish a grievance procedure for claims of sex discrimination—as opposed to Title VII, which merely recommends it—and because colleges and universities are making efforts to raise awareness of sexual harassment, litigation may increase as students become aware of their rights. Students, therefore, may be more likely to challenge academic sexual harassment in the courts as the scope and extent of Title IX relief becomes clearer. (See *Franklin,* above.)

Alexander v. Yale (1980)

Alexander v. Yale has earned a place in legal history as the first federal case alleging sexual harassment brought under the auspices of Title IX. The case is particularly interesting because its plaintiffs alleged a variety of claims—both *quid pro quo* and hostile environment—as well as the lack of appropriate grievance procedures, as required by Title IX. The students asked for injunctive relief in the form of the development of an appropriate grievance procedure at the University. In the Connecticut District Court where the case was first heard in 1977, the court held that the plaintiff who alleged that she received a low grade because she refused to cooperate sexually with her professor did indeed have a "justiciable" claim. This established, for the first time, that *quid pro quo* harassment of students violates Title IX. The court explicitly rejected the claims of her co-plaintiffs—who alleged that they were harmed by the sexually intimidating and hostile atmosphere at Yale—holding that environment and atmosphere were "imponderables" not contemplated by Title IX. The students' further allegation, that Yale's failure to establish appropriate grievance procedures for claims of sexual harassment contributed to the offensive environment and was tantamount to official policy condoning harassment, was also rejected.

On appeal, the Second Circuit affirmed the decision of the lower court, further confirming the right to sue for *quid pro quo* harassment under Title IX. Other issues were left undecided. For example, the court did not address the hostile environment issue which had become moot due to the graduation of the complainants. In addition, Yale had in the interim established a grievance procedure. Thus, although the decision leaves significant questions unanswered, it did firmly establish that a student claim of sexual harassment by a professor lies within the purview of Title IX, at least when the student can claim that she has suffered some tangible educational harm (see R. Schneider, 1987, for a thorough discussion).

Moire v. Temple University School of Medicine (1986) and Lipsett v. University of Puerto Rico (1986)

In *Moire,* the second federal suit brought under Title IX, a woman medical student brought a hostile environment claim alleging that she had failed her third-year psychiatric clerkship due to sexual harassment by her supervisor. Moire raised no *quid pro quo* allegations, asserting rather that she had been subjected to harassment on the basis of her sex, and that the university had conspired to protect the supervisor. Although the district court did not find the evidence in Moire's case to be convincing, it did allow the claim, which was based solely on an allegation of environmental harm. A very similar case, and decision, can be found in *Lipsett v. University of Puerto Rico* (1986). In combination with the Supreme Court's decisions in *Franklin* and *Meritor,* these strongly suggest that hostile environment cases may significantly increase in the near future. [Elgart & Schanfield, (this volume) argue that the future of hostile environment theory under Title VII is still unclear; interested readers should consult their article for a complete discussion.]

Implications for Institutions of Higher Learning

The recent Supreme Court decision in *Franklin v. Gwinnett County Public Schools* (February 26, 1992) is the most significant ruling under Title IX. It clearly establishes that money damages are available to students and other victims of intentional gender discrimination (in this case sexual harassment). It has broad implications for college and universities including:

- The decision is likely to be construed as expanding significantly the remedies previously understood to be available under two federal anti-discrimination statutes—Title VII of the Civil Rights Act of 1964 and Section 504 of the Rehabilitation Act of 1973, which prohibits discrimination by recipients of federal funds on the basis of race and disability. *Franklin's* recognition of more extensive remedies under Title IX almost certainly means that courts will determine that the same remedies are available under Title VII and Section 504.

- Because money damages are now available, plaintiffs suing under Title IX will be entitled to jury trials.

- The expanded remedy that *Franklin* establishes is limited to cases involving intentional discrimination. The extent to which discriminatory activity of an employee can be imputed to the educational institution will assume ever greater significance in new cases.

- Colleges and universities are well advised to put preventive programs in place and to review internal practices and procedures aimed at minimizing exposure to liability such as that allowed by *Franklin*.

In the most complete analysis of academic sexual harassment so far available in the legal literature, Schneider

(1987) notes the paucity of applicable federal cases and offers an analysis extrapolated from Title VII jurisprudence and applied to the faculty/student case. She offers a definition that tracks the EEOC definition of harassment in the workplace, suggests the use of the "reasonable student" standard for determining whether an environment is hostile, accepts the proposition that hostile environment harassment requires a pattern of behavior whereas *quid pro quo* can be triggered by a single incident, and generally suggests a theory consistent with the guidance recently offered by EEOC (1990) with respect to workplace harassment. She cautions, however, that some distinctions are relevant. For example, the notion of hostile environment may prove even more powerful in academic situations. She writes: "A nondiscriminatory environment is essential to maximum intellectual growth and is therefore an integral part of the educational benefits that a student receives . . . . Any diminution or deprivation of such an academic benefit on the basis of sex violates Title IX" (p. 551). She argues further that a higher standard should be imposed upon faculty members' behavior toward students than upon employers' behavior towards workers. "The student-faculty relationship encompasses a trust and dependency that does not inherently exist between parties involved in a sexual harassment claim under Title VII" (p. 551). Noting that Title IX mandates a grievance procedure for allegations of sex discrimination, whereas Title VII does not, she suggests that "the inclusion of such prophylactic measures in Title IX may suggest that Congress perceived a need for broader protection against discriminatory behavior in the academic context" (p. 545).

Schneider is not alone in suggesting that the courts may hold faculty to a higher standard than employers. In their chapter in this volume on campus policies and sexual harassment law, Little and Thompson, state: "In the world of work, actionable harassment must be severe and pervasive. [Recent legal decisions] suggest that this standard does not apply to the professional members of an academic community. The courts maintain high standards of conduct for academia. Indeed, these standards are often more strict than the law requires."

Summary

Although the sexual harassment of students by faculty has only recently become a subject of litigation, the federal cases that have been decided indicate that both *quid pro quo* harassment and hostile environment harassment are cognizable claims under Title IX. In addition, there is reason to believe that the courts may take an even stronger position on academic harassment than on its workplace counterpart, holding institutions of higher learning to a stricter standard than that previously applied to employers. The scope of institutional liability suggests the desirability of a proactive stance on this issue, including but not limited to strong anti-harassment policies, clear grievance procedures, and active programs to inform and educate both faculty and students.

GROUNDS FOR DISCIPLINE OF FACULTY

Although colleges and universities have not often pursued discipline against tenured faculty members for sexually harassing students, Cole (1986) stated, "Courts appear willing to defer to the academic judgment of college administrators in their attempts to discipline offending faculty. The courts regard the college's protection of students from such abuse as an important duty with concomitant responsibility and liability such as colleges have not seen since the demise of *in loco parentis*" (p. 17). In this context, it is important to note that tenure has proven to be no immunity in cases where institutions have determined that a faculty member is guilty of serious sexual harassment. Three recent cases demonstrate the courts' willingness to support faculty discipline.

Cockburn v. Santa Monica Community College (1984)

Cockburn, an instructor at Santa Monica Community College, was terminated from his position for sexual harassment. He sued the college, alleging that the punishment was too severe. Cockburn admitted to grabbing and kissing a student employee, but denied allegations by several other students that he had made lewd comments and fondled them against their will. A psychologist examined Cockburn and testified that he could be rehabilitated. Despite this testimony, the court upheld the termination, stressing that the personnel commission that made the decision had a "grave responsibility . . . to the (college) and their personnel, the professors, instructors, students . . . and the general public" (p. 597).

Korf v. Ball State University (1984)

Korf is instructive on several accounts. The case demonstrated that same-sex harassment is accorded the same treatment as heterosexual cases; in addition, the court rejected the arguments that consent provides a defense in cases of faculty/student sexual harassment, and supported the faculty member's termination (even though Ball State did not have any explicit policy prohibiting faculty/student sexual relationships), finding instead that Korf's behavior constituted an unethical exploitation of students. In *Korf,* the university committee charged with hearing the case determined that Korf's advances to male students, consensual or not, involved unethical conduct, as defined in the *Faculty Handbook,* and recommended first probation, then, on remand, dismissal. Korf offered the defense that a student in question had initially consented to the relationship and that, in any event, the university had violated his constitutional right to due process. Since Ball State had no explicit policy covering these matters, Korf argued that he had inadequate warning concerning the consequences of his conduct.

The court held that the student's consent or lack of consent was not the issue, as the complaint against Korf was "exploiting students for his private advantage." It relied explicitly on the fiduciary nature of the professor-student relationship and noted "University professors occupy an important place in our society and have concomitant ethical obligations" (p. 1227). Despite the absence of an explicit policy, the court noted that common sense and good judgment should have warned Korf that his conduct was inappropriate. The court cited, with approval, the AAUP Statement on Professional

Ethics that admonishes the professor to demonstrate respect for the student and "adhere to his proper role as an intellectual guide and counselor."

Levitt v. University of Texas at El Paso (1986)

Levitt is another case that demonstrates, once again, that tenure does not protect faculty members from the professional consequences of their actions. Levitt, a tenured professor of chemistry, was terminated by the University of Texas at El Paso based on complaints of pervasive sexual harassment of female students. In challenging the decision, Levitt offered a due process argument, claiming that the university's disciplinary procedures were biased against him and had violated his rights of due process. The strategy was not successful. The Fifth Circuit held that even though the institution had failed to follow its own rules exactly, it did not deny Levitt any constitutional guarantees.

Naragon v. Wharton, et al (1984)

Naragon is another case where a decision to discipline a university employee (in this case a female graduate assistant), involved in a relationship with a female student was made and upheld not on the basis of the assistant's sexual orientation but on the belief of the university that the relationship with the student was a breach of professional ethics and undermined Naragon's effectiveness with other students. Naragon sued the university based on a violation of her constitutional rights under the First and Fourteenth Amendments when she was removed from teaching and her assignment changed, although she suffered no loss of pay. The court found that it was the relationship with the student and not Naragon's homosexuality that occasioned the discipline and that there was no need to examine the issue of any violation of her constitutional rights.

Summary

As this review of relevant court cases makes clear, the courts grant considerable deference to academic institutions' right to discipline faculty members for sexual harassment. Although care must obviously be taken when preparing and pursuing a case where serious penalties may ensue, universities need not avoid vigorous disciplinary measures for fear of possible retaliatory legal action. Universities that have based discipline and dismissal of faculty accused of sexual harassment on professional standards internal to the institution rather than on external or legal standards have found support in the courts.

POSTSCRIPT

Two major legal developments occurred in 1993: the appearance of the EEOC's supplement (U.S. Equal Employment Opportunity Commission, 1993) to its original Sex Discrimination Guidelines (see discussion above) and the Supreme Court's decision in *Harris v. Forklift Systems, Inc.* Although neither development took place within the specific context of higher education, it is likely that each will have implications for colleges, universities and other institutions of higher learning.

Harris v. Forklift Systems, Inc. (1993)

Harris represents the second statement issued by the Supreme Court on the topic of sexual harassment. Like *Meritor,* its predecessor at the highest level of review, *Harris* was a hostile environment case and was expected to resolve conflicts among the lower courts on two major points: the appropriate standard of severity in hostile environment cases and the issue of whose perspective (i.e., reasonable person, reasonable victim, etc.) should be dispositive. Unfortunately, most observers agree that only the first of these issues was clearly resolved.

Theresa Harris worked as a manager at Forklift Systems, Inc., a rental equipment company in Tennessee. She sued her employer, claiming that the conduct of Charles

Hardy, the company's president, constituted an abusive working environment because of her gender. Among other facts, Harris alleged that Hardy made frequent sexual innuendoes, insulted her in front of other employees (e.g., "You're a woman, what do you know?"), and required her and other female employees to behave in demeaning ways (e.g., asking them to remove coins from his front pants pocket, throwing objects on the ground and asking them to pick them up). Deciding what they acknowledged to be a "close case," both the Magistrate who made the original decision and the 6th Circuit Court of Appeals who confirmed it concluded that Hardy's behavior did not create an abusive environment because it was not "so severe as to ...seriously affect [Harris'] psychological well-being" or lead her to "suffer injury.". The Court reversed and remanded, holding that psychological injury is not required to establish that sexual harassment has occurred. Delivering the opinion for the unanimous Court, Justice Sandra Day O'Connor remarked somewhat dryly . . . "Title VII comes into play before the harassing conduct leads to a nervous breakdown." The decision makes it considerably easier for plaintiffs to make their cases without the necessity of laying open their psychological history for public scrutiny, although evidence of psychological injury continues to be relevant to damage awards.

　　With respect to the second issue, the Court's consistent use of the "reasonable person" terminology appeared to retain the traditional, theoretically sex-blind, perspective despite urgings to do otherwise [some appellate courts, notably the 9th Circuit, have adopted a "reasonable woman" standard, whereas several *amicus* briefs in the case (e.g., the American Psychological Association) argued for the use of "reasonable victim"]. Indeed by requiring both an objective standard (i.e., reasonable person) and a subjective standard (i.e., the victim must also perceive the environment as hostile), the Court appears to have posed a contradiction or, at the least, avoided the issue for the present. It is virtually certain that we have not heard the last of this issue.

REFERENCES

Alexander v. Yale University, 631 F.2d 178 (2d Cir. 1980).

Barnes v. Costle, 13 F.E.P. Cases 123 (D.D.C. 1974), rev'd, 561 R2d 983 (D.C. Cir. 1977).

Bundy v. Jackson, 641 F.2d 934 (D.C. Cir.1981).

Cockburn v. Santa Monica Community College District Personnel Commission, 207 Cal. Reptr. 589 (Cal. App. 2 Dist. 1984). 20 Ed. Law Rep. 1178 (1984).

Cole, E. K. (1986). Recent developments in sexual harassment. *Journal of College and University Law, 13,* 267-284.

Cole, E. K. (1990). Sexual harassment on campus: A legal compendium (2nd ed.). Washington, DC: National Association of College and University Attorneys.

Connolly, W. B., Jr., & Marshall, A. B. (1989). Sexual harassment of university or college students by faculty members. *Journal of College and University Law, 15,* 381-403.

Corne v. Bausch & Lomb, 390 F. Supp. 161 (D. Ariz, 1975), vacated and remanded, 562 F. 2d 55 (9th Cir. 1977).

Ellison v. Brady, 924 F.2d 872 (9th Cir. 1991).

Equal Employment Opportunity Commission (1980). Guidelines on discrimination because of sex. *Federal Register 45,* 74676-74677.

Equal Employment Opportunity Commission (1990). Policy guidance on current issues of sexual harassment. Reprinted in E. K. Cole (1990). Sexual harassment on campus: A legal compendium (2nd ed.). Washington, DC: National Association of College and University Attorneys.

Fitzgerald, L. F., & Ormerod, A. J. (1991). Perceptions of sexual harassment: The effect of gender and context. *Psychology of Women Quarterly, 15,* 281-294.

Franklin v. Gwinnett County School District. 112 S. Ct. 1028 (1992).

Harris v. Forklift Systems, Inc; 976 F.2d 733, (6th Cir. 1992). No. 92-1168 S. Ct. (1993)

Henson v. City of Dundee, 682 F.2d 897, 908n.18 (11th Cir. 1981).

Korf v. Ball State University, 726 F.2d 1222 (7th Cir. 1984).

Levitt v. University of Texas at El Paso, 759 F.2d 1224 (5th Cir. 1985), cert. denied, 106 S. Ct. 599 (1986).

Lipsett v. University of Puerto Rico, 864 F.20 881 (1st Cir. 1988).

MacKinnon, C. A. (1987) Feminism unmodified: Discourses on life and law. Cambridge, MA: Harvard University Press.

Meritor Savings Bank, FSB v. Vinson, 477 U.S. 57, 106 S. Ct. 2399 (1986).

Miller v. Bank of America, 418 F.Supp. 233 (N.D. Cal. 1976), rev'd and remanded, 600 F. 2d 211 (9th Cir. 1979).

Moire v. Temple University School of Medicine, 613 F. Supp. 1360 (E.D. Pa. 1985), aff'd, 800 F. 2d 1136 (3d Circ. 1986).

Naragon V. Wharton, 737 F.2d 1403 (5th Cir. 1984).

Neville v. Taft Broadcasting Co., 42 FEP Cases 1314 (W.D.N.Y. 1987).

Robinson v. Jacksonville Shipyards, Inc., 760F.Supp. 1486 (M.D. Fla. 1991).

Schneider, R.G. (1987). Sexual harassment and higher education. *Texas Law Review*, 65, 525-583.

Tomkins v. Public Service Electric & Gas Co., 422 F.Supp. 553 (D.N.J. 1976), rev'd, 568 F.2d 1044 (3rd Cir. 1977).

U.S. Equal Employment Opportunity Commission (1993). Proposed harassment guidelines. *Federal Register, 58*, 51266.

9

INSTITUTIONAL POLICIES AND PROCEDURES

by Louise F. Fitzgerald

> The best means by which a university can protect itself . . . is to draft, implement, and enforce a sexual harassment policy.
> —Connolly & Marshall, 1989

There is general agreement that the most important action a university can take is to establish a strong policy against sexual harassment and a clearly articulated grievance procedure for handling complaints. Unions also have a role to play in ensuring a discrimination-free workplace as discussed by others in this book. Not only does Title IX mandate that institutions of higher learning establish procedures for resolving complaints of discrimination on the basis of sex, but the *Meritor* decision establishes the importance of such procedures in adjudicating Title VII claims as well. This chapter will examine what is currently known about institutional policies and review relevant policy recommendations concerning their establishment and maintenance.

EXTENT AND NATURE OF POLICIES

The most extensive analysis of academic sexual harassment policies to date was provided by Robertson, Dyer, and Campbell (1988). With funding provided by the U. S. Department of Education through the Women's Educational Equity Act, these authors surveyed nearly 700 American colleges and universities—approximately 10% of all American institutions of higher learning—concerning: (1) their methods for handling sexual harassment complaints; (2) the content of

An earlier version of this chapter appeared in *Sexual Harasment in Higher Education: Concepts and Issues* (pp. 36-44). Washington, DC: NEA, 1992.

their institutional policies and procedures; and (3) their assessment of the effectiveness of various types of university responses to the problem.

Sixty-six percent of the respondent institutions had formal sexual harassment policies and 46% had specific grievance procedures for dealing with complaints. These overall figures obscure some interesting patterns, however. When the sample was divided into public institutions (which tended to be large) and private institutions (which tended to be small) a clearer picture emerges. Nearly 80% of public schools had policies and 54% had grievance procedures. In comparison, slightly over 50% of private schools had policies and only 38% had procedures. In general, private schools were less likely to have addressed the problem vigorously. For example, fewer private schools had conducted sexual harassment self-studies and many tended to underestimate the number of complaints they received, compared to the average number provided by those who kept formal statistics. The Robertson study found that much of the difference between public and private institutions could be attributed to religious institutions, which tended to have few equity policies of any kind.

With respect to actual complaint resolution, the most frequent outcome was an informal process in which the complainant was given advice about handling the situation. Official investigations were relatively rare and actual formal sanctions against faculty almost nonexistent. The authors note: "It seems that, faculty fears to the contrary, institutions seldom have levied career-damaging sanctions for sexual harassment. Most cases are handled and resolved informally" (Robertson et al., 1988, p. 799). Nevertheless, many respondents reported that considerable apprehension surrounded the institution of sexual harassment policies. The most commonly expressed fear was of false complaints (78%), which was linked to concern about possible damage to faculty careers. Faculty were also concerned that confidentiality would not be appropriately safeguarded, or that their freedom of speech or association would be abridged.

Noting that fear of false accusations is a major source of resistance to the implementation of sexual harassment policies and procedures, the authors calculated the maximum number of complaints that could be classified as false and reported: "A rough extrapolation from the numbers given would make the false complaints less than one percent of the annual complaints. This is a maximum estimate that does not take into account that some complaints listed as false by administrators may have been genuine." (p. 800).

These researchers also examined the actual policies established by the responding institutions. They reported that most of these were based to some degree on the EEOC Guidelines (1980), particularly the portion attempting to prohibit forced sexual relations through the misuse of power or authority (*quid pro quo*). They note, however, that definitions including the notion of "hostile environment" were much less widespread. Many of the institutions that used the Guidelines as a model had modified—that is, weakened or eliminated—this section, apparently because of apprehension concerning the possible implications of allowing the offense to be at least partially defined by the victim's perceptions of the environment. Given that the Robertson data were collected in 1984, when the EEOC Guidelines and sexual harassment litigation were both relatively new, it is likely that current policies are more likely to incorporate a "hostile environment" element into their definitions of sexual harassment. The recent success of a hostile environment claim at the highest level of judicial review (i.e., *Meritor*) suggests it would be prudent for institutions to do so.

THE ROLE OF THE UNION

It is important to mention the special role played by unions. As Gluck (this volume) has noted, few issues are as fraught with contradictions for unionists—particularly feminist unionists—as sexual harassment. For faculty members and other employees who belong to a union, the problem raises additional issues of due process, contractual enforcement, and above all, moral dilemmas that are specific to union members. First and foremost, the association should be involved in the formulation of procedures for handling sexual harassment complaints to ensure protection and due process for its members, whether accused or accuser. There is also a need to educate members about sexual harassment. In the face of proposed institutional sanctions, the union is often called on to defend an accused perpetrator whose actions, if proven, are clearly abhorrent to the membership. Conversely, because standard contractual language includes a non-discrimination section, and given that sexual harassment is defined as sex discrimination, unions may be held liable for violation of their "duty of fair representation" if they are presented with a case and do nothing to assist the member who has been subjected to harassment.

Such dual responsibilities can create dilemmas, but also often yield creative solutions. Gluck describes just such a situation at California State University-Northridge, whose union-supported Women's Council has developed a procedure in which the Faculty Rights Committee assists the accused perpetrator through the necessary process, while other committee members offer support and assistance to the complainant. This dual process makes clear that, although the union will protect faculty rights to due process, it also opposes sexual harassment and will support complainants. The most important message here is that unions must work with the administration, the Faculty Senate and other such bodies to establish a strong anti-harassment policy and clear, workable procedures for acting on complaints. Public support of the union, when added to that of the administration, the Senate, and other campus organizations, can contribute enormously to eradicating harassment in both the classroom and the academic workplace.

GRIEVANCE ARBITRATION

Arbitrators under collective bargaining agreements have been addressing sexual harassment issues on a limited, but regular, basis since at least 1977. Monat and Gomez (1986) reviewed 36 arbitration cases on the topic and found that "the issue of sexual harassment virtually always arises in arbitration where a grievance has been filed by the alleged harasser after discipline has been imposed" (p. 26). Most arbitrators have cited or followed the EEOC Guidelines on the conduct necessary for a finding that harassment occurred. Arbitrators have found actionable harassment occurred when offensive remarks and leering went on for a period of time, when "accidental" touching of female students' breasts, arms, and legs happened during instruction, and when obscene drawings were posted where they could be seen by employees.

Arbitrators have also upheld the employer's right to impose discipline in cases of harassment. Discharges were upheld by arbitrators where it was proven that the sex-related conduct had occurred over a long period of time, where the harassment was accompanied by a threat of rape or assault, and where the employer, such as a hospital or nursing home, had a special need for sensitivity. In other cases, employees were suspended for a short time, ordered to obtain therapeutic counseling, and/or given final warning and a long-term suspension. Thus, in an increasing number of cases, arbitration may prove a practical alternative to the prospect of extended litigation.

PROCEDURES FOR RESPONDING TO COMPLAINTS

There is considerable guidance available to institutions that wish to establish or revise their procedures for responding to sexual harassment. Information is also available for unions that wish to negotiate contractual language on non-discrimination. Cole (1990a) has developed an extensive outline giving a step-by-step procedure that scrupulously attends to the legal rights of all parties, as well as to the practicalities involved in conducting an investigation and grievance resolution. In addition, R. G. Schneider (1987) and Connolly and Marshall (1989) discuss various aspects of procedures from a legal perspective, and Remick et al. (1990) provide guidance from the administrative point of view. In general, institutions should keep in mind the following principles.

1. Procedures should be designed in such a way that reporting is encouraged. It is sometimes difficult for colleges

and universities to recognize that receiving a number of complaints of sexual harassment indicates that their program is not effective. Given the nature of sexual harassment, it is natural for institutions to be troubled when a number of students or employees report that they are being exploited, demeaned or in other ways harassed by other members of the academic community. However, given that there is no reason to believe that any institution is immune to this problem, lack of student complaints is no reason for self-congratulation. Rather, it probably implies that the procedures for making such complaints are unknown, unclear or ineffective.

On a practical level, this principle means that colleges and universities should identify, train, and publicize the existence of persons whom students and employees can feel comfortable contacting concerning problems they are having with sexual harassment. Although each campus culture is different, it seems reasonable to suggest that multiple avenues should be open for students to access the grievance system. Experience suggests that female contact persons are viewed more positively by complainants. However, both male and female individuals should be available for complainants, as male victims do exist, and it is likely that victims will find it easier to discuss their experiences with someone of the same sex. Students should be encouraged to talk with whomever they find most comfortable; it is critical that they be offered a procedure that does not require them to go through an official of their department, to confront the harasser personally before making a complaint, or to sign a formal statement before any resolution procedure can be initiated. Likewise, faculty or staff should have access to an official outside the normal academic hierarchy within their department or college.

2. Both formal and informal procedures should be available. Informal observation, formal research, and common sense all confirm that students or employees will use informal complaint mechanisms, but that they are reluctant to sign formal complaints (Meek & Lynch, 1983). Unfortunately, many institutions make the mistake of assuming that there is nothing to be done unless they are presented with a written, signed

statement. Yet, the law is very clear that institutions are liable for sexual harassment of which they have knowledge, whether the student signs a formal complaint or not. As Remick et al. (1990) point out "Should a person refuse to sign a statement, then later sue, claiming that the institution knew of the situation but did nothing to keep it from continuing, the institution would be hard pressed to say that it has a policy on the issue, knew of this complaint, but did not act because their procedures for formal complaints were not exactly followed" (p. 196).

These authors argue that legal requirements do not rule out informal actions. They differentiate between formal and informal procedures, not by whether there is a signed complaint, but rather by the outcome and whether there is an investigation. Whether or not there is a written statement, informal complaints can result in a variety of actions. The alleged harasser may agree to apologize, change his behavior, reverse an educational decision made about the complainant, or even accept actions such as leaves of absence, counseling, demotions or resignation—all without formal disciplinary procedures being invoked. Care should be taken to ensure due process in both informal *and* formal hearings or investigations. A formal procedure requires a complaint that is written out and signed and an investigation into the facts, and results in formal disciplinary action if the complaint is supported.

In general, informal procedures are sufficient when the harasser agrees that the incident(s) alleged did take place—although the harasser may offer a different interpretation, or even be surprised and embarrassed that the behavior was considered offensive. If the professor denies the behavior occurred, then a formal process—including an investigation—will need to be initiated if the situation is to be resolved. A formal process is also indicated if there have been previous complaints against the professor, or if the behavior is particularly serious or severe. Thus, informal procedures are designed to be educational, whereas formal procedures are more legal in nature. Individuals experienced in the area of harassment agree that the overwhelming majority of complaints can be resolved informally and that students generally do not wish to pursue action against a faculty member. Rather, they simply want the behavior to stop and to continue their education undisturbed.

3. **Procedures should be appropriate and accessible for faculty and staff as well as students.** Most discussions of sexual harassment in the university focus on the difficulties experienced by female students. But, as we have seen, women who are employed in academia are at least as equally, at risk as their student counterparts. It is important that universities design and publicize their policies and procedures in such a way that they are accessible and appropriate for faculty and staff as well as students. In practice, this likely requires— among other things—that multiple channels be available for reporting. Universities like other organizations have well-developed institutional subcultures, and the nuances of life in academia suggest that a woman carpenter or custodian may not see a faculty committee as particularly relevant or helpful. Similarly, the Affirmative Action Office, situated outside the traditional academic hierarchy, may not be seen as an appropriate resource by women faculty. Finally, the emphasis on harassment of students common to most university brochures and informational posters often creates the appearance that institutional priorities and programs are not concerned with faculty and staff.

A particularly well-designed program that specifically addresses these concerns is that of the University of Illinois, whose informational brochure clearly designates separate resource offices for students, faculty and staff. As an additional alternative, the office of the University Ombudsman serves as a resource for any member of the campus community. The narrative makes clear that campus policies apply to both students and employees, and the brochure includes a wide range of relevant examples. Materials such as these ensure that institutional programs and resources are available to all individuals who need them.

4. **Publicize policies and procedures widely.** The strongest policies and most carefully designed procedures will

be ineffective unless the university community is familiar with and educated about them. Over the last several years, institutions have developed a number of effective methods for educating faculty and students about sexual harassment. One of the most effective is to develop and distribute a brochure outlining the institutional policy. Brochures should include the university's definition of sexual harassment, a strong statement that such behavior is illegal, unprofessional and will not be tolerated, and information concerning whom to contact for advice, information, or to make a complaint. In addition, many institutions publish their policies in the schedule of classes, as well as in the course catalogue. Articles in the student newspaper have been found to be very effective for raising the issue and educating the campus community.

One of the most effective educational strategies is to offer workshops for faculty and staff. These require an initial investment of time and money, but are ultimately well worth the cost. Robertson et al. (1988) indicated that 64% of institutions responding to a survey item concerning educational methods had instituted workshops. Those institutions reported that they were among the most effective strategies available. Many schools have made such workshops mandatory, particularly for staff and administrators. For educating students, guest lectures and presentations in classes and student meetings are generally considered very successful.

To be effective, schools should use multiple methods of publicity and education. Robertson et al. (1988) found that the average number of methods used was 5.3 for those using any method, with large schools using more. Additionally, it is important for the education program to be ongoing. Students are a transient group, new faculty and staff arrive every year, post-doctoral fellows come for a year or two and then move on, and policies as well as the names and phone numbers of ombuds officers change. Thus, brochures should be distributed every year and updated periodically. Articles in the newspaper should be published on an annual basis, and workshops should be made available regularly. Successful eradication of sexual harassment requires that institutions make an authentic and substantial commitment to the process.

Symbolic gestures, one-shot programs and other cosmetic devices are ineffective and, worse, generate cynicism among the campus community concerning the administration's intentions and commitment.

5. Publicize statistics on harassment complaints and their outcomes. To be effective, policies and procedures must have credibility within the campus community. Students and faculty need to be made aware that complaints are taken seriously, handled expeditiously, and treated fairly by the institution. In addition to developing credibility for the university's efforts, such a procedure serves as a deterrent as it gives public notice that the institution will take action.

The American Council on Education (1990) strongly recommends such reporting procedures as part of its guidelines for developing effective campus programs. One of the leaders in this area has been the University of Minnesota, which has developed a useful format for such reporting. Complaints of harassment are identified by the status of the complainant and respondent, the date and nature of the complaint, and the date and nature of the outcome; names are not used. Formal and informal complaints are reported separately, and summary statistics for all complaints and inquiries are reported as well. Examples of the Minnesota report can be found in Cole (1990b).

6. Publicize institutional support for preventive and remedial programs. Finally, and most importantly, the central administration should take a strong and public stand in support of institutional efforts to eradicate sexual harassment. All institutions reporting successful sexual harassment programs indicate that strong support from the top administration was critical to their success (Robertson et al., 1988). In addition, it is extremely helpful to have the support of the union, and Faculty Senate, or a similar governance body that has credibility with faculty members.

Summary

The American Council on Education (ACE, 1990), in its policy statement concerning campus sexual harassment policy and educational programs, suggested that effective programs contain the following elements:

1. A basic definition of sexual harassment;

2. A strong policy statement indicating that it will not be tolerated;

3. Effective information channels for informing the university about the campus policy;

4. Effective educational programs designed to help all members of the campus community to recognize and discourage sexual harassment; and

5. An accessible grievance procedure that offers multiple methods of initiating complaints, procedures to protect the rights of all individuals involved, and prompt investigation and resolution of grievances.

ACE notes that "Each institution has the obligation, for moral as well as legal reasons, to develop policies, procedures and programs that protect students and employees from sexual harassment and to establish an environment in which such unacceptable behavior will not be tolerated" (ACE, 1990).

REFERENCES

American Council on Education. (1990). Sexual harassment on campus: Suggestions for reviewing campus policy and educational programs. In E. K. Cole *Sexual harassment on campus: A legal compendium* (2nd ed.). Washington, DC: National Association of College and University Attorneys.

Cole, E. K. (1990a). How to handle the investigation of sexual harassment claims. In E.K. Cole (1990). *Sexual harassment on campus: A legal compendium.* (2nd ed.). Washington, DC: National Association of College and University Attorneys.

Cole, E. K. (1990). *Sexual harassment on campus: A legal compendium.* (2nd ed.). Washington, DC: National Association of College and University Attorneys.

Connolly, W. B., Jr., & Marshall, A. B. (1989). Sexual harassment of university or college students by faculty members. *Journal of College and University Law, 15,* 381-403.

Equal Employment Opportunity Commission (1980). Guidelines on discrimination because of sex. *Federal Register, 45,* 74676-74677.

Meek, P., & Lynch, A. Q. (1983). Establishing an informal grievance procedure for cases of sexual harassment of students. *Journal of the National Association for Women, Deans, Administrators, and Counselors, 46,* 30-33.

Monat, J. S. & Gomez, A. (1986). Sexual harassment and the grievance arbitration option. *The Arbitration Journal, 41,* 24-29.

Remick, H., Salisbury, J., Stringer, D., & Ginorio, A. (1990). Investigating complaints of sexual harassment. In M.A. Paludi (Ed.)., *Ivory power: Sexual harassment on campus.* Albany, NY: SUNY Press.

Robertson, C., Dyer, C. C., & Campbell, D. A. (1988). Campus harassment: Sexual harassment policies and procedures at institutions of higher learning. *Sings, 13,* 792-812

Schneider, R. G. (1987). Sexual harassment and higher education. *Texas Law Review, 65,* 525-583.

10

CAMPUS POLICIES, THE LAW, AND SEXUAL RELATIONSHIPS

by Doric Little and John A. Thompson

State legislation and judicial interpretations of federal Equal Employment Opportunity Commission (EEOC) guidelines have focused increased attention on sexual harassment in the workplace and, in response, most academic institutions now have sexual harassment policies in place. These policies tend to protect faculty and staff from sexual harassment. But few of them address the potential problems posed by administrator/faculty-student relationships.

There is today a growing concern about the legality of "unwelcome" though possibly consensual faculty-student sexual relationships. Colleges and faculty organizations such as NEA need to keep the legal and ethical propriety of such relationships under continuous scrutiny. This chapter summarizes the case law on sexual harassment and analyzes the responses offered by a sample of colleges and universities.

The U.S. Supreme Court first ruled on a sexual harassment case in *Meritor Savings Bank, FSB v. Vinson* (1986). The Court ruled in *Meritor* that sexual advances by co-workers (or by analogy, professors) that created a "hostile work environment" are a form of sex discrimination that is actionable under Title VII. The decision stated:

> Relevant to the charges at issue in this case, the guidelines provide that sexual misconduct constitutes prohibited "sexual harassment," whether or not it is directly linked to the grant or denial of an economic *quid pro quo*, where "such conduct has the purpose or effect of unreasonably interfering with an individual's work performance or creating an intimidating, hostile, or offensive working environment."

An earlier version of this chapter appeared in *Thought and Action,* Spring 1989, 5 (1), 17-24.

The Court then addressed the "welcomeness" of the advances:

> But the fact that sex-related conduct was "voluntary," in the sense that the complainant was not forced to participate against her will, is not a defense to a sexual harassment suit brought under Title VII. The gravamen of any sexual harassment claim is that the alleged sexual advances were "unwelcome". . . . The correct inquiry is whether respondent by her conduct indicated that the alleged sexual advances were unwelcome, not whether her actual participation in sexual intercourse was voluntary.

The Court also determined that the legal concept of *respondeat superior* made commercial institutions such as Meritor liable for damages as a remedy for the harassment. The liability of private colleges depends upon the position that state courts have taken on whether charitable institutions have immunity from lawsuits. In some states, the concept of sovereign immunity protects public institutions and would probably shift liability for damages to the individual harasser. Regardless of whether or not the institution could be sued, the potential jeopardy to faculty could be most serious.

The cases that directly involve faculty members have been adjudicated on a somewhat different basis than the *Meritor*-type decisions. Typically, an institution has terminated the contract of a faculty member for involvement in sexual relationships with students. The key cases in this issue were heard before *Meritor*. In *Cockburn v. Santa Monica Community College District* (1984), the state court said:

> Community college district personnel commission did not abuse its discretion by dismissing an instructor who embraced and kissed his student laboratory assistant once, and attempted to do so again, despite her resisting his attempts to do so again, notwithstanding psychologist's opinion that the instructor could be rehabilitated without presenting a danger to himself and others.

These activities, said the court, created a "hostile employment environment," the existence of which is crucial to many private sector cases.[1]

Two cases address the "welcomeness" of sexual advances. *Naragon v. Wharton* (1984) addressed consent in a lesbian relationship between a student and a teaching assistant. The university was found within its rights to change the duties of the assistant. In *Korf v. Ball State University* (1984), the plaintiff asserted that a student had consented to a sexual relationship. Testimony suggested that "submission" rather than consent characterized the relationship. One witness said: "You had to be very assertive to get away from Dr. Korf's amorous advances." The appeals court rejected the defense of consent (welcomeness) and found the university had acted properly in dismissing the professor.

Before *Meritor* and the promulgation of the EEOC guidelines, academicians may have felt secure when they engaged in a consensual relationship with a student. Today, consensuality may no longer be a viable defense.

Current faculty and administrator concern about sexual relationships between their colleagues and the students they teach has resulted in the revision of sexual harassment policies or the promulgation of newly adopted codes of ethics.

We recently examined sexual harassment policies or codes of ethics, including faculty/administrator–student sexual relationships, at a randomly selected sample of 118 doctoral-level institutions and 230 baccalaureate-level institutions. Some 87 doctoral institutions and 103 baccalaureate institutions replied to the study survey, a combined return of 54%

The survey found that 16 universities and 16 colleges had policies or codes of ethics that discussed faculty/administrator–student relationships. Fifteen public and 17 private institutions had sexual harassment policies; 72 public and 85 private institutions did not. The responses were divided into groups based upon governance (public v. private) and size (large v. small). The returns showed 14 large and 18 small institutions had sexual harassment policies, while 72 large and 86 small colleges did not.[2]

Chi-square tests were applied to each of the three groupings: doctoral and baccalaureate, public and private, and large and small. The tests determined whether there was a difference between those institutions that had policies and those that did not. The tests found no statistically significant ($p = .05$) differences in the institutions by type, governance, or size.

These findings allow us to evaluate all institutional policies together.

The sexual harassment policies adopted by institutions in our sample addressed both the "unwelcomeness" standard and the professionalism expected of faculty and administrators. These policies repeatedly discussed the unequal relationship between faculty/administrators and students. They warned that the "unwelcomeness" of such a relationship is always subject to question. The policies also emphasized the importance of a professional relationship between academicians and their students.

The policies of 14 doctoral institutions discussed the professional expectations of faculty while seven discussed the power differential between faculty and students that results in "unwelcomeness." The baccalaureate institutions mentioned both issues 10 times. Only two baccalaureate policies mentioned neither standard. The policies were thus written, at least in part, in response to legal decisions.

All the institutional policies in our sample were assigned an overall rating of strength (weak, adequate, and strong) based upon five categories:

- who is prohibited.
- the nature of the relationship.
- whether the relationship is specified.
- type of grievance procedure.
- the term used to caution or condemn.

A chi-square technique determined that, save for one category, the policies of baccalaureate and doctoral institutions did not differ in strength. These institutions did differ in the term used to caution or condemn. The terms of caution or condemnation used by doctoral institutions—predominantly large, public universities—were stronger than those used by baccalaureate colleges, which were small and primarily privately funded. To illustrate, the most frequent admonition used by the doctoral institutions surveyed was "shall not" whereas the most frequent advice given to baccalaureate faculty was "sensitive to." Doctoral institutions may not be the pioneers in sexual harassment policy development that the literature on this subject suggests. However, they do use significantly stronger terms to censure faculty administrator/student sexual relationships.

Just how may an institution or an individual faculty member be held liable in what began as a consensual relationship between one of its faculty members and a student? An institution may be liable in at least three ways. First, welcome conduct can become unwelcome, and the student can then claim sexual harassment. In *Korf v. Ball State University,* the court indicated that the defense of equal choice in the sexual relationship does not exist when one partner (the faculty member or administrator) has power over the other (the student). Second, the parents of the student may contend that a "consensual" relationship is unprofessional.

Third, classmates of a student having a sexual relationship with an instructor may claim unequal treatment—a violation of EEOC guidelines. In all three cases, the institution and the faculty member are vulnerable to a sexual harassment charge.

Five of seven recent sexual harassment court cases that involve collegiate institutions provide evidence of an expectation of professional behavior on the part of academicians. *Korf v. Ball State* (1984) elaborates on this expectation:

> In any event, while there is no evidence that the young student Dr. Korf admitted having a sexual relationship with did not consent to engage in sexual activity with him, Dr. Korf's conduct is not to be viewed in the same context as would conduct of an ordinary "person on the street." Rather, it must be judged in the context of the relationship existing between a professor and his students within an academic environment. University professors occupy an important place in our society and have concomitant ethical obligations.

In the world of work, actionable harassment must be severe and pervasive. *Korf* suggests that this standard does not apply to the professional members of an academic community. The courts maintain high standards of conduct for academia. Indeed, these standards are often more strict than the law requires.

In *Korf v. Ball State University* (1984) the institution relied upon a "Statement on Profesional Ethics" incorporated into the faculty handbook. The court interpreted a statement that faculty should not exploit their students for private advantage to include sexual exploitation. It upheld the dismissal of the faculty member. The courts have not considered the *strength* of a policy or code of ethics in their decisions on sexual harassment. But an institution with no policy or code of ethics may find itself unable to take action against an employee whose personal behavior was unprofessional.

The guide for development of a policy on sexual relationships set forth in Figure 10.1 may facilitate selection of an appropriate institutional policy. The user may select the strength of the desired policy across five categories: who is prohibited, the specific types of relationships prohibited, the terms that are used to caution or condemn, the nature of the relationship, and whether or not a grievance procedure is provided. The courts frequently cite these categories in their decisions.

From this guide, an academic institution may create a suitable policy. Many institutions mix the strength of the categories. That is, an institution may use strong terms and specify relationships that cover all employees with power, but provide no grievance procedure. This guide should make development of a sexual harassment policy more feasible, practicable, and consistent. If an institution wishes to adopt a policy that cautions faculty about the sexual exploitation of students, the institution would use terms similar to those at the top of the chart. To construct a moderate policy, the college would select from terms in the middle area. A strong policy would come from the bottom row. If an institution wished to enact a compromise policy, it would mix strong and weak categories, as necessary.

There are at least two reasons for the current interest in sexual harassment policies. First, the *Meritor* decision will undoubtedly be widely applied to postsecondary institutions. Second, there is a widespread realization that academic institutions must have a policy or code of ethics that delimits the parameters of sexual relationships on campus to ensure a high standard of professional conduct.

An institution that refuses to define acceptable profes-

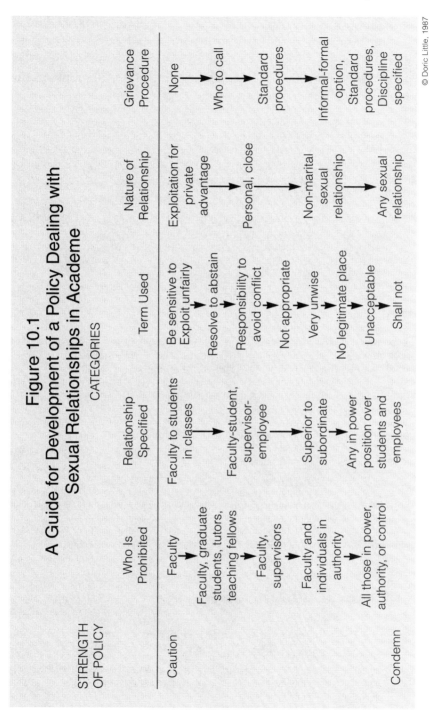

Figure 10.1
A Guide for Development of a Policy Dealing with
Sexual Relationships in Academe

© Doric Little, 1987

sional conduct may be open to the charge that it lacks professional judgment. Judicial interest in sexual harassment cases leads enlightened institutions and faculty members to publish a collegially developed, thoughtfully crafted statement on this sensitive matter.

NOTES

1 In another case, *Moire v. Temple University School of Medicine* 613 F. Supp. 1260 (D.C. PA. 1985) the defendant was unable to establish that a professor had harassed her and created a hostile environment.

2 The American Council of Education's text *American Universities and Colleges*, 12th edition, lists institutions by governance and size by enrollment. An enrollment of 5,000 was selected to divide the sample into large and small groups. That number represented the median enrollment of all the academic institutions listed in the volume.

REFERENCES

Alexander v. Yale University. 459 F. Supp. (D. Conn. 1977), revised by *Alexander v. Yale University*, Civil Action No. 77-277, D. Conn. (July 2, 1979) and affirmed No. 79-7547, 2nd Cir. (September 22, 1980).

Cockburn v. Santa Monica Community College Dist. 207 Cal. Reptr. 589 (Cal. App. 2 Dist. 1984).

Korf v. Ball State University. 726 F. 2d 1222 (7th/Cir. 1984).

Levitt v. University of Texas at El Paso. 759 F. 2d 1224 (5th Cir. 1985).

Meritor Savings Bank FSB v. Vinson. 1206 S. Ct. 2399 (1986).

Moire v. Temple University School of Medicine. 613 F. Supp. 1360 (D. C. Pa. 1985).

Naragon v. Wharton. 737 F. 2d 1403 (5th Cir. 1984).

SUGGESTED READINGS.

Benson, D. J. and G. E. Thomson, "Sexual Harassment on a University Campus: The confluence of authority relations, sexual interest and gender stratifications," *Social Problems, 29* (March, 1982): 236-251.

Cole, E. K., "Recent legal developments in sexual harassment." *The Journal of College and University Law, 13*, No. 3 (Winter, 1986): 267-284.

Crocker P. L. "Annotated bibliography in sexual harassment in education."

Women's Rights Law Reporter. Rutgers Law School 7, No. 2 (Winter, 1982).

Dziech, B. W., and Linda Weiner. *The lecherous professor: sexual harassment on campus* (Boston: Beacon Press, 1984).

Glaser, R. D., and J. S. Thorpe. "Unethical intimacy; A survey of sexual contact and advances between psychology educators and female graduate students," *American Psychologist, 41* (1986): 43-51.

Kennevick, J. "The significance of the Vinson decision on corporate employees." *Journal of Contemporary Law 12* (Winter, 1986): 163-176.

McMillen, L. "Seeking balance: Many colleges taking a new look at policies on sexual harassment," *The Chronicle of Higher Education 33* (December 17, 1986): 1, 16.

Monat, J. S., and Angel Gomez. "Sexual harassment: The impact of Meritor Savings Bank v. Vinson on grievances and arbitration decisions." *The Arbitration Journal 41* (December, 1986): 24-29.

Quinn, R. E. "Coping with cupid: The formation, impact and management of Romantic relationships in organizations." *Administrative Science Quarterly 22* (March, 1977): 30-45.

Robinson, R. K., D. J. Kirk, and E. G. Stephens. "Hostile Environment: A review of the implications of Meritor Savings Bank v. Vinson." *Labor Law Journal 38* (March, 1987): 179-183.

Schoenheider, K. J. "A theory of tort liability for sexual harassment in the workplace," *University of Pennsylvania Law Review 134* (July, 1986): 1461-1497.

Weber-Burdin, E., and P. H. Rossi. "Definition of Sexual Harassment on Campus: A Replication and Extension." *Journal of Social Issues 38* (1982): 111-120.

11

SEXUAL HARASSMENT: FACULTY, STUDENT CONSIDERATIONS

by Doric Little

The hearings on the nomination of Clarence Thomas to the U.S. Supreme Court point to the current significance that charges of sexual harassment now hold in America. This has not always been the case. Before the mid-1980s, encounters of a sexual nature involving young female students and aging male instructors were seldom regarded as serious or taken as a cause for concern. Most male faculty—when they chose to discuss a situation—referred to their aging peers as either lecherous old fools or lucky devils.

The 1990s are totally different. The "sexual climate" of the academic community has drastically changed. Any faculty who date current students are walking on thin ice. "In my opinion," the provost of a community college in Hawaii recently told faculty, "a faculty member who engages in sexual harassment is committing professional suicide."

What does this change in attitude mean to members of the academic community? Should a faculty member have a sexual relationship with a student? When may an overture be construed to be sexual harassment? The answers are not simple nor are they clear-cut.

BRIEF HISTORY

As a legal issue, sexual harassment developed from Title VII of the Civil Rights Act of 1964. Title VII prohibited discrimination on the basis of race, color, religion, national origin, and sex. Many believe that the term "sex" was added the night before the Act was approved by Congress. There was no discussion of harassment.

An earlier version of this chapter appeared in *Thought and Action*, Spring 1992, *8* (1), 5-12.

The term "sexual harassment" was coined in 1974. Professor Lin Farley and other women at Cornell University settled on "sexual harassment" as an appropriate label for the activity that now, unlike then, can make national headlines. Interestingly, the pronunciation of this term is currently undergoing change. Many dictionaries now acknowledge "ha*rass*" as the more common pronunciation rather than the traditional "*harass.*" Most women consider the "ha*rass*" pronunciation as the harsher sounding and the more indicative of the feelings of the "ha*rassed.*"

Courts began hearing cases involving sexual harassment in 1964. Most of these cases were brought to the courts as a form of sex discrimination under Title VII. Some cases were heard as a violation of Title IX of the 1972 Education Amendments, which prohibit gender discrimination in federally funded programs. In November 1980, as sexual harassment cases were on the increase, the Equal Employment Opportunity Commission (EEOC) issued legal guidelines for courts to use in sexual harassment cases.

The first Supreme Court case on sexual harassment was heard in June 1986. The Supreme Court decision in *Meritor Savings Bank v. Vinson* set a judicial precedent. The increase in court cases dealing with sexual harassment then so overwhelmed the EEOC that by March 1990 officials had updated the EEOC legal guidelines on sexual harassment three times. Sexual harassment law continues—at the federal level—to be made in the courts, not in the legislature. Many states, on the other hand, have passed statutory laws on this subject.

LEGAL DECISIONS AND HIGHER EDUCATION

The Supreme Court's decision in *Meritor* (1986) determined that what makes a case actionable is whether or not the activity is "welcome." Prior to *Meritor,* defendants could claim that their accuser had gone along with the sexual activity. In other words, the "voluntariness" of the victim served as a defense for the accused.

The behavior of the principle character in a recent

novel, *Professor Romeo* (Bernays, 1989), best illustrates the impact *Meritor* has had on higher education. In the novel, Professor Romeo considers his female students the "perks" of his professional position. Each semester, Professor Romeo enjoys selecting the young female students who will be recipients of his sexual favors. The *Meritor* decision ultimately costs Professor Romeo his job. After a complaint by one of his "perks," the university finds Professor Romeo's previous behavior actionable under Title VII.

The *Meritor* decision has a direct impact on professors who, in the past, used "voluntariness" as a defense for their sexual activities with their students. A number of other federal and Supreme Court cases also illustrate that the courts expect professional behavior from the academic community. In *Korf v. Ball State University* (1984) and *Naragon v. Wharton* (1983), the courts enunciated their high standards for academicians and supported academic institutions that disciplined faculty members for sexually exploiting students.

Certainly, that the courts have historically deferred to academic decision making (*Board of Curators, University of Missouri v. Horowitz*, 1978, and *Regents of University of Michigan v. Ewing*, 1985) and have ruled against academic decisions only if they were found to be arbitrary and capricious (*Connelly v. University of Vermont*, 1965) has contributed to this expectation of a high standard of professional behavior. With the deference that the courts give academicians comes a concomitant expectation of professional behavior.

CONCERN IN ACADEME

There are some in the academic community who believe that all sexual relationships between faculty and students should be prohibited. Realistically, such a prohibition would be unenforceable on most campuses. Actually, the few campuses that have such policies come from a religious tradition that also bans smoking and drinking alcoholic beverages.

On the other hand, there are many in the academic community who contend that sexual relations between consenting adults on college campuses, even those who are in a faculty-student relationship or supervisory-subordinate relationship, are perfectly acceptable. There are at least three reasons why this contention, if acted upon, may lead to serious problems.

First, what may begin as a welcome, consensual relationship may become unwelcome. It is more than a cliché to say that the course of true love may not always run smooth. When a student decides that a sexual relationship is over and claims harassment, who is the guilty party? The answer most often is the person in power. In the academic community, that person is usually the one who gives the grade. Second, students are not the only complainants. The parents of a student may complain. This was the case in *Naragon v. Wharton* and, even though in this case the student was over 18 years of age, disciplinary action was taken and upheld by the courts. Finally, classmates of a student who is having a sexual relationship with an instructor may legally claim unequal treatment as a violation of Equal Employment Opportunity Commission guidelines.

RECENT LEGAL DEVELOPMENTS

The Hill-Thomas confrontation, while not a legal proceeding, illustrates the importance of credibility in cases of sexual harassment. Credibility has played an important role in past sexual discrimination cases. The federal district court case in *Heelan v. Johns-Manville Corp,* (1978) shows how courts review sexual harassment cases:

Much of the testimony in this case is conflicting, not only in pivotal areas but in areas of marginal relevance as well. This case is based largely upon the court's view of the credibility of the witnesses, i.e., their worthiness of belief.

We have carefully scrutinized all testimony and the circumstances under which each witness has testified, and every matter in evidence which tends to show whether a witness is worthy of belief. For example, we have taken into account each witness' motive and state of mind, strength of memory and demeanor and manner while on the witness stand.

Three federal court decisions in the 1990s may offer guidance to the faculty member who wishes to comply with the standards enunciated by the courts. A significant decision was made by the Ninth Circuit Court in San Francisco in 1991 in the case of *Ellison v. Nicholas.* The standard presented for the first time in this case is called the "reasonable woman" standard. The court ruled that a previous standard "the reasonable person" standard was not necessarily appropriate in sexual harassment cases because it tends to present the male view of what is reasonable.

In the *Ellison* case, lengthy love letters written by a fellow employee whom Ellison had lunch with once were considered sexual harassment. The court ruled that a "reasonable woman" would consider such behavior by a co-worker harassing. Within a month after the *Ellison* decision, another judge ruled in favor of the plaintiff in a sex discrimination case. Judge King, in *Kay Austen v. University of Hawaii* referred to the *Ellison* standard in his decision.

Another significant decision—one of particular importance to vocational instructors—was made in Florida in the case of *Robinson v. Jacksonville Shipyards* in 1991. The court ruled that nude or partially nude pictures, displayed in the workplace, can constitute sexual harassment.

In *Robinson v. Jacksonville Shipyards*, the workplace was a shipyard and the plaintiff a female welder. Despite her numerous complaints of harassment, nude posters (many with her hair color and length of hair) were displayed in areas where she worked. The United States District Court ruled in favor of Robinson.

A 1990 case, *Jew v. University of Iowa*, (1990) involved the behavior of university professors. Dr. Jew, an anatomy professor, had complained for over 15 years that several faculty had spread lies about her sexual habits and her sexual relationship with her supervisor. The court found the university and the accused professors guilty of sexual harassment and sex discrimination. The financial penalties to the defendants in this case were considerable. Ironically, the University of Iowa has one of the strongest sexual harassment policies in the nation.

Two significant actions that allow monetary damages beyond backpay—not previously available under Title VII or IX—were taken in 1991. The Civil Rights Act of 1991—signed into law on November 21—creates a right of action for compensatory and punitive damages for victims of intentional discrimination under Title VII.

In December 1991, the Supreme Court heard arguments in the case of *Franklin v. Gwinnett County Public Schools* and decided in February 1992 that schools and colleges may be required to pay compensatory damages for violations of Title IX. The Civil Rights Act of 1991 and the *Franklin v. Gwinnett* decision should put all campuses on notice that sexual harassment is both illegal and can prove to be exceedingly expensive.

In January 1992, a federal judge ruled that a Minnesota sexual harassment lawsuit filed by three women who work at Eveleth Mines may proceed on behalf of all women who work in the mines (*Jenson v. Eveleth Taconite Co.*). This is the first class-action sexual harassment lawsuit ever allowed in a federal court. The implication of such a ruling is that women may be more willing to step forward as a group than as individuals. In the academic community, as in the world outside, individuals who file sexual harassment suits must frequently deal with character assassination and retaliation not unlike the attacks that rape victims face. The *Jenson* case was decided in May 1993. The Federal District Court found in favor of the plaintiffs on two claims: (1) sex discrimination in promotions to step-up foreman and foreman and (2) sexual harassment. The impact of this favorable ruling in the first federal class-action sexual harassment lawsuit may be signigicant. Time will tell.

The third Supreme Court case dealing with sexual harassment, *Harris v. Forklift Systems, Inc.,* decided on November 9, 1993, resolved a conflict among the various circuits regarding the requirements of a sexual harassment case. In a unanimous decision, Justice O'Connor stated that "so long as the environment would reasonably be perceived and is perceived as hostile or abusive . . . there is no need for it also to be psychologically injurious." While Justice O'Connor did not specify the "reasonable woman" test, the Sixth Circuit, which had decided the case under appeal, ruled that "a reasonable woman manager under like circumstances would have been offended."

GUIDELINES FOR PROPER CONDUCT

What does the change in attitude toward sexual harassment mean to the academic community? Academics, it is clear, need to behave carefully at all times. The person in a power position—the position of the academic in relation to the student—is the person who is liable in a charge of sexual harassment.

Should a faculty member have a sexual relationship with a student? A "yes" answer involves a substantial risk. That risk may be nullified if the faculty member waits until the student has completed his or her course or the faculty member is no longer in a supervisory position to the student.

Finally, when may an overture be construed to be sexual harassment? This is the question for which no clear guidelines exist. Generally, if one has power over another person, it would be wise not to enter into a sexual relationship or to make sexual overtures.

Recent court cases discussed in this chapter do offer some guidance for the academic community. For example, one way to determine whether sexual harassment is occurring would be to try to view the situation as a reasonable woman would. There can be little doubt that posting nude or partially nude pictures is a potentially dangerous activity. And, clearly, spreading lies regarding the sexual habits of others in the academic community can be very expensive. Certainly, a credible reputation is a critically important element in a sexual harassment hearing. Therefore, unless "professional suicide" is your goal, use caution in your interactions with students and those you supervise. Don't take chances. Behave professionally. How can academicians, legally or ethically do anything less?

REFERENCES

Austen v. University of Hawaii, 759 F. Supp. 612 (D. Haw. 1991).

Bernays, A. (1989). *Professor Romeo.* New York: Penguin Books.

Board of Curators, University of Missouri v. Horowitz, 435 U.S. 78 (1978).

Connelly v. University of Vermont and State Agricultural College, 244 F. Supp. 156 (D. Vt. 1965).

Ellison v. Nicholas, 924 F.2d 872 (1991).

Franklin v. Gwinnett County Public Schools, 112 S. Ct. 1028 (1992).

Harris v. Forklift Systems, Inc. No. 92-116 8, Supreme Court of the United States. (1993) U.S. Lexis 7155.

Heelan v. Johns-Manville Corp., 20 FEP251 (D. Colo. 1978).

Jenson v. Eveleth Taconite Co., 62 EPD & 42 469 (D. Minn. 1993).

Jew v. University of Iowa, 749 F. Supp. 946 (S.D.Ia. 1990).

Korf v. Ball State University, 726 F. 2d 1222 (1984).

Meritor Savings Bank v. Vinson, 106 S. Ct. 2399 (1986).

Naragon v. Wharton, 572 F. Supp. 1117 (M.D. La. 1983).

Regents of University of Michigan v. Ewing, 474 U.S. 214 (1985).

Robinson v. Jacksonville Shipyards, Inc., 760 F. Supp. 1485 (M.D. Fla. 1991).

12
SEXUAL HARASSMENT OF UNIVERSITY STUDENTS

by Lloyd D. Elgart and Lillian Schanfield

Sexual harassment has recently become the focus of public attention—the subject of federal guidelines as well as a major U.S. Supreme Court decision. But redress—such as it has been—has largely been limited to equal employment opportunity and has not effected similar attention in higher education.

Despite the considerable documentation and publicity on the sexual harassment of students and despite grim forecasts of future litigation, we contend that the most victims have achieved is a right without a remedy. Our contention does not make sexual harassment any less a critical issue; in a sense this reality makes sexual harassment more critical. The less reliance on the law that can be expected, the more responsibility there is on the university and its various stakeholders to act in an ethical manner.

In short, whatever one's feelings may be about the failure of the legal system to deal with the problem, we believe that sexual harassment in American higher education is currently a problem of ethics and values rather than a problem of law. Consequently any meaningful remedy for the student victim must be created and implemented by the institution.

DEFINING A TRANSGRESSION THAT RESISTS DEFINITION

Sexual harassment, a long-time fixture in the work force as well as the university, has only recently been identified. In fact, before the women's movement, there was no label for sexual harassment. Harassment essentially passed,

An earlier version of this chapter appeared in *Thought and Action,* Spring 1991, 7 (1), 21-42.

and still to a great extent does, under the guise of so-called natural male behavior.

When we speak of sexual harassment in this chapter, we are talking about relationships between male faculty and female students, by far the most common setting for harassing behavior. We acknowledge that there are other variations—homosexual harassment, the female harassment of males, senior/junior faculty harassment—but our focus is on the form of harassment whose prevalence renders it virtually invisible to some people. Given the cultural context of male and female sexuality in this country, the possibility that women might harass men in return for academic or economic favors is statistically so remote as to distort the weight of the evidence and to unjustly dilute the damage wrought by male sexual harassment of females.

Various institutions have developed their own definitions of sexual harassment: the Equal Employment Opportunity Commission (EEOC), the Office for Civil Rights of the Department of Education, the National Advisory Council on Women's Educational Programs, the American Psychological Association, and a host of universities, including Harvard, Yale, and the University of California. These definitions can be classified as more or less restrictive. The more restrictive the definition, the easier it is to identify and—we might add—the easier to deal with in legal or other ways. By the same token, the more restrictive the definition, the fewer violations it can meaningfully take into account.

The discrete behaviors that constitute sexual harassment can be arranged on a continuum that extends from the most blatant and overt at one end—assault, touching, bribery, demands for sexual favors, threats, exposing of self—to more subtle forms that include undue attention, statements about physical appearance, flattery, embraces, gestures, accidental bodily contact, flexibility in grading, favoritism, the disclosure of inappropriate aspects of one's personal life, sexist joking, an overemphasis of sexuality in unnecessary contexts, as well as disparaging attitudes about women, verbal abuse, sexist joking, and so on. Leering, ogling, and lechery—while difficult for nonindulgers to visualize—have a particularly lascivious ring!

This list of behaviors is not exhaustive, nor can any definition ultimately include all harassing behaviors. Therefore, it is important to try to identify a key element that distinguishes sexual harassment from other discriminatory or (merely) annoying behavior. In all cases there is a power imbalance—dominance and subordinance—with the harasser taking advantage of his institutional authority. The vehicle of the harassing behavior is always the emphasis on (in one way or another) the sexual identity of the harassed. Clearly, a faculty member would not be in a position to harass were he not employed as faculty in the first place. This is the reason that students may flirt, annoy, hassle, provoke, and even pursue, but it is our view that as subordinates in the power dyad they cannot harass a faculty member.

It is worth noting (sadly) that the harassing behaviors listed above may distress those among us who are both male *and* friendly, tactile, helpful, kind, caring, thoughtful mentors—but not sexual harassers. Unfortunately, there are signs all around that we may have to modify our personal styles of interacting with students.

We humans are generally beset with semantic difficulties as we struggle to describe things accurately, fairly, and truthfully through language. Crocker (1983) emphasizes the difficulty of definition and the need for definition to be flexible and designed from the victim's perspective. For example, how does one define "substantial" interference (used in Rutgers University's definition) or "grossly objectionable" (in Tulane University's)? The question is: how "substantial" is "substantial" and how "gross" is "gross?" Adjectives render other definitions equally subject to the connotative aspects of language and hence personal, subjective interpretation. How do we define an act that is "deliberate," "unwanted," "intentional," "repeated," or "pervasive?" Similarly, the very word "harass," by definition, connotes an act that is repeated, yet according to Tulane's definition a one-time "grossly objectionable" act would certainly constitute sexual harassment.

A still more problematic impediment to definition is the cultural context in which sexual harassment occurs. Androcentrism, a term coined in this century, literally means "male-centered" and generally refers to male bias. It is best seen as a filter or a lens through which experience is unconsciously viewed, onto which learned values, attitudes, and expectations are projected, and through which much discourse becomes suspect.

Androcentrism accounts for the fact that sexual harassment was invisible for so long because only the non-androcentrentic vision was able to give the behavior a name and confirm reality. Sexual harassment flourishes because of the "nexus of power and sexual prerogative of men with formal authority over women (Benson & Thompson, 1982)."

The fellow faculty member who shrugs off an incident of alleged sexual harassment with the attitude that "a man's a man for a' that" is demonstrating this kind of masculinist thinking. "After all," the unconscious premise goes, "men will be men. It's only natural." And so on. Here we confront the difficulty of truly seeing a problem that never seemed to be a problem before—and indeed for many still does not.

An example of this, and still vivid in our minds is about the case of "The Dirty Don," also dubbed "The Sex Pest Don" by the university newspaper during our sabbatical year at the University of Oxford. Several female students brought charges against a male faculty member for fornication, impregnation, insistence on abortion, as well as threats about academic status and future postgraduate work. What seemed most disturbing to us was the collegial closing of male ranks around the alleged harasser by his individual college and fellow faculty. One of his colleagues, a nationally renowned legal authority (in matters other than sex discrimination) and involved in some measure with the "investigation" of the matter, expressed the idea in conversation that romantic interactions between dons and female students constituted expected behavior (more or less) in the natural course of male-female relationships.

Such masculinist attitudes draw on myths in Western culture that die hard. One of them is the misogynistic depiction of the female as a temptress—an Eve, a Delilah, or a Cleopatra—who tempts man to his fall with her beauty or her wiles. This perspective, of course, absolves Adam, Samson, and Caesar of responsibility in the matter and places most of the onus on the female. At worst, the male is guilty of being weak. Furthermore, the locker room tradition—not without some pride—would have us believe that male sexuality is beastly, unrestrainable, and insatiable—the male in constant readiness and pursuit like the lover on Keats' urn, forever unsatisfied, forever yearning.

Astonishingly, androcentrism is a cultural filter for women as well as men. And lest we think that the myth of the seductive female is not still among us, one need only cite Phyllis Schlafly, who unfortunately claims to speak for women. In 1980 she sanctimoniously proclaimed to the Senate Labor and Human Resources Committee that "virtuous women are seldom accosted by unwelcome sexual propositions or familiarities, obscene talk, or profane language" and that sexual harassment only happens when "a nonvirtuous woman gives off body language which invites sexual advances but she chooses to give her favors to Man A and not to Man B and he tries to get his share too" (Tuana, 1985).

Finally, to muddy the waters of definition still further is the semantic difficulty of describing "what actually happened." In a court of law one is enjoined to tell "the truth and nothing but the truth." Philosophers, artists, and poets have apparently had a harder time deciding what Truth or Reality is than has the legal mind. In fact, the poetic imagination has had to resort to figurative language or multiple perspectives to render so fundamental an aspect of human experience. In Faulkner's (1936) *Absalom, Absalom!,* for example, the act dredged up from the painful archival memories of a family in the American Deep South cannot be articulated as it "really" happened but must be filtered through the consciousness and changing memories of several characters. Indeed, the very theme of *Absalom, Absalom!* becomes the difficulty of remembering and expressing reality.

It is fairly easy for an aggressor, especially one trained to communicate his thoughts in an articulate manner, to make light of an instance of sexual harassment, to claim that it was not serious, or to deflect the blame onto the victim. Often women report that they feel ashamed, embarrassed, or even unable to articulate the experience. In fact, a woman may not even be sure that "it" took place (Sandler & Associates, 1981). Needless to say, we are suspicious of the reams of surveys and statistics on the subject that purport to quantify events that are often "too deep for words."

SEXUAL HARASSMENT AND THE LAW

How can undefined behavior be proscribed or dealt with legally? The American legal system has been struggling with this dilemma since the early days of the first Civil Rights Act. The courts and administrative agencies have dealt extensively with the issue of sexual harassment in the context of employment, but not in academe between faculty and students. Aside from dicta contained in the oft-quoted case of *Alexander v. Yale University* (1980),[1] there has been no direct indication that such a cause of action exists in federal courts for students, as it clearly does for university employees, who benefit from the overlapping jurisdiction of the EEOC under the Civil Rights Act of 1964 and the Office for Civil Rights of the U.S. Department of Education under Title IX of the Education Amendments of 1972.

In its "Guidelines on Discrimination because of Sex the EEOC (1980) clearly states that harassment on the basis of sex is a violation of the Civil Rights Act. This, the only official government definition of sexual harassment, has been adopted by the Supreme Court as the standard. The proscribed conduct includes unwelcome sexual advances, requests for sexual favors, and other verbal or physical conduct of a sexual nature under the following conditions:

(1) Submission to such conduct is made either explicitly or implicitly a term or condition of an individual's employment.

(2) Submission to or rejection of such conduct by an individual is used as the basis for employment decisions affecting such individual.

(3) Such conduct has the purpose or effect of unreasonably interfering with an individual's work performance or creating an intimidating, hostile, or offensive working environment.

The federal courts have been divided on how these guidelines should be applied and whether or to what extent coercive conduct described in (1) and (2) above (called *"quid pro quo"* harassment) should be treated differently from conduct that simply pollutes the atmosphere as described in (3) (called "hostile environment" harassment).

In its first opinion on the subject, in *Meritor Savings Bank v. Vinson*[2] (1986), the U.S. Supreme Court attempted to resolve this conflict by adopting the EEOC definition of harassment and upholding as actionable both the *quid pro quo* and hostile environment theories. Speaking for the majority, Justice Rehnquist refused to endorse strict liability for employers but did hold them responsible for a supervisor's *quid pro quo* harassment of a subordinate (with or without notice of such conduct) when the supervisor is given authority over the terms and conditions of the subordinate's employment.

In cases based on the hostile environment theory (as in *Meritor*), the Court required that harassment be "unwelcome" as well as "sufficiently severe or pervasive to alter the conditions of [the victim's] employment and to create an abusive working environment." Furthermore, the employer must have either actual or constructive notice of the alleged misconduct. The EEOC interpreted and reinforced *Meritor* in new guidelines issued on October 25, 1988.

It should be pointed out that in the case of *quid pro quo* harassment, the employee's remedies may include back pay, lost wages or benefits, and injunctive relief when appropriate. But in cases of offensive environment harassment, only injunctive relief is available. In neither case will the court award damages for mental or emotional injury.

The only federal laws addressing faculty harassment of students are contained in Title IX of the Education Amendments. This statute provides that no person in the United States shall "on the basis of sex, be excluded from participation in, be denied the benefits of, or be subjected to discrimination under any education program or activity receiving federal financial assistance." The term "sexual harassment," it should be noted, has not been mentioned here nor does it appear in any regulation promulgated by the Office for Civil Rights or the Department of Education.

In *Alexander v. Yale University* (1980), the first federal case to date on the accountability of a university for a professor's alleged sexual harassment of a student (not also employed by that university), Judge Lumbard found in favor of the defendant university, declaring:

> In a Title IX suit, it is the deprivation of "educational" benefits which, once proven, allows the courts to afford relief. The statute recognizes that loss of educational benefits is a significant injury, redressable by law. Where the alleged deprivation, however, relates to an activity removed from the *ordinary educational process, a more detailed allegation of injuries* suffered as a result of the deprivation is required. . . . [emphasis added] (p. 184).

Although this language seems to support a claim of sexual harassment under Title IX, it is so vague that it offers no help in determining the quantities of proof necessary to prevail. For example, what is meant by "ordinary educational process" or "more detailed allegation of injuries?" It is difficult to understand how so many authors have concluded that this opinion constitutes a judicial acknowledgment of sexual harassment as an available cause of action under Title IX.

In the case of *Lipsett v. University of Puerto Rico* (1988), the U.S. Court of Appeals (1st Circuit) dealt with the complaint of a female surgical resident at the university hospital who sought to hold the university responsible, *inter alia,* for both *quid pro quo* and hostile environment harassment, allegedly committed by fellow residents and supervisors, that resulted in her termination as an employee and a student. This case is interesting because of the plaintiff's hybrid standing as both a student and employee. The court confirmed that the Title VII standard for proving discriminatory treatment should apply, but specifically limited this holding to "the context of employment discrimination" (p. 897). Based on the fact that the plaintiff was partly an employee in the program, the court found "no difficulty extending the Title VII standard to discriminatory treatment by a supervisor in this mixed employment-training context" (p. 897). This opinion may be encouraging to faculty members who are harassed by fellow faculty members, supervisors, or the university itself on the basis of sex, but it appears to offer no consolation to non-employee students.

In another Court of Appeals Case, *Bougher v. University of Pittsburgh* (1989), the court specifically declined to deal with the question of "whether evidence of a hostile environment is sufficient to sustain a claim of sexual discrimination in education in violation of Title IX" (p. 77). Given all of the above, it does not appear that federal courts are currently prepared to apply Title VII concepts to disputes involving faculty-student sexual harassment.

The agency charged with the responsibility of enforcing the prohibition against sex discrimination under Title IX is the U.S. Department of Education, Office for Civil Rights (OCR), with nine regional offices located throughout the United States. There have been no guidelines issued by this agency, and the only basis for enforcement known at this time is a policy memorandum issued by the OCR in 1981 that defines sexual harassment as "verbal or physical conduct of a sexual nature, imposed on the basis of sex, by an employee [e.g., faculty] or agent of a recipient [i.e., an institution that receives federal aid] that denies, limits, provides different, or conditions the provision of aid, benefits, services or treatment protected under Title IX."

There are a number of constraints upon the OCR that hamper any effort on its part to deal with faculty/student harassment complaints. First, no mention is made of sexual harassment even though the regulations governing this section deal specifically with a number of educational discrimination issues and mandate the establishment by institutions of a grievance mechanism. Secondly, the proscription against sex discrimination under Title IX covers only those institutions that are recipients of "federal financial assistance." And, thirdly, there is the failure to provide the OCR with realistic and effective penalties as a tool for enforcement.

Before the controversial U.S. Supreme Court case of *Grove City College v. Bell* (1984), "federal financial assistance" was broadly interpreted to include an entire institution when only a single program was aided. As a result, OCR had jurisdiction to investigate complaints wherever they arose since most institutions of higher education received federal assistance of one kind or another. This was reversed by the U.S. Supreme Court's Grove City doctrine. The court held that only the programs receiving federal financial assistance were covered by Title IX, thus narrowing almost to obscurity the influence of OCR in the field of discrimination in education. The Grove City decision was attacked on a wide political front.

Representatives James Jeffords and Gus Hawkins introduced into Congress a bill known as the Civil Rights Restoration Act, which became law over the veto of President Reagan (Public Law 100-259, March 22, 1988), and the broad interpretation of institutional coverage under Title IX was restored. Still, no mention of sexual harassment was made by either house of Congress.

The gravest weakness of Title IX in the area of gender discrimination, as mentioned earlier, is its failure to provide the OCR with realistic and effective penalties as a tool for enforcement. Under current law, universities are required by the regulations to "adopt and publish grievance procedures providing for prompt and equitable resolution of student and employee complaints alleging any action which would be prohibited" by law. These relate to discrimination in areas such as admission, recruitment, housing, and financial assistance, but do not address sexual harassment.

The most that the agency can do after investigating and documenting a violation is to recommend that the institution's federal funding be withdrawn. As a practical matter the OCR will use persuasion and pressure, which are often successful, but if not, the matter is referred to the Justice Department where no further action is taken. We have found no reported case of the withdrawal of federal funds from a college or university as a result of its failure to deal with sexual harassment.

It would seem that the only federal constraint against faculty/student sexual harassment, if one exists at all, must be drawn from Title IX.[2] Since this is so ineffective, the only real hope for student victims can be found in grievance procedures specifically aimed at sexual harassment and voluntarily initiated by their institutions.

Once such procedures are in place, the federal courts have been extremely supportive of a school administration's right and power to discipline a guilty faculty member, even to the extent of contract termination.[3] In *Korf v. Ball State University* (1984), a case involving homosexual males, Circuit Judge Coffey, citing the university handbook and the American Association of University Professors Statement on Professional Ethics, rejected the defendant professor's argument that the sexual relationships complained of were consensual. Upholding the right of the institution's Board of Trustees to terminate the defendant's contract, the court commented that "Dr. Korf's conduct is not to be viewed in the same context as would conduct of an ordinary 'person on the street.' Rather, it must be judged in the context of the relationship existing between a professor and his students within an academic environment. University professors occupy an important place in our society and have concomitant ethical obligations" (p. 1227).

Such language may sound encouraging, but a caveat to the optimists is warranted. The fact that some federal courts have upheld disciplinary action by institutions against professors harassing students does not ensure that these same courts will uphold complaints by students under Title IX. This is not inconsistent, since Title IX does not provide students with any clear-cut protection against faculty harassment. The courts are free to support university administrations that choose to do so. We maintain, therefore, that the burden of protection falls squarely upon the institution, not as a matter of law but of ethics.

CAVEAT PROFESSOR

Faculty in higher education have more independence, self-direction, power over others, and professional latitude than most professionals. But this combination, especially the freedom from close supervision, is too easily clothed with the protective veneer of academic freedom, which in turn is too easily invoked as a clarion call against the questioning of conduct.

Besides teaching, academics interact with students in other ways: they advise, counsel, direct theses, make recommendations, and mentor. That most full professors and/or tenured faculty in America are male deserves mention in this context.[4] In many descriptions of sexual harassment, the teachers in question have been in roles of "gatekeepers," standing between the student and her aspirations in the form of degree, thesis completion, grants, fellowships, even future jobs. In the case of undergraduates, the offending faculty have been described as persons of great influence on the student's growth, self-esteem, and future prospects.

In spite of the drastic changes that have taken place in the university/student relationship since the 1960s, we believe that it is morally incumbent upon the faculty member, as well as the institution, to fulfill in part the *in loco parentis* role and help students in the maturation process. We believe that the dynamics of teaching places a male faculty member in a position of a fiduciary or a trustee, who receives faith, trust, and confidence and who, in turn, owes his students the exercise of good faith in the performance of his professional duties. More dramatically, we would draw the analogy to the duty owed a patient by a psychotherapist. The latter is obliged to recognize, *as the former cannot,* that the inherent process of psychotherapy reinforces dependency and renders the patient susceptible to certain forces that come into play, particularly those that foster respect, admiration, acceptance of authority, and even worship. The arena in which teaching is carried on can too easily become a platform for self-aggrandizement at the expense of others and—it bears adding—without fear of challenge.

Finally, because of all that the above implies, we see faculty/student sexual relationships as exploitation of students—even if the student is the one who is aggressor. The aggressiveness is in the end only an illusion. The faculty member is the professional. Relationships with female students that are something other than academic should be proscribed because they represent a conflict of interest. The teaching and learning community consists of faculty and scholars, professionals and students, counselors and counseled, even parents and children—but not male adults and female adults.

It need hardly be pointed out that a faculty member performing any of the harassing behaviors itemized earlier can scarcely be said to be more interested in his female students' intellectual growth than he is in their sexuality. And without meaning to cast any gloom on those wonderful marriages that may have emerged from faculty/student relationships (we all know a few), let us reiterate that as long as a romantic relationships exists, it interferes with the scholarly one. Margaret Mead (1980) once suggested that mandating as taboo sexual relationships between men and women who work together would be more effective than legal remedies and bureaucratic procedures and would in fact empower women in "the new society we are struggling to create."

The burden of responsibility, as well as sensitivity and awareness, must clearly be on faculty, regardless of perceived or real provocation. Codes such as the one generated by the University of California, Santa Cruz implicitly acknowledge the difficulty of defining anything but the most blatant forms of sexual harassment but demonstrate a sensitivity to the real issues. The Santa Cruz code prohibits "only unreciprocated and unwelcome relations." But it accords importance to the dynamics of power by stipulating the following: "Persons in positions of power/authority/control over others should be aware of and sensitive to problems which may arise from those relationships which are *apparently* mutual. Given the pervasiveness and depth of sexism in *both men and women,* such relationships often involve dynamics which extend far beyond simple mutual attraction. Thus, individuals are urged to examine such relationships before engaging in them especially in terms of *emotional health, self-esteem, and respect for the independence* of the persons involved" (Emphasis added) (Crocker, 1983, p. 702).

The consequences for faculty of sexual harassment charges can indeed be dire: embarrassment, negative publicity, the upsetting of personal lives, suspension, dismissal, perhaps even loss of career. Such charges are likelier to occur in the current climate of women's heightened awareness—and even militancy. Feminists come in all degrees of persuasion (with some of our best feminists being men). But "caveat" the professor who underestimates the zeal of feminists like those who constituted WOASH, Women Organized Against Sexual Harassment, at the Berkeley campus of the University of California. An assistant professor of sociology was accused of sexually harassing several female students and, as a result of the dogged efforts of the group, he finally left the university for a teaching post in Tunisia, claiming that he was a victim of discrimination by "people . . . looking for a cause (Dzeich & Weiner, 1984)." The days of cavalier, locker-room acceptance of harassive behavior are apparently over.

THE STUDENT BODY

Contrast the power inherent in the position of faculty to the inherent subordination and powerlessness of the student, this in spite of the watershed of the 1970s. Students may appear very sophisticated to us, especially in the context of our memories about ourselves at their age. We are told to consider them adult consumers, so we no longer patrol dormitories, send grade reports home to parents, or prescribe courses.

The sexual revolution, we are all aware, has occurred. Student dress, both male and female, is casual and revealing; to some, it might even appear provocative. Young women sometimes appear unable to distinguish between mere talking and flirting. But in discussing the sexual harassment of female university students, it is more realistic, a lot wiser, and (we might add) more ethical to think of students as vulnerable, unprotected, often alone for the first time, divorced from familiar sources of support and—most emphatically—less sophisticated than they may appear to be. Unfair charges of sexual harassment are possible. But we should keep in mind that some students are immature, overly sensitive, misguided, afraid, or angry. The power of faculty may in fact be real, but it may also be magnified through misperception. Tremendous damage can be done to a faculty member who is perceived as a sexual harasser.

Women students are particularly vulnerable to being

sexually harassed because the very faculty-student relationship is a model for that of dominance and subordinance. Despite a great deal of noisy rhetoric to the contrary, things are clearly not equal for females as they grow up. Told that they have the ability as well as the opportunity to compete as equals in the world of work, girls are raised in a world that reinforces their self-image of "otherness" or secondary status. Studies demonstrate the unfortunate consequences of this conditioning: the public world demands qualities that often conflict with those learned by women since childhood and which some would even characterize as "feminine": docility, inexperience with competition, passivity, deference to authority figures (usually male); from these often follow lack of self-confidence, fear of failure, and even fear of success. Young women learn to respect their superiors, not to challenge them. They may even regard their professors, as one writer of a popular magazine piece on the topic breezily put it, with a "dash of awe" ("Fighting lechery. . .," 1980). A student may confuse feelings of dependence and submission with the illusion of being professionally and psychologically nurtured. Insidious though it may be, we venture the observation that women are so used to being "harassed" that they can confuse harassment with attentive, concerned, and respectful male behavior.

This is not intended to stereotype either the modern American woman or the modern male professor, but it ought to suggest the unequal psychological and social preparation for the competitive terrain into which women are emerging. We maintain that sexual harassment, whatever form it takes (including those behaviors from the most subtle range of the continuum), reaffirms to women themselves the image of "woman-as-object" and obviously unequal contenders in the new world. The experience for a student can be extremely traumatic, and the damage may be permanent. Academic plans may change; future careers may be sabotaged; self-confidence can be seriously damaged. This was the contention in the Yale case, though as the outcome of that trial demonstrated, damages are almost impossible to assess and, as indicated earlier, an androcentric bias may make true comprehension extremely difficult.

Interesting but superficial is the argument by some feminists against the need for guidelines and procedures on sexual harassment and "amorous relationship statements such as those issued by various universities proscribing such attachments (Harvard, for example, and the University of California). The contention is that such documents actually extend the system of paternalism from which female adults have liberated themselves and abridge their rights as adults to form whatever social connections they may choose to form (Hoffman, 1986).

We understand the logic of such arguments, particularly in the context of the patriarchal tradition of protecting dependent women, and we agree that ultimately to regard the university *in loco parentis* to female adult students is indeed a contradiction in terms. But in the end the argument strikes us as casuistic because it fails to *meaningfully* take into account the years of injustice that have preceded and the inequities that continue to constrain adult females. This contention takes a superficial, somewhat insensitive (though optimistic) approach to the reality of women's experience. Indeed, if there is any *in loco parentis* relationship to be considered, we maintain that it is not gender specific but rather exists between the university and *all* students.

THE INSTITUTION

The academic institution is the only agent in this web in a position to moderate among the various elements and to set standards, adequately communicate them, and create a mechanism for discipline and the redress of legitimate grievances. Positioned sensitively with equal responsibility to students and faculty, the institution may find itself in the sticky position of trying to discern between a faculty member's academic freedom and that same faculty member's interference with the rights of others. Despite the changes in the university *qua* parent role, we maintain that the institution's ethical responsibility for the well-being of a student extends at the very least into the classroom and other sites where faculty/student interactions occur because the university is the agent ultimately responsible for bringing faculty and students together.

The courts have always avoided interference in university, faculty, and student relationships, and it is difficult to see how, given the complex nature of the problem, recourse to the courts will offer relief to the aggrieved or effect justice. At best the courts will be forced to invoke the narrowest, most physical definition of harassment—but as this chapter has tried to suggest, the damages wrought at the "softer" end of the continuum are extremely difficult to identify, probably unassessable, and virtually impossible to redress, particularly in their subtle reaffirmation of a patriarchal ideology of woman's "secondness." It is for this reason that the academic institution owes serious attention to this ethical dilemma and should acknowledge its importance through policy statements, grievance procedures, awareness programs, and information distribution. In the spirit of truly caring, an institution's procedures and statements should be characterized by informality, simplicity, succinctness, and clarity.

The law lacks the ability to define sexual harassment in its fullest meaning, but the university does have the power to define what *it* means by sexual harassment, even though that definition may vary from one institution to another. The violation of an institution's definition can be enforced and to some extent redressed; in fact, only then are the courts willing to provide support in the redress process. The academic institution's character, its values and ethics, its commitment to its various stakeholders—remain the best line of defense for everybody.

CONCLUSION

The most valuable lesson any parent can teach a child may be the ability to be independent and take care of oneself. This may also apply to the university and its students, particularly the undergraduates. There are some situations, however, that do not lend themselves to self-help and that require intervention by one of society's more powerful forces in order to prevent or redress a wrong. So it is with sexual harassment—a wrong visited upon those who are often not capable of helping themselves with the potential of causing its victims grievous mental and emotional harm. Under Title IX, sexual harassment may be construed as a form of sexual discrimination. No one disputes the right of any female student to enjoy an academic environment free of unwanted verbal and physical pollution, but her inability to handle a situation where such pollution is encountered in the form of a sexist or even lecherous professor can effectively deny her that right.

We have tried to show that courts, legislatures, and administrative agencies do not offer a remedy to most student victims of sexual harassment and probably never will. Only the university can promulgate a set of standards that protects everyone. The university alone has both the credibility and resources to reach the potential victim with its message before the damage is done. It alone has the power to impose awesome penalties upon those who choose to ignore these standards. In addition, once the university has set such a mechanism in motion, it will be supported completely by the courts, an even more powerful deterrent to the offensive practices in question. The exact nature of such mechanisms is beyond the scope of this chapter and, in our opinion, must be treated on an individual basis taking into consideration the traditions and general culture of each university.

Consistent with the law and with principles of ethics, the time has come for educational institutions that have not already done so to act: fairly, even-handedly, and decisively.

NOTES

1 Decided by the U.S. Court of Appeals, Second Circuit.

2 It should be pointed out that this chapter deals with legal remedies for faculty/student harassment arising only under federal law. Constraints may be found in the laws of some states, however, affording students causes of action directly against offending faculty members based, for example, upon theories such as intentional infliction of emotional distress. This could result not only in compensatory but also punitive damages against an offending faculty member, but the burden of proof in such cases would fall squarely upon the student. Furthermore, much of the injury and loss inflicted on student victims of sexual harassment cannot be redressed adequately with money damages.

3 See e.g., *Korf v. Ball State University,* 726 F .2d 1222 [7th Cir. 1985], *Levitt*

3 See e.g., *Korf v. Ball State University*, 726 F .2d 1222 [7th Cir. 1985], *Levitt v. University of Texas at El Paso*, 759 F. 2d 1224 [5th Cir. 1985], cert. denied, 106 S. Ct. 599 [1986]; *Naragon v. Wharton*, 737 F. 2d 1403 [5th Cir. 1984]).

4 Benson and Thomson: 95 percent; National Center of Educational Statistics, 1980-81: over 90 percent; 76.3 percent of all tenured faculty are male (*The Chronicle of Higher Education*, Aug. 25, 1993, pp. 47-119).

REFERENCES

Alexander v. Yale University. 631 F2d 178. 2nd Cir. (1980).

Association of University Professors. (1984). *Sexual harassment: Suggested policy and procedures for handling complaints* (AAUP Policy Documents and Reports). Washington, DC: Author.

Bougher v. University of Pittsburgh. 882 F2d 74. 3rd Cir. (1989).

Benson, D. J., & Thomson, G. E. (1982). Sexual harassment on a university campus: The confluence of authority relations, sexual interest and gender stratification. *Social Problems, 29*, 236-251.

Buek, A. P. (1978). *Sexual harassment: Fact of life or violation of law? University life under Title IX*. Washington, D.C.: The National Advisory Council on Women's Educational Programs.

Chronicle of Higher Education (1993, Aug. 25). Almanac Edition, pp. 47-119.

Civil Rights Restoration Act. Public Law *100-259*. 22 March 1988.

Cockburn v. Santa Monica Community College District Personnel Commission. 161 Cal. App. 3d 734. (1984).

Cole, E. K. (1986). Recent legal developments in sexual harassment. *Journal of College and University Law, 13*, 267-284.

Crocker, P. L. (1983). An analysis of university definitions of sexual harassment. *Signs, 8*, 696-705.

Durham, M. (1988, May 11). "Sex pest don' gag on cherwell." *The Daily Telegraph*, p. 2.

Dziech, B. W., & Weiner, L. (1984). *The lecherous professor: Sexual harassment on campus*. Boston: Beacon Press.

Equal Employment Opportunity Commission (1980). Guidelines on discrimination because of sex, *Federal Register, 45*, 74676-74677.

Faulkner, W. (1936). *Absalom, Absalom!* New York: Random House.

Federal Register. 45 (9 May 1980). No. 92. 30955-30965.

Fighting lechery on campus. (1980, February 4). *Time*, p. 84.

Grove City College v. Bell. 104 S. Ct. 1211. (1984).

Hoffman, F. L. (1986). Sexual harassment in academia: Feminist theory and institutional practice. *Harvard Educational Review, 56,* 105-121.

Korf v. Ball State University. 726 F2d 1222. 7th Cir. (1984).

Levitt v. The University of Texas at El Paso. 759 F2d 1224. 5th Cir. (1985).

Lipsett v. University of Puerto Rico. 864 F2d 881. 1st Cir. (1988).

Mead, M. (1980). A proposal: We need taboos on sex at work. In D. A. Neugarten & J. M. Shafritz (Eds.), *Sexuality in organizations: Romantic and coercive behaviors at work.* Oak Park, Ill.: Moore Park Co., Inc.

Meritor Savings Bank v. Vinson. 106 S. Ct. 2399. (1986).

Naragon v. Wharton. 737 F2d 1403. 5th Cir. (1984).

Oxford University Women Tutors' Group. (1988). *Sexual harassment: Draft code of practice.* Unpublished manuscript.

Project on the Education and Status of Women. (1980). *Title VII sexual harassment guidelines and education employment.* Washington, DC.: Author.

Sandler, B. R. & Associates. (1981). Sexual harassment: A hidden problem. *Educational Record, 62,* 52-57.

Tuana, N. (1985). Sexual harassment in academe: Issues of power and coercion. *College Teaching, 33,* 53-63.

U.S. Department of Education-Office for Civil Rights. (1987). *Title IX grievance procedures: An introductory manual.* Washington, DC: Author.

U. S. Department of Education-Office for Civil Rights. (1984). *Sexual harassment: Its not academic* (Reprinted 1986, December). Washington, DC: Author.

13
CONSENSUAL AMOROUS RELATIONSHIPS

by Louise F. Fitzgerald

I resent horribly the exploitation of female students by male faculty. Too many male teachers use (this place) as a sexual supermarket, and I grieve for my female students who are (rightly) awed by these men, whom they see as so wonderfully appreciative of their minds, only to find out that this man simply gets off on the adoration of 19-year-old women. It's still offensive to see aging male faculty members with nubile pregnant wives who are former graduate students, many of whom will never finish. . . .
—Female professor, quoted in Fitzgerald and Weitzman (1990)

As the issue of sexual harassment has become widely recognized as a serious social problem, some universities have gone beyond establishing prohibitions against the more commonly recognized problems and developed policies addressing what have come to be known as consensual relationships—situations where women students "willingly" enter into a sexual relationship with a professor; in this context, "willing" is taken to imply the absence of bribery, coercion or any form of threat or inducement whether direct or subtle.

Keller (1988) provides an extensive analysis of such policies from a legal perspective. She argues that the constitutional right to privacy, grounded in the penumbra of various constitutional amendments, offers some protection for consensual relationships between faculty and students at public institutions. She notes, however, that "[this right] is not absolute. As with any constitutionally guaranteed individual right, compelling state interest permits certain infringements of that right. Laws which limit the fundamental freedoms of an indi-

An earlier version of this chapter appeared in *Sexual Harassment in Higher Education: Concepts and Issues* (pp. 45-48). Washington, DC: NEA (1992).

vidual must serve a compelling state interest and also must be narrowly drawn to serve only that interest. *The context of an educational institution may reveal such a compelling interest"* (pp. 33-34).

After reviewing relevant case law, Keller concludes that faculty-student relations within the "zone of instruction"— when the student is in the professor's class, when he is her thesis director, or in some supervisory capacity—can legitimately be prohibited on the grounds that the element of coercion can never be completely eliminated when the faculty member has such power over the student. She notes that such associations "carry the presumption of coercion and render the consensual nature of the relationships suspect. . . .the university may legitimately proscribe all such associations" (p. 40).

If, however, the faculty member does not supervise the student in any way, the institution has no basis to question her consent, nor would any favoritism be implied. Thus, according to Keller, the state has no compelling interest that would justify such a prohibition. She proposes a "bright line" test for determining when a university may legitimately prohibit faculty-student relationships: "namely, when the faculty member academically supervises the student. Intimate consensual relationships falling outside the instructional context are constitutionally protected from university interference" (p. 41).

At first reading, Keller's logic seems compelling. But readers familiar with life in academia will realize immediately that the bright line she proposes is neither as bright nor definitive as she would have us believe. Even with respect to strictly formal power, any professor will realize that he does not have to directly teach, supervise or advise a student to be able to influence or even determine her fate, for good or ill. This is particularly true within the somewhat intimate confines of graduate departments where a professor may not academically supervise a student in any way and have no authority over her, and yet still be in a position of considerable authority and influence. Although there may certainly be cases where the professor and student are so far professionally removed from one another that his power is minimal or trivial, Keller's bright line distinction will not serve to identify them.

Zalk, Paludi, and Dederich (1990) offer a thoughtful analysis of the psychological power differentials inherent in any faculty-student relationship. Their analysis seems particularly suited for illuminating the situation of undergraduate women who become involved with professors. They write:

> The bases of the faculty member's almost absolute power are varied, and range from the entirely rational into broad areas of fantasy. Professors give grades, write recommendations for graduate schools, awards and the like, and can predispose colleague's attitudes toward students. But it goes beyond that.
>
> Knowledge and wisdom are power—particularly in the academy, the setting within which the student must effectively operate. While superior knowledge, and thus presumably greater wisdom, are often ascribed to faculty members by society at large, the students' adolescent idealism exaggerates its extent. The knowledge and experience ascribed to age add to this source of power. The extension of the power of knowledge is often made into the realm of values and students often accept, uncritically, as true or right what the professor espouses (Stimpson, 1988).
>
> It is easy to see how this imbalance of power exacerbates the vulnerability of all students. One can also understand what a heady experience it is for the student who is singled out as "special" by a professor (pp. 109-110).

As a practical matter, universities that have consensual relationship statements have tended to incorporate Keller's distinction between supervisory and non-supervisory academic relationships. For example, the strongest policy to date on consensual relationships is that of the University of Iowa, which states *"No faculty member shall have an amorous relationship (consensual or otherwise) with a student who is enrolled in a course being taught by the faculty member or whose academic work (including work as a teaching assistant) is being supervised by the faculty member."* The policy goes on to say that consensual relationships outside the instructional context, can lead to great difficulties, particularly when the individuals are in the same or related departments. It cites problems with appearances of favoritism, possible conflicts of interest, and so forth.

Other statements, although not formally proscribing such relationships, indicate that they are generally inappropriate or problematic. The University of Wisconsin, Illinois, Pennsylvania, and Harvard, among others, have policies of this sort. Most of these policies also point out that if subsequent charges of harassment are brought, they will be extremely difficult to defend.

SUMMARY AND RECOMMENDATIONS

As our knowledge and understanding of the dynamics of sexual harassment have developed and expanded, so too have the policy statements designed to address it. Currently, colleges and universities are beginning to confront the difficult legal, moral, and ethical issues raised by apparently consensual sexual relationships between faculty and students.

Although history and custom have traditionally inhibited institutions from formally proscribing such relationships, such prohibitions are both advisable and legally defensible, at least within the instructional context broadly defined. The courts have ruled that faculty have no right to "exploit students for personal gain" whatever the student's consent may or may not have been (*Korf v. Ball State University*, 1984), and universities themselves should do no less.

POSTSCRIPT

Of all the issues raised by the problem of sexual harassment in higher education, none has proved thornier for colleges and universities than that of supposedly "consensual" relationships between faculty and students. In contrast to the progress that has been made on other aspects of the problem, attempts to address this particular issue continue to be met with resistance from a variety of sources. Even fairly conservative policies such as that recently implemented by the University of Virginia (which prohibits faculty members from dating students who are enrolled in their classes) are frequently opposed by those who argue that they infringe on professors' rights of privacy and association. The UVA Faculty Senate debate on the policy attracted national media attention, including attempts at live television coverage, front page headlines, and lengthy (and frequently sarcastic) features in magazines such as *Newsweek*. Some elements within the media and academia have delighted in ridiculing the issue as "political correctness" run amok, and even some feminist academicians (e.g., Hoffman, 1986) have argued that such policies patronize women by suggesting that they cannot make informed decisions about their personal lives.

Much of this resistance appears to represent a disproportionate (albeit well meaning) emphasis on the rights (as opposed to the responsibilities) of faculty combined with a certain innocence about professorial power and influence. However, as Rollo May (1972) pointed out some time ago "we need only ask any graduate student whether his [sic] professors have power over him, and he will laugh at our naiveté. The perpetual anxiety . . . as to whether they will be passed or not is proof enough. The professor's power is even more effective because it is clothed in scholarly garb. *It is the power of prestige, status, and the subtle coercions of others that follow from these"* (p. 102, emphasis added).

Consider the following scenario: Professor X meets and becomes attracted to Graduate Student Y when she takes his seminar in medieval ecclesiastical history. Scrupulously ethical, he waits until the end of the semester before he asks her out, but shortly after that, they become a couple. They go everywhere together, including departmental social events and faculty dinner parties. It becomes commonplace for her to interact on a personal and social level with the rest of the faculty, who are still her professors. She never takes another course from Professor A, and indeed, is specializing in a totally different historical period. In short, they are a fixture of departmental life. Everyone knows they plan to marry.

The following year, Student Y attempts her qualifying exam. To everyone's consternation, she does not do particularly well; a rewrite is required. This is somewhat embarrassing for all concerned, but not a major problem—after all, these things happen. Unfortunately, the rewrite is only marginally better. The committee is in a quandary. The unspoken theme that haunts their deliberations: how can they fail this woman who is, after all, their friend and engaged to their colleague? Finally, with much rationalization and some discomfort, she is passed and admitted to candidacy.

The following year, while beginning to work on her thesis, things begin to go quite wrong for Student Y. Her relationship is not going well; Professor X is restless, distracted, somewhat distant. After several weeks of quarrels, he breaks down and tells her that he doesn't want to get married—and, in fact, he has met someone else, a woman professor in his own area of expertise. He feels badly, but there it is. Student Y is devastated, crushed—she can't believe it's over. She calls him constantly, leaves notes in his mailbox. She is obsessed with the breakup of the relationship, and feels somehow betrayed in ways she only vaguely understands. Her advisor, who plays squash with Professor X, feels awkward, caught in the middle, and begins to dread working with her. Soon, the department is polarized; many feel sorry for Professor X, who is being "harassed" by a distraught, hysterical woman. Others feel badly for Student Y who is, after all, a friend of theirs and is now unable to get her work done and cries a great deal of the time. The undergraduates in the survey course she teaches complain that she is disorganized and missing class. At the end of the semester, to everyone's relief, she takes a leave of absence; the next year, her former advisor's wife runs into Student Y at a bookstore/coffeehouse where she is working— no, she doesn't plan to come back to school right now—it's still too painful. Maybe someday. End of story.

This story, and others like it, play themselves out every day in graduate departments all over this country and no doubt would pass Keller's (1988) "bright line" test for a protected consensual relationship. *But what Keller's analysis ignores is that there are many forms of power, and the professor has them all—whether he acknowledges it or not, or even wishes to or not. It is a fact of life that all of us in academia recognize, if we are truthful, but often wish or choose to ignore.* It is disingenuous to pretend that because we do not chair someone's dissertation committee, act as advisor, or have the opportunity to give a grade in a particular class, a sexual relationship has no influence on a student's academic life, for good or ill. The truth is, of course, that such a relationship colors not only all of her professional interactions with her "partner," but also with every other professor in (at least) her academic department. Academic and professional opportunities and decisions that should depend solely on her talent and performance will be inappropriately enlarged or constricted for all the wrong reasons. Fellow students will sometimes fall silent when she enters the room. Is she a colleague or a "faculty fink?" Did she receive her fellowship because of her brilliant thesis proposal, or because she is sleeping with the most powerful professor in the department; did she *not* receive it because the thesis wasn't good enough or because the committee, with many deserving proposals to choose from, wished to avoid any suspicion of favoritism? The status lines are hopelessly confused. And, these are the consequences of so-called successful relationships, although "of course, nearly every observant academic admits that most teacher-student liaisons are temporary and that few end on an upbeat note?" (Wagner, 1993, p. B2).

Wagner (1993) argues that such relationships can have tragic consequences not only for the individuals involved but, in the post-Franklin era, can be extremely costly for institutions as well. She notes "Given the current case law on sexual harassment, the conclusion is inescapable: Colleges and universities whose federal funding brings them under Title IX cannot tolerate a faculty-student sexual relationship, regardless of the student's age, . . . willingness to enter such a relationship, undergraduate or graduate status, . . . [or] whether the student comes under the direct supervision of the teacher or not." Although there are certain to be those who disagree, her logic is compelling.

REFERENCES

Fitzgerald, L. F., & Weitzman, L. M. (1990). Men who harass: Speculation and data. In M. A. Paludi (Ed.). *Ivory power: Sexual harassment on campus.* Albany, NY: SUNY.

Hoffman, F. L. (1986). Sexual harrassment in academia: Feminist theory and institutional practice. *Harvard Educational Review, 56,* 105-121.

Keller, E. A. (1988). Consensual amorous relationships between faculty and students: The constitutional right to privacy. *Journal of College and University Law, 15,* 21-42

Korf v. Ball State University, 726 F.2d 1222 (7th Cir. 1989).

May, R, (1972). *Power and innocence.* New York: Dell.

Wagner, E. N. (1993). May 26, Fantasies of true love in academe. *The Chronicle of Higher Education* (p.B.2).

Zalk, S. R., Paludi, M. A., & Dederich, J. (1990). Women students assessment of consensual relationships with their professors: Ivory power reconsidered. In E. K. Cole (Ed.), *Sexual harassment on campus: A legal compendium* (2nd ed.). Washington, DC: National Association of College and University Attorneys.

PART IV

CONSEQUENCES AND REMEDIES

14
SEXUAL HARASSMENT AND ACADEMIC POWER

by Loralee MacPike

Sexual harassment is a prevalent and elusive misuse of academic power. Indeed, its very elusiveness is inherent in the nature of the university. But although I have harsh words for the university as an institution, I believe that attention to sexual harassment signals a change in the nature of the university itself. This change will be the biggest single help in eliminating harassment, not only in the academic world but in all arenas of social contact.

I wish that the amount and quality of education gathered in a university faculty was a safeguard against stereotypical beliefs or rigid inegalitarian structures of thought. Unfortunately, the hypereducated status of most faculties is a major reason for the prevalence of harassment in academic communities. We are all socialized to share ideas regarding the nature of an educated person and of "education" that are grounded in the hierarchy of values of Western culture. These cultural values are based on a particular privileging of certain events and products that represent the predominance of white, middle-class, heterosexual male existence. Former Education Secretary William Bennett's (1984) list of the great books whose mastery (pun intended) was the stamp of education included events such as wars, presidencies, and scientific "discoveries," and products such as arts (over crafts) and nuclear warheads (over children).

Most disciplines traditionally view women and their activities as less important. Quilts are not "art," letters and diaries are not "literature," childrearing is not "history." Women most often appear as sex objects (mistresses of emperors, for example) or nurturers (mothers of emperors, for example).

An earlier version of this chapter appeared in *Thought and Action,* Spring 1989, 5 (1), 49-52.

The casting of women into primarily sexual roles devalues them as actors in our cultural heritage and leads inescapably to their devaluation as individuals. And in a culture in which power confers right, the power of the superior justifies the benefits of using the inferior. Sexual harassment is part of higher education because higher education (and "lower" education as well) is based on the presumed inferiority of women.

None of us can escape being socialized to view women as inferior. As an educated American, I have been trained for years to accept privileged, white, middle-class male events and products as ultimately valuable. So has Mr. Bennett; so have the readers of *Thought & Action.* We cannot help this, for such acceptance is the basis of our Euro-American culture. University education is not grounded in day-to-day human interrelations but instead in the reification of those interrelations into ideas (philosophy, history, psychology, literary criticism, indeed even biology). Because of this grounding, we in the academic world are *more* likely to have developed a complex, intricate, and often unassailable structure of thought about those interrelations, a structure which is based on masculine values and which devalues women.[1]

Women's studies has demonstrated the overwhelming predominance in university management and classrooms of values, beliefs, methodologies, and conclusions that Western culture associates with the masculine. The privileging of war over social relations in the field of history, or psychology's studies of life cycles based on data from male lives, are two of many examples of masculine-dominant structuring of academic disciplines. In both disciplines, exposure of these male biases led to new questions and new methodologies that changed their natures. Psychologists know they must confine pronouncements about their results to the groups on whom they base those results. It is irresponsible to claim for "people" a trend that has been proven only for *male* people. The field of social history, the fastest-growing in the discipline, has required a major shift in methodology and materials, with the result that the discipline of history as a whole has changed.

My view of sexual harassment as a function of the university's masculine bias leaves me not surprised about its prevalence.

The attention we now pay to sexual harassment is related to changes in the disciplines. These changes result from the findings of women's studies that expose that bias.[2] We know that within a "feminine" (or feminist) context, people's ideas and actions change.[3]

These findings lead me to be optimistic about changes in university policies and practices regarding sexual harassment. "Surface changes" *can* create structural changes. Two examples from the field of linguistics illustrate this point. The Sapir-Whorf hypothesis (Whorf, 1941) suggests that the language we use is embedded in social constructs and can help shape our thought processes. The work of MacKay and Fulkerson (1979) on the generation of pronouns suggests that we choose linguistic constructs based on our pre-existing categories of thought. Thus, by defining certain acts as harassment, we create a thought structure within which a perpetrator must eventually think of certain acts as harassment. As we develop a category of thought about what constitutes harassment, we produce acts in conformity with that category of thought. In other words, we stop harassing. People are already saying: "I don't think that's harassment, but I see that my colleagues do, and so I'll have to be careful not to do the acts they think of as harassment."

Truax (this volume) believes that harassment is "behavior" and that behavior is learned. Harassers understand that there are boundaries, but do not yet realize that the boundaries of acceptable behavior have changed. As Truax notes, we no longer associate harassment with the benign idea of eccentricity, so it loses its apparent benignness and is thus freed to accept the more harmful (and, for the perpetrators, shameful) associations connected with that new term and concept: "sexual harassment." As we develop language to name events and our feelings about them, we create new social structures to deal with those events and feelings.

Having the term "sexual harassment" means that no one can dismiss the acts that constitute harassment as friendliness, flattery, or "just part of the job." Harassment victims have thus changed everyone's view of these encounters. In this way people begin to create a better world.

Such change is the finest function of the university: to

give birth to more truly "universal" structures of thought — in this case to a structure in which women are not victims, are not inferior, but claim their voices and gain the right to be heard. The magnitude of this change is great, because it signals a shift away from exclusively white, male middle-class, heterosexual values and toward a universal choir of human values whose preservation and celebration is the university's true purpose.

POSTSCRIPT

As I had predicted nearly five years ago, the issue of sexual harassment has become a contested site, an arena of discourse in which we see, played out on a small stage, the outlines of the current interesting struggle for the definition of the university. When I wrote for *Thought and Action* in 1989, I saw a possibility that the shift in discourse I perceived occurring might signal a more multivocal construction of academic reality. That multivocality would, I predicted, take the form of harassers interpreting their actions (previously seen as harmless or flattering) from the standpoint of the unwilling recipients of those actions. They would begin to say, "I don't think that's harassment, but I see that my colleagues do, and so I'll have to be careful not to do the acts they think of as harassment." Such a realization would cause an actual change in perception, a small shift of standpoint, which would simply and directly translate into a change in behaviors and a concomitant change in university climate.

In one way I was right, I think: a new arena of discourse has been created. But I was premature to think that this new discourse would be the solution. For in the intervening five years I have seen more, not less, struggle for control of this new discourse arena. Most immediate and most alarming is the very visible attempt to reframe the discourse to blame or impugn the victim(s): denial that the events occurred; retreat to a legalistic insistence that without witnesses nothing could be proved; the suggestion (as with Anita Hill) that the alleged events actually occurred only in the victim's desires; or a counteraccusation that the accusers are using the rubric of sexual harassment to discredit falsely those whose power they (illegitimately) covet and challenge. Today sexual harassment is harder than ever to prove because its victims' complaints are dismissed as imaginary and the victims themselves transmuted into sex-obsessed powermongers. To me these are signs of contested discourse. And if they become hegemonic, we're in trouble.

Directly related to the phenomenon of blaming the victim is the claim of "reverse discrimination."[4]   There has been an alarming tendency for members of the university community to accede, albeit sometimes uneasily, to the supremacy of the rights of the individual. Certainly no one wants people punished for crimes they did not commit. But that belief is getting translated into another: that no person should suffer pains to which that person is not habituated. If such a belief becomes conflated with absolute moral rights, then we are doomed to maintaining the existing structures of white, male, middle-class, heterosexual dominance so that those categories of people need never temper their present privilege by listening to or ceding space to "outsiders." And certainly sexual harassment is one such privilege.

Ironically, though, even this alarming attempt to redirect the discourse exposes (as do all such redirections) what is really at stake. The immediate response of denial and attack discloses another layer of the gendered construction of culture within the university.[5] Seen thus, it becomes clear that solving the problem of sexual harassment requires solving a whole lot of other problems in which some people have privilege and others do not. And I believe that unless we peel off the layers until we reach the core of human equality and dignity, sexual harassment will continue under one rubric or another. What we need to do, I think, is to be very clear about our insistence that blaming the victim or crying reverse discrimination are simply deflections from the real issues. We cannot become so mesmerized by the right of individuals to do whatever they want that we are coopted.

Ultimately, I believe the threatened backlash against strong sexual harassment policies is related to the simmering issues of "political correctness" and its mirror image, "hate speech." Badly put, the accusation of political correctness is an attempt to disempower ideas or people who appear too threatening to the status quo.[6] The cry of political correctness comes when minorities and women and gays and the disabled are finally becoming more visible both as consumers and as dispensers of higher education, and I see it as a direct attack on the gains made by these and other marginalized groups. It also comes at a time when the public is actively and vocally resentful of higher education. As James W. Carey (1992) puts it, "Political correctness' is an effective political attack because it acts as a condensation symbol that names and coalesces growing resentments against higher education and the academic establishment" (pp. 58f.). Under the rubric of political correctness, it is possible to dismiss the concerns of the nonprivileged by disqualifying them as ideologically motivated, in opposition to the "unideological" foundations of, for instance, the First Amendment.[7] It is not fanciful to see the privileging of First Amendment rights as partly parallel to reverse discrimination—certain people's rights assume priority over other people's rights. If we allow the goals of the prevention of sexual harassment to be subsumed under an unexamined ideological privileging, we will fail once again to accord full human rights to every person. Indeed, one of the major problems with allowing the issue of sexual harassment to become conflated with or sucked into the pseudodebate about political correctness is that such conflation separates *beliefs* about sexual harassment from the *ends* of sexual harassment policies (Whitney & Wartella, 1992). We must above all never lose sight of the ultimate goal, which is a university free of the disempowerment through sexuality of its students and workers.

Hate speech works exactly inverse to political correctness. In order to preserve the rights of a few to say what they want, the rights of others to live in an atmosphere free of direct verbal assault is sacrificed. In the case of political correctness, some people are silenced by impugning the motives of their speech. In the case of hate speech, some people are vocally empowered by claiming exemption from a similar examination of motives. This comparison suggests that much vaunted First Amendment rights are *always* placed in context and *always* serve political and ideological ends. If we do not see and make explicit those ends, we will lose control of yet another frame of discourse.

So I believe with Molefi Asante (1992) that "The attack on political correctness [and by extension on sexual harassment policies and on the protection of hate speech] . . . is merely the anticipated reaction to the expansion of dialogue and extension of discourse to the least visible populations in the society" (p. 147). If we know this; if we refuse to be deflected into pseudodebate within discourse frameworks that make us invisible; if we understand that the solution is to continue to insist on the expansion and extension of discourse to include everyone—only then will we really begin to change the cultural discourse community by which sexual harassment, hate speech, sexism, and economic oppression are constituted.

When all is said, however, I find I haven't lost my optimism. The issue of sexual harassment will be key in the turf battle I see going on over how moral behavior will be defined, and by whom. I hope that campuses that are serious about eliminating sexual harassment will see the connections among a strong affirmative action policy, an ongoing requirement that students study gender and race, a campus atmosphere in which hate speech is not helplessly condoned, healthy women's studies and ethnic studies and lesbian and gay studies programs, and a refusal to gloss over sexual harassment. The hegemony of thought that has characterized university education over the past two or three centuries will not easily yield. Part of its strength is its ability to reconstitute the discourse that determines how a threatening topic like sexual harassment will be viewed.

But if we understand the battle for discourse and remain focused on what we really want, we will be able, eventually, not only to eliminate sexual harassment as in any way a protected category of behavior, but also to move simultaneously on all fronts toward a society in which all people are truly equal in both opportunity and treatment.

NOTES

1 I choose the word "masculine" here to indicate a set of social constructs artificially associated with gender. I do not believe there is any innate connection between sex (i.e., maleness in individuals) and these gendered social constructs. I will hereafter use the word "masculine" to indicate gendered rather than sexual connections. Truax (this volume) wrongly assigns sexual harassment to "men." It is true that most harassers are men, but I doubt there is a biological connection. Sexual harassment seems to be connected not with gender per se but with power. Women who harass are more likely to occupy traditional male positions and adopt masculine philosophies and prerogatives. These women may take on the belief that people in "lower" power positions exist for their convenience or pleasure, too. Therefore, the preponderance of male harassers results from the way our culture empowers and privileges men. Women who assume masculine power and privilege all too often help sustain a system of which sexual harassment is an intrinsic part.

2 I am convinced that the issues of race and class are inextricable from and integral to the changes I describe. The change in social constructs that I believe we are undergoing results from any new ways of viewing human realities, of which women's studies is only one.

3 See Cathryn Adamsky's (1976) study on self-esteem in relation to use of a generic "she," or Wendy Martyna's (1978) findings on the relation between language use and imaginings of personal power.

4 In fact, "reverse discrimination" cannot exist; discrimination requires that the group discriminating be in a position of general cultural and economic dominance over the group discriminated against. The fact that one member of a dominant group suffers does not constitute discrimination so long as the group to which that member belongs retains its dominance.

5 This construction of culture is also racial, ethnic, age-related, disability-related; all these (and other) categories display the hierarchy on which sexual harassment (and other dominations) are based. My focus here on gender merely allows for clarity and brevity.

6 There's an extended discussion of political correctness in "Symposium: Communication Scholarship and Political Correctness," *Journal of Communication 42*, No. 2 (Spring 1992), pp. 56-149. See also *Signs: Journal of Women in Culture and Society 17*, No. 4 (Summer 1992), pp. 779-805; and *Social Policy 22* (Summer 1991), pp. 16-40.

7 For an excellent analysis of why the Fourteenth Amendment protection of equal treatment under the law should take precedence over First Amendment rights, see Asante (1992).

REFERENCES

Adamsky, Cathryn (1976). *Changes in pronominal usage among college students as a function of instructor use of she as the generic singular pronoun.*" Paper presented at the American Psychological Association conference.

Asante, Molefi K. (1992). The escape into hyperbole: Communication and political correctness," *Journal of Communication 42*, 141-47.

Bennett, William J. (1984). *To Reclaim A Legacy.* Washington DC: National Endowment for the Humanities.

Carey, James W. (1992). Political correctness and cultural studies. *Journal of Communication 42*, 47-59.

MacKay, Donald and David C. Fulkerson (1979). "On the comprehension and production of pronouns." *Journal of Verbal Learning and Verbal Behavior 18*, 661-73.

Martyna, Wendy (1978). What does 'he' mean? *Journal of Communication 28*, 131-38.

Whitney, Charles and Ellen Wartella. (1992). Media coverage of the 'political correctness' debate." *Journal of Communication 42*, 88-95.

Whorf, Benjamin L. (1941). "The relation of habitual thought and behavior to language," in *Language, Culture, and Personality: Essays in Memory of Edward Sapir.* L. Spier (Ed). Menasha, WI: Sapir Memorial Publication Fund, pp. 75-93.

15
THE FEMINIST-UNIONIST DILEMMA

by Sherna Berger Gluck

Few issues are as fraught with contradictions for feminist unionists in the academy as the handling of sexual harassment. Sexual harassment is both a product of and expression of sexism. In fact, the attempt to fight sexism has led to the redefinition of formerly socially acceptable behaviors as sexual harassment. But as unionists we also uphold and believe in academic freedom, due process, and the enforcement of our contracts. At times, the commitments to fight sexism and to protect faculty members collide.

This clash is most evident during the complaint/punishment process, but troubling questions even arise at the definitional stage. Most observers agree on the egregious forms of sexual harassment, and even on less obvious forms, such as comments about physical attributes. Most feminist literature on sexual harassment assumes that the victim must set the standard. Indeed, women must set the standards since sexual harassment is a form of sexism.

The definition of sexual harassment is more problematic when we consider behavior that creates a hostile or intimidating learning environment. Do we include passive messages, like the artwork we hang in our offices? After all, our offices are public spaces. Can each student use her own standard of morality to define a hostile learning environment? Given the diversity of our students, perhaps it is not wise to decorate our offices with anything but bland art. But this is an inappropriate answer to a vexing question, and it also hovers on a violation of academic freedom. Instead of engaging in philosophical debates on this aspect of sexual harassment, perhaps it is wiser to seek practical solutions. For example, a sexual harassment policy may give students the right to

An earlier version of this chapter appeared in *Thought and Action,*
Spring 1989, 5 (1), 45-47.

request meetings in an alternative space if there is material that they find offensive in an office. The same right would, of course, also apply to faculty and staff women.

The classroom use of sexist and gendered language is much more pernicious and widespread than the passive messages that office decorations communicate. When a professor uses the generic male pronoun to refer to humanity, our women students receive an active message: they are secondary, they are irrelevant. This message creates a hostile and intimidating learning environment. Universities must develop and publicize policies on the use of sexist and gender-neutral language. Students and faculty must learn these policies, as well as the ways that sexist and gendered language create hostile and intimidating learning environments.

Faculty unionists must play an active role in these definitional discussions—not just because we abhor sexual harassment. The lack of specificity creates problems when we must defend alleged faculty perpetrators in the grievance process. We should include a range of occurrences in any definition. Feminist legal writers suggest that broad inclusion makes faculty aware of all the actions for which they are accountable. Taking this step also alerts students to their rights (Crocker, 1983).

After engaging in definitional discussions, we must assure that our procedures are fair and reflect the principles of progressive discipline. Perpetrators must be held accountable, and the victims of harassment must have a nonthreatening complaint procedure. But I am troubled when sanctions are meted out on the basis of informal complaints. This practice forces the union to defend perpetrators of sexual harassment. The more we work *with* the administration and campus women's groups to establish good procedures for hearing and acting on complaints, the less often will we have to defend alleged perpetrators.

Despite our groundwork, we will continue to defend alleged perpetrators because of procedural errors. This is where our feminist and union politics directly conflict. We must support both the contractual rights of faculty members *and* the well-being of our students and our women colleagues. How do we avoid the appearance of favoring the perpetrators of sexual harassment?

California State University at Northridge (CSUN) has a strong, union-supported Women's Council that devises creative solutions to this dilemma. The Faculty Rights committee helps the "defendant" through the necessary process. But other committee members offer support to the harassed student, staff, or faculty member. This "two-headed beast" gives a clear message to the campus community. The union will protect faculty due process and contractual rights. It will also fight sexual harassment and support sexual harassment complaints. This workable solution raises some secondary problems. Do men process the grievances of the alleged perpetrators while women support the victims? What message does this practice give to the campus? As odious a task as it might be, women must also process the grievances.

It is not always easy to fight sexism and to defend faculty rights. But to make faculty unions strong and principled, and to assure that they represent the best interests of women, we must actively participate in other organizations that are concerned about sexual harassment. Once we have union structures that deal with both faculty rights and victim rights, we have to wait to be called. As former CSUN chapter president Pat Nichelson noted: "Even the Equalizer (television's avenger for hire) waits for a phone call."

POSTSCRIPT

The vexing dilemma we feminist union activists face has been mitigated, to some extent, by the burgeoning awareness of sexual harassment. Anita Hill made the phrase part of the popular vocabulary, and academic administrators have scurried to protect their campuses from legal actions. Notices defining and condemning sexual harassment are posted and distributed, and procedures are now clearly articulated for filing complaints. Nevertheless, because students are still reluctant to come forward to file official complaints, the common practice of encouraging informal, anonymous complaints continues to threaten due process.

We have yet to tackle effectively ways to deal with sexist speech in the classroom. Many faculty senates and women's commissions continue to hammer away at the problem, producing handbooks that ever so gently prod faculty into using nongendered language. But, having made only the slightest dent on this front, the clamor about feminist "thought police" has caused many campuses to retreat from the effort totally.

REFERENCES

Phyllis L. Crocker, (1983) An analysis of university definitions of sexual harassment, Signs: Journal of Women in Culture and Society, 8, 696-705.

16
SEXUAL HARASSMENT ON CAMPUS AND A UNION'S DILEMMA

by Rachel Hendrickson[†]

Sexual harassment is illegal discrimination and, as such, may already be prohibited by nondiscrimination or equal opportunity clauses in higher education bargaining agreements. Institutions of higher education have developed extensive policies covering various aspects of reporting alleged incidents of harassment, providing confidentiality for accused and accuser, and setting up investigation and discipline procedures. However, where a collective bargaining agreement exists, such procedures may come into direct conflict with contractual due process standards, information disclosure requirements, and disciplinary clauses.

Sexual harassment cases provide dilemmas for the union and its advocates. The first dilemma a union faces is whether to include a section on sexual harassment in its contract, to leave one out but influence the development of campus policies, or to allow those policies to be developed and implemented with the contract functioning as a court of last appeals through its grievance and arbitration process in any disciplinary action that might be taken against a unit member.

On the one hand, a union is charged with the responsibility of advocating for all its members and, under most contracts, ensuring that standards of due process are followed. On the other hand, as we understand more about the negative consequences of sexual harassment, and as we see stories featured in *The Chronicle of Higher Education* about cases on

An earlier version of this chapter was originally presented at the Baruch Conference on Collective Bargaining in Higher Education, 1992.

†[Dr. Hendrickson is a staff member of the National Education Association in its Office of Higher Education, Constituent Group Relations. This chapter reflects the view of the writer and not that of the NEA. Where NEA policy is mentioned, it is identified as such.]

campus, about attempts to prohibit all sorts of consensual relationships, and about recent decisions such as *Franklin* defining the potential liability of institutions that do not take adequate care to protect their students or employees, unions need to rethink their positions. Unions need to consider whether they should develop protections and language within their contracts both to ensure their members are protected during complaint procedures and to ensure that there are no reprisals taken against either the complainant or the accused.

This volume represents an effort by NEA to educate itself and its members on various aspects of sexual harassment on the campus. Research is also being conducted into contract clauses and language in higher education bargaining agreements. Those contracts provide information on how some units have approached the issues raised in the previous paragraphs.

There are few higher education contracts in the NEA data base that address the issue of sexual harassment in any great detail. While there are institutions with effective complaint and investigation procedures, some of which can be found in the Appendix of an NEA monograph by Louise Fitzgerald (1992), not many are translated into contractual language. Those that have attempted to handle the issue within the contract have some elements in common; they follow the definitions of *Meritor Savings Bank FSB v. Vinson* (1986) and the Equal Employment Opportunities Commission (EEOC); they appear to attempt to keep the issue on campus by providing a forum there, instead of through the EEOC, state agencies, or the courts.

Among those contracts that handle the issue of sexual harassment, some provide extensive clauses and procedures, but the majority provide only limited mention of the issue, usually by adding a brief section on policy by referring the issue to an institution handbook or by adding a reference to the standard nondiscrimination clause or to a section on discipline. For example, Oakland Community College's 1990-92 contract had, at the end of a routine equal opportunity section, the clause "nor will sexual harassment be tolerated, in its employment practices." The 1992-95 contract maintains that and adds "and/or educational programs or activities." This clause has the effect of including both Title VII and Title IX protections in the contract.

The McHenry County College contract states, "The Board shall adopt a progressive discipline standard and denote which infractions are subject to which penalties. Except as specifically noted (e.g., assault, theft, inebriation on the job, sexual harassment, etc.), warnings shall be given and an opportunity rendered to remediate any deficiency notes." An example of a policy section comes from Shawnee State University; "It is the policy of Shawnee State University and the Association to maintain an educational and employment environment that is free from sexual harassment and hostility. If there is a complaint of sexual harassment against a faculty member, the provisions in the agreement shall be followed" (Sec. 7). (The provisions referred to are those concerning discipline.)

The Skagit Valley College contract simply references the college policy: "Sexual harassment matters shall be handled in accordance with the Sexual Harassment Policy...and applicable terms of this Agreement." The Clark College agreement is much more comprehensive in its coverage of the issue. The Agreement first covers the issue of due process and representation for the accused. For general "offenses," there is a statute of limitations on records of the event or reprimand—3 years. After 3 years, the personnel file is purged of all information on complaints. The two exceptions are for instances of drug/alcohol abuse and sexual harassment.

Clark College also includes a fairly extensive section on the definition of sexual harassment and procedures for filing a complaint. The initial language of the contract defining sexual harassment basically follows *Meritor* or the EEOC guidelines, but links the problem directly to the academic setting. Defining the issue as a situation that "involves the inappropriate introduction of sexual activities or comments that demean or otherwise diminish one's self-worth on the basis of gender into the work or learning situation," the contract extends the EEOC criteria to educational settings, that is, when the implicit or explicit submission to or rejection of conduct of a sexual nature affects academic standing or when the hostile or intimidating environment creates an offensive working or educational environment.

The Clark contract combines in its definitions both discriminatory relationships involving faculty and students and faculty and other faculty or peers:

> Sexual harassment often involves relationships of unequal power and contains elements of coercion—as when compliance with requests for sexual favors becomes a criterion for granting work, study, or grading benefits. However, sexual harassment may also involve relationships among equals, as when repeated sexual advances or demeaning verbal behavior have a harmful effect on a person's ability to study or work.

Thus, the contract combines both Title IX and Title VII issues, defining discrimination against faculty *and* students. Faculty are allowed to elect which complaint procedure to follow—either the College's sexual harassment grievance procedure or the contractual grievance procedure. Fitzgerald (this volume) notes the importance of multiple channels for complaint. Here is an instance where the faculty member has a choice of two.

The final section in the harassment portion of the Clark contract provides for confidentiality for both the accused and the complainant, although it provides no further guidance than the warning that it must be maintained. Because of the college's strong policy on due process rights, under the contract, the burden of proof in any discipline case rests with the college. The college has an additional responsibility—that of pursuing the issue "in a timely manner." Once any complaint about any potential disciplinary concern is brought forward, the college is required to call it to the attention of the faculty member in a timely manner or it may not be used as the basis for any disciplinary action. A college that ignores complaints cannot later use them.

The Youngstown University Professional Staff agreement provides for reporting all allegations of discrimination to the Affirmative Action Office. It limits the extent of the processing of the allegations to the third step of the grievance procedure. Thus it appears that no binding resolution exists under the agreement.

The Florida State University System (FSU) has one of

the most extensive sections on sexual harassment found in the data base. It covers intent, policy, definition, investigation, and election of remedies. The FSU sexual harassment policy is contained within its nondiscrimination article. The "Statement of Intent" within the article expresses a firm commitment on the part of both union and university: "They desire to assure equal employment opportunities within the SUS (State University System) and recognize that the purpose of affirmative action is to provide equal opportunity to women, minorities, and other affected groups to achieve equality. The implementation of affirmative action programs will require positive actions that will affect terms and conditions of employment and to this end the parties have, in this Agreement and elsewhere, undertaken programs to ensure equitable opportunities for employees to receive salary adjustments, tenure promotion, sabbaticals, and other benefits."

The policy section first defines its nondiscrimination thrust, then moves to a specific discussion of sexual harassment from a legal and precedential view and then a philosophical view. Sexual harassment is defined by incorporating into the contract sections of the *Meritor* decision, citing both *quid pro quo* and hostile environment harassment. The agreement also explores the issue of consensual relations within the academic context: "In addition to the parties' concern with respect to sexual harassment in the employment context, the parties also recognize the potential for this form of illegal discrimination against students. Relationships between employees and students, even if consensual, may become exploitive, and especially so when academic or athletic endeavors are supervised or evaluated by the employee... These relationships may also involve a conflict of interest." Thus, while consensual relationships are not forbidden, the warning is clear that such relationships might result in a violation of other sections of the contract.

The issue of consensual relations is, indeed, a thorny one, as exemplified by the recent controversies on various campuses. The NEA has established policy on personal relationships that it encourages its units to follow:

The National Education Association recognizes that in institutions of higher education adult students and educators may establish personal relationships. However, such relationships should be voluntary and not be used to coerce or influence others for personal advantage. Thus, the Association believes that sexual relationships between a faculty member and student currently enrolled in the faculty member's course, or under the supervision or direction of the faculty member are unprofessional. The Association urges its affiliates in institutions of higher education to establish strong policies declaring such relationships unprofessional.

The FSU contract provides for access to all relevant documents except for those protected by law. It also provides for an election of remedies. The parties express their intent to resolve any complaints under the grievance procedure of the contract rather than through the courts or under other procedures. The Union agrees "not to process cases arising under this Article when alternate procedures to Article 20 [the Grievance Article] are initiated by the grievant." Thus, a grievant must elect either to use the grievance process in the contract or use the court, but cannot immediately do both. Presumably, once a person alleging sexual harassment has completed the grievance procedure under the contract, he/she is not barred from then seeking redress through the courts if not satisfied with the outcome. The Supreme Court ruled in *Alexander v. Gardner-Denver* that, in cases of discrimination, a complainant may pursue two remedies.

Should a bargaining unit decide to include provisions concerning sexual harassment within its contract, what are the elements that need to be considered for inclusion in the collective bargaining agreement?

1. I like the concept of a statement of intent or of philosophy. If sexual harassment is to be eradicated on the campus, both parties to an agreement should affirm clearly their belief that harassment is wrong. Both should make a statement, similar to that of FSU's, concerning their determination not to tolerate harassment.

2. What constitutes sexual harassment needs to be defined within the contract for two reasons. First, faculty and staff need to know the boundaries of acceptable conduct and

understand when those boundaries have been breached, either when it is pointed out to them through a disciplinary process or informal consultation, or when they believe they have been harassed. Second, where arbitration processes exist, there are inherent problems in asking an arbitrator to define a situation as harassment if the parties themselves have not done so or are unable to do so. Parties need to be able to weed out inappropriate over-reactions. While definitions and parameters of sexual harassment are still evolving, the parties need to ensure that rude or obnoxious behavior is addressed as such and not as sexual harassment.

3. Standards of due process need to be defined. Since sexual harassment is illegal discrimination under external law, some of the more traditional due process clauses where there is no concern about self-incrimination may not fit the situation. Confidentiality is an issue—both for the accused and the complainant, particularly in a campus environment where gossip is part of the culture. While it is not a contractual issue but an internal union issue, when both parties are members of the bargaining unit, great care must be taken to ensure that the rights of both members are protected. It might be appropriate to define the standards to be used during an investigation and both the burden and quantum of proof. Care in the investigation will assure that a harasser will not later be returned to the educational community by an arbitrator because of a defective procedure, will assure that false claims are weeded out, and will assure that the person being harassed also has protection.

Where a separate investigation process exists under a faculty handbook, the union should consider how limited or defined in scope any campus hearing arising out of an investigation should be. It would be a travesty of due process if a faculty member were to be hauled before one tribunal in which no standards of evidence or process as we understand them are used, found "guilty," terminated or disciplined, then to have to go through another whole grievance and arbitration process where the administration might use evidence or testimony from the first hearing. A union should consider very carefully if or under what limitations it is willing to agree to alternate or additional hearing processes.

4. I have the personal belief that there should be no clause providing for election of remedies or delay of filing. Sexual harassment *is* covered under external law and under any contract that has a nondiscrimination clause, whether it is explicitly mentioned or not. There are different standards of proof in arbitration than in a federal agency or courtroom. There may be different definitions of what constitutes sexual harassment on a campus. There clearly are different remedies available from the courts than from the arbitration process. Arbitrators are seldom permitted to award damages beyond a "make whole" in a contract. The recent *Franklin* decision increased the potential liability for institutions that fail in their responsibility to their students. What should be clear in the contract are the standards an arbitrator is to use in ruling on the presence or absence of harassment. Some arbitrators use EEOC standards in their decisions; some may use a "reasonable woman" standard; some are left to flounder. It is up to the parties to craft the standards by which an accusation should be judged, discipline imposed, or redress offered. Also to be considered is the type of information that may be entered into the hearing. For instance, there is some evidence that some arbitrators do take the complainant's prior sexual activities into consideration. The parties should also agree on the parameters of discipline or redress involved, so an arbitrator has good guidance in crafting a remedy.

5. Along with no election of remedies, a union might want to consider having multiple channels of complaint available to its members. If we assume that most victims of harassment simply wish it to stop and not to be subject to retaliation, then alternatives to an immediate formal grievance or complaint procedure might have the desired effect before positions become hardened in hearings. The Affirmative Action Officer or campus committee charged with investigation or mediation, a campus ombudsperson, a committee constituted by the union, or some other form of a joint committee are all potential channels.

6. The parties should be clear on what the actual offense is and how it fits into contractual traditions of tenure or just cause. It might be appropriate to class offenses accord-

ingly. Is an action to be considered sexual harassment? Is it to be considered exploitation of students? An abuse of authority? Unprofessional behavior? Simple rudeness? Is it considered an offense warranting institution of proceedings for removal under tenure or one for lesser disciplinary action?

7. Most of the above observations revolve around the assumption that a faculty member has been accused of harassment. Provisions need to be made to protect a faculty member who is being harassed—either by another faculty or staff member or by a student. If the institution and union have both agreed to actively eliminate harassment, both have a responsibility to protect the victim who may be a member of the same union as the accused. Another option to explore is, if the institution does not take steps to protect the victimized faculty member, the availability of a procedure within the contract for the union to file a grievance against the institution and its administration on behalf of a faculty or unit member who is being harassed.

8. I suggest that the parties keep in mind that one of their most important goals is to ensure that sexual harassment does not occur in the first place. Therefore, my final suggestion is that the parties agree to institute training for all current supervisors and faculty and to provide it on an ongoing basis. While the institution of training does not necessarily have to appear in a contract, its presence signals to the academic community that union and administration are serious about their responsibilities

NEA President Keith Geiger wrote in the preface to Fitzgerald's (1992) monograph that "Sexual harassment is a matter of particular concern to the academic community. Students, faculty, and staff must rely on bonds of intellectual trust and dependence. Sexual harassment can damage careers, negatively impact the educational experience of those harassed, and upset the well-being of the faculty, staff, and students. It. . . damages the integrity of the academic enterprise." I suggest that it is crucial for union and administration to work together, through collective bargaining, to ensure that academic integrity remains intact.

POSTSCRIPT

On November 9, 1993, the United States Supreme Court announced its decision in the *Harris v. Forklift Systems, Inc.* case (No. 92-1168). The actual decision, which was quite short, reaffirmed the *Meritor* (1986) definition of what constitutes a hostile environment. The *Harris* decision also affirms that "to be actionable, as 'abusive work environment' harassment, conduct need not 'seriously affect [an employee's] psychological well-being' or lead her to suffer injury.

Justice O'Connor's decision provides the following guidelines in determining hostile environment harassment:

This standard, which we reaffirm today, takes a middle path between making actionable any conduct that is merely offensive and requiring the conduct to cause a tangible psychological injury. As we pointed out in *Meritor*, "mere utterance of an ...epithet which engenders offensive feelings in an employee," does not sufficiently affect the conditions of employment to implicate Title VII. Conduct that is not severe or pervasive enough to create an objectively hostile or abusive work environment—an environment that a reasonable person would find hostile or abusive—is beyond Title VII's purview. Likewise, if the victim does not subjectively perceive the environment to be abusive, the conduct has not actually altered the conditions of the victim's employment, and there is no Title VII violation.

But Title VII comes into play before the harassing conduct leads to a nervous breakdown. A discriminatory abusive work environment, even one that does not seriously affect employees' psychological well-being, can and often will detract from employees ' job performance, discourage employees from remaining on the job, or keep them from advancing in their careers. . .

That is not, and by its nature cannot be, a mathematically precise test...But we can say that whether an environment is 'hostile' or 'abusive' can be determined only by looking at all the circumstances. These may include the frequency of the discriminatory conduct; its severity; whether it is physically threatening or humiliating, or a mere offensive utterance; and whether it unreasonably interferes with an employee's work performance. The effect on the employee's psychological well-being is, of course, relevant to determining whether the plaintiff actually found the environment abusive. But while psychological harm, like any other relevant factor, may be taken into account, no single factor is required.

REFERENCES

Alexander v. Gardner-Denver Co., 1994. S. Ct. 1011 (1974).

Fitzgerald, Louise. (1992), *Sexual harassment in higher education: Concepts & issues*. Washington, D.C., The National Education Association

Franklin v. Guinnett County School District. 112-S. Ct. 1028 (1992).

Harris v. Forklift Systems, Inc. No. 92-1168 S. Ct. (1993)

Meritor Savings Bank, FSB v. Vinson, 477 U.S. 57, 106 S. Ct. 2399 (1986)

The following labor contracts are cited in the above article. The dates indicate the year of expiration. Unless otherwise specified, the contract covers the faculty bargaining unit.

Clark College, Washington, 1993
Florida State University System, 1994
McHenry County College, Illinois, 1993
Oakland Community College, Michigan, 1992
Oakland Community College, Michigan, 1995
Shawnee State University, Ohio, 1993
Skagit Valley College, Washington, 1995
Youngstown State University, Professional Staff, Ohio, 1994

17
ETHNICITY, SEX, AND SEXUAL HARASSMENT

by Michele A. Paludi

The nature, range, and impact of sexual harassment in college/university settings may be suggested by the words of women who have been victimized (Project on the Status and Education of Women, 1978; Till, 1980).

> I see male colleagues and professors chum it up and hear all the talk about making the old boy network operate for women, so I thought nothing of accepting an invitation from a . . . professor to attend a gathering at his house. Other graduate students were present. . . . The professor made a fool out of himself pursuing me (it took me a while to catch on) and then blurted, "You know I want to sleep with you; I have a great deal of influence. Now, of course, I don't want to force you into anything, but I'm sure you're going to be sensible about this." I fled.
>
> Playboy centerfolds were used as Anatomy teaching slides . . . In slides, lectures, teaching aids and even our own student note service, we found that nurses were presented as sexy, bitchy, or bossy but never as professional health care workers.
>
> When people treated me differently in college because I was Black and female in things like counseling me . . . or making comments about my background or about Blacks, I wondered what was wrong with me.

As these women's accounts affirm, sexual harassment in colleges and universities is a major barrier to women's professional development. Women's performance in course work suffers, and many drop out of school altogether (Paludi, 1990; Paludi & Barickman, 1991). Stress reactions invariably follow sexual harassment. These stress reactions—depression, tension, anger and fear, insomnia, headaches, feelings of help-

An earlier version of this chapter appeared in *Thought and Action,* Winter 1993, *8* (2), 105-116. Portions were presented at the NEA Higher Education Conference, February 1992, San Diego, California as part of the Symposium, "Sexual Harassment on Campus: Concepts and Issues."

lessness and embarrassment, decreased motivation—constitute what Rabinowitz (1990) calls the Sexual Harassment Trauma Syndrome.

For ethnic minority women who have been sexually harassed, economic vulnerability is paramount. These women are frequently dependent on financial aid to fund their education; as graduate students, they have loans more often than research or teaching assistantships (Blackwell, 1981; DeFour, 1990).

POWER PLAYS

Sexual harassment involves the confluence of authority (power) relations and sexism in a culture stratified by sex. This power or authority can be either formal or informal; it can be achieved or ascribed. Formal power is derived from a formal role—research supervisor, for instance, or professor. Informal power is derived from men's sexual prerogative.

Informal power suggests that men have a right to initiate sexual interactions or assert the primacy of a woman's sex—or race, class, age, or sexual orientation—over her role as student. As Fitzgerald (1990) has commented: "It is this prerogative, a sort of psychological *droit de seigneuer*, that accounts for the mystification that often leads women to misperceive and mislabel their experiences of harassment" (p. 38).

Women feel powerless, not in control, afraid, not flattered, by sexual harassment. Women who have been harassed react emotionally and physically like the victims of rape, incest, and domestic violence. They are not engaging in "courtship behaviors."

Barickman, Paludi, and Rabinowitz, (1992) have found that, for certain groups of women, professors are particularly powerful:

- Graduate students, whose future careers are often determined by their association with a particular faculty member.
- Students in small colleges or small academic departments, where the number of faculty is limited.
- Women of color, especially those with "token" status.

- Women in male-populated fields like engineering.
- Students who are economically disadvantaged and work part-time or full-time while attending classes.

Women in these situations find that the structure of the academy interacts with psychological dynamics to increase women's vulnerability to all forms of sexual harassment.

A professor's greatest power lies in the capacity to enhance or diminish student self-esteem. This power can motivate students to learn course material or convince them to give up. The tone and content of the student-professor interaction is especially important. Is the student encouraged or put down? Do the faculty members use their knowledge to let students know how "stupid" they are or to challenge their thinking? As Zalk, Paludi, and Dederich (1991) point out, this is *real power.*

IT HAPPENS ALL THE TIME

The documentation of harassment in academe is widespread. Dziech and Weiner (1984) have reported that 30% of undergraduate women suffer sexual harassment from at least one of their instructors during their four years of college. When definitions of sexual harassment include sexist remarks and other forms of "gender harassment," the incidence rate in undergraduate populations nears 70% (Paludi, 1990).

Research by Adams, Kottke, and Padgitt (1983) shows that 13% of women students have avoided taking a class or working with certain professors because of the risk of being subjected to sexual advances. A 1983 study conducted at Harvard University indicates that 15% of the graduate students and 12% of the undergraduate students who had been harassed by their professors changed their major or educational program because of the harassment.

In work by Bailey and Richards (1985), of 246 women graduate students in their sample, 13% indicated they had been sexually harassed, 21% had not enrolled in a course to avoid such behavior, and 16% indicated they had been directly assaulted.

Bond (1988) reported that 75% of the 229 women members of the division of community psychology of the American Psychological Association who responded to her survey experienced jokes with sexual themes during their graduate training, 69% were subjected to sexist comments demeaning to women, and 58% experienced sexist remarks about their clothing, body, or sexual activities.

HARASSMENT AND ETHNICITY

Research in progress by Paludi, DeFour, and Roberts (1992) suggests that the incidence of academic sexual harassment of ethnic minority women is even greater than that reported with white women. Tong (1984) reported that:

> In those cases where their harassers are white men, [B]lack women generally observe that their harassers use sex as an excuse not only to control their individual bodies but also to exercise power over all of them as a class of persons: as women (sexism) or [B]lacks (racism) or as disadvantaged [B]lacks (classism). . . . That [B]lack women's reports of sexual harassment by white male superordinates reflect a sense of impunity that resounds of slavery and colonization is, in this connection, highly significant (p. 165).

DeFour (1990) suggests that ethnic minority women are more vulnerable to receiving sexual attention from professors. Ethnic minority women are subject to stereotypes about sex, achievement motivation, and career development. All women students are vulnerable to some degree, but male faculty tend to select those who are most vulnerable and needy.

Stereotypes Don't Help

Sexual harassment victims may experience a second victimization when they attempt to deal with the situation through legal and institutional means. Stereotypes about sexual harassment and women's victimization blame women for the harassment. These stereotypes treat sexual harassment as a form of seduction. Women, these myths would have us believe, secretly want to be sexually harassed and do not tell the truth. As DeFour (1990) comments:

> The images and perceptions of women of color also increase their vulnerability to harassment. These images either portray the women as weak and thus unlikely to fight back if harassed, or they are perceived as very sexual and thus desiring sexual attention. Hispanic women have been described as hot-blooded . . . Asian women have been described as . . . submissive. However, they are also viewed by some as the exotic sexpot who will cater to the whims of any man (pp. 48-49).

IMPLICATIONS FOR EDUCATION, ADVOCACY, AND PRACTICE

Several kinds of intervention may be instituted to challenge attitudes that perpetuate harassment. As Biaggio, Watts and Brownell, (1990) suggest, key individuals within organizations can be targeted—residence hall advisors in dormitories, department chairs—for attendance at workshops at which they can be informed about the institutional policy and procedures dealing with harassment. In addition, new faculty and student orientations are another arena for disseminating information about institutional policies that prohibit sexual and gender harassment. Items relating to gender and sexual harassment can also be placed on teaching evaluations.

Sandler (1988) has also offered suggestions for meeting this goal. She advises colleges to establish policy statements that make it clear that differential treatment of professional women on campus will not be tolerated. Colleges, notes Sandler, should also establish permanent committees to explore and report on professional climate issues and publish an annual report on women's progress on campus.

Barickman, Paludi, and Rabinowitz (1992) recently offered advice for counselors, advocates, and educators in the area of academic sexual harassment. Among the recommendations were:

- Acknowledge women's courage by stating how difficult it is to label, report, and discuss sexual harassment.
- Encourage women to share their feelings and perceptions.

- Provide information to women about the incidence and psychological impact of academic sexual harassment.
- Assure women that they are not responsible for their victimization.
- Work with women in their search for the meaning in their victimization; support them while they mourn their losses.
- Work with women in monitoring their physical, emotional, academic, and interpersonal responses to academic sexual harassment.
- Provide a safe forum for women's expression of anger and resentment.

A student, faculty, or staff peer counseling group can be an important resource for women who are understandably wary of an entire institution as a result of their sexual harassment by a member of that institution.

A CASE IN POINT

Hunter College of the City University of New York has been involved in several intervention programs in the area of academic sexual harassment. Hunter College is a large, coeducational, four-year liberal arts institution. It was founded by Thomas Hunter in 1870, as a Normal School, to educate women whose career goals included teaching children and adolescents.

Today, Hunter has approximately 20,000 students and remains a college where women predominate: 73% of the students are women. This figure is higher than the average of 53% for four-year, public institutions in the middle states region. This percentage of women undergraduates has not varied since 1985. Approximately 53% of Hunter's student population are minorities.

Hunter established a *sexual harassment panel* in 1982. The panel currently has three components: research, education/training, and the investigation of complaints of sexual harassment. In collaboration with the Employees Assistance Program, the sexual harassment panel has facilitated a four-part series on sexual harassment for staff, faculty, and administrators. These "workshops" include case studies, role playing, and presentations on legal issues involved in sexual harassment. The program objectives include learning:

- how informal and formal power or authority in the university setting is perceived by students and faculty.
- the politics involved in such nonverbal gestures as touch, body position, and personal space.
- the social meanings attributed to behaviors that legally constitute sexual harassment.

The Hunter panel also publishes an informational booklet for faculty, "*The Student in the Back Row*," which notes several techniques to help eliminate sexual discrimination in the classroom, ranging from choosing nonsexist course material to not assuming a heterosexist model when referring to human behavior. Information about sexual harassment is also presented in faculty meetings.

In all of these programs, considerable time is devoted to discussing the legal definitions of sexual harassment. Case studies that raise legal and ethical issues are presented to stimulate personal reflection and generate discussion. These case studies illustrate issues that may not be addressed by policy statements and laws. Case studies often disclose certain moral conflicts. The responses to the ethical dilemmas posed by the case studies require for their resolution a mode of reasoning that is contextual rather than abstract. Women center their responses on their responsibility to relationships. The moral imperative that emerges repeatedly in research with women who are discussing sexual harassment is an injunction to care (Fuehrer and Schilling, 1988). For male faculty members, the moral imperative usually appears as an injunction to protect the power differential (Paludi, 1990).

WHAT SHOULD BE DONE?

Paludi and Barickman (1991) provide questions for campuses to address concerning academic sexual harassment:

- Are there policies and effective procedures for dealing with academic sexual harassment? For workplace sexual harassment? Do the policies forbid peer harassment behaviors or are they limited to harassment by faculty, administrators, and other staff?
- Are the policies forbidding sexual harassment well publicized? Are the policies circulated periodically among students, staff, faculty, and administrators? .
- How do individuals in the campus community learn whom they should see to discuss sexual harassment?
- Are there specific individuals to whom individuals can go for help with sexual harassment?
- Are remedies clear and commensurate with the level of violation?
- Does the campus have procedures to inform new faculty, staff, and students about sexual harassment?
- What services are available to individuals who have experienced sexual harassment?

Paludi and Barickman also suggest the following educational interventions, based on their work at Hunter:

- Include information about academic sexual harassment in faculty and student orientation materials.
- Hold a "Sexual Harassment Awareness Week" and schedule programs around the issue of lesbian and gay harassment.
- Require that student leaders attend workshops on sexual harassment.
- Encourage sororities and fraternities to present programs on sexual harassment.
- Include information on sexual harassment in packets for transfer students.
- Report annually on sexual harassment.
- Encourage faculty to incorporate discussions of sexual harassment in their courses.

Education, however successful, is not sufficient in itself to prevent sexual harassment or offer remedies when it occurs (Paludi, 1990). Because sexual harassment occurs in a context of institutional power, individuals who have been victimized are often, understandably, reluctant to use the ordinary channels in the college or university for resolving complaints. This is especially true because sexual harassment is disorienting. A victim may experience the sort of self-doubt, self-blame, and sense of degradation common to victims of rape, incest, and battering. It is important, therefore, that the means of hearing and resolving complaints of sexual harassment should be distinct from regular departmental and administrative hierarchies.

The panel operating at Hunter College since 1982 has successfully met this requirement. The members are appointed by the president of Hunter College, and the panel reports to both the president and the vice president for student affairs/dean of students, but it is independent of the administrative structures of the president's office and the Office of Student Services.

The Hunter panel guarantees that all procedures will be confidential and further guarantees that the individual bringing the original complaint will be the person who decides whether a formal complaint is filed. This encourages individuals to contact panel members to discuss the problems they may have encountered. Unless faculty, staff, and students feel they have these protections, they will seldom report the sexual harassment they have experienced. Research findings fully support this conclusion. Obviously, individual complaints cannot be resolved and the pervasive injury done to the college community by sexual harassment cannot be remedied unless complaints are actually reported.

To promote the effective and equitable resolution of problems involving sexual harassment, it seems necessary to have:

- an explicit policy adopted by the organization in compliance with the provisions of Titles VII and IX, applicable to all units of the system. Such a policy allows the organization to uphold and enforce its policies against sexual harassment within its own community (including such severe penalties as loss of pay, position or tenure) without requiring victimized individuals to undertake the laborious, protracted, and costly process of seeking redress from the courts under Titles VII and IX.

- one body of individuals, delegated by and responsible to the president of the organization, who are specially educated about the nature of sexual harassment and trained to deal with sexual harassment fairly, sensitively, and confidentially.

- a body representative of the entire organization. For example, under Hunter's policies, a person may contact any member of the panel for initial, informal discussion. To make access to the panel as easy and as comfortable as possible, the panel represents the community in terms of sex, sexual orientation, academic program, and all ranks and racial and ethnic backgrounds. Research has indicated, and the panel's experience has confirmed, that many individuals feel more comfortable contacting someone they identify as a peer, so that the more diverse the composition of the panel in terms of status, sex, race, and so forth, the more access the panel provides the community it serves.

- common definitions of sexual harassment and common procedures for resolving conflicts applied equitably throughout an organization, regardless of the status of the complainant or the person complained against. Without a common procedure, inequities can easily occur in the effort to protect individuals' rights under Titles VII and IX.

Definitions of sexual harassment can educate a community and promote discussion and conscientious evaluation of behavior and experience. Employers can then shape their understanding of the problem in ways that direct their actions on individual inquiries and complaints. A definition of sexual harassment sets the climate for the organization's response to these incidents.

As Mead (1978) has argued, a new taboo is needed on

campus that demands that faculty make new norms, not rely on masculine-biased definitions of success, career development, and sexuality. What is also needed is an ethic of care— and the restructuring of academic institutions so that caring can become a central and active value (Stimpson, 1988). This suggests changes in the present mentor-protege relationships that dominate the college and university system.

POSTSCRIPT

Procedures for investigating complaints of sexual harassment must take into account the psychological issues involved in the victimization process, including individuals' feelings of powerlessness, isolation, changes in social network patterns, and wish to gain control over their personal and professional lives. Research has suggested that individuals who experience sexual harassment frequently exhibit the following responses to the harassment: confusion and/or embarrassment, helplessness, anger, worry.

I therefore recommend that the investigative process take into consideration these emotional responses to assist the complainant's path to recovery from the trauma of sexual harassment. For example:

Complainant's Response: Confusion

Investigator's Response: Help with labeling of experiences; provide behavioral definitions of sexual harassment

Complainant's Response: Helplessness

Investigator's Response: Discuss complainant's power in handling case, focus on ways individual is powerful in other aspects of her/his life

Complainant's Response: Anger

Investigator's Response: Discuss confidentiality of investigative process; focus on ways to rebuild career; offer support systems

Complainant's Response: Worry

Investigator's Response: Discuss due process, sanctions against retaliation, confidentiality of investigative process

With respect to education/training programs in sexual harassment, successful training programs have incorporated the following into their design and implementation:

- Support of the highest-ranking official
- Attendance at the training session must be mandatory
- Training sessions are provided for groups of individuals working together in a department or unit
- Resources must be provided for participants in training sessions
- Training sessions must be held annually
- Training sessions must be at least 3 hours in length and involve more than a recitation of individuals' rights and responsibilities and what the law and campus policy require; training also requires dealing with individuals' assumptions and misconceptions about sexual harassment with their anxieties about the training itself
- Training programs should include women and men as participants

These suggestions are based on research and my work as a consultant for colleges and organizations throughout the United States and Canada. They are related to changing the organization. From my work as an expert witness in investigative hearings and court cases in sexual harassment, I would like to call for researchers to pursue the following lines of inquiry so as to provide valuable information for court cases and investigative hearings and alleviate the double bind that many victims now face as they take their cases to court.

First, research should include women from general populations as well as specific populations, e.g., victims who have filed law suits or complaints with the Human Rights Commission, victims who have sought counseling regarding the harassment. Within this framework, mediating and moderating variables must be outlined in order to elucidate the conditions under which sexual harassment leads to the Sexual Harassment Trauma Syndrome. Examples of such variables include: age, perception of the meaning of the trauma, duration, response to the harassment, availability of resources to assist victims, social support, and campus or organizational climate.

In addition, we need studies that document lesbian women's experiences with sexual harassment. Mary Kay Biaggio (1993) has recently noted that lesbian women may experience sexual harassment differently and may be exposed to some unique forms of sexual harassment. For a lesbian woman, sexual harassment may be experienced as an affront to her sexual orientation and may reinforce her sense of being an outsider. Biaggio also contends that while most victims of sexual harassment are often worried about being believed by others and about possible retaliation if they take formal steps to protest the behavior, this may be an especially salient obstacle for lesbians. Those who are not out to other co-workers or to family members may be worried that perpetrators could retaliate by informing others of their sexual orientation. Such disclosure may result in rejection by family, friends, and co-workers. Furthermore, the large majority of lesbian employees in this country are not protected from employment discrimination on the basis of their sexual orientation.

Third, we need additional research on the reasons why men sexually harass women. The man who engages in sexually harassing behavior appears to be one who emphasizes male social and sexual dominance and who demonstrates insensitivity to other individuals' perspectives. In addition, men are less likely than women to define sexual harassment as including jokes, teasing remarks of a sexual nature and unwanted suggestive looks or gestures. Men typically view sexual harassment as a personal, not an organizational issue. Men have also been found to be significantly more likely than women to agree with the following statements, taken from my "attitudes toward victim blame and victim responsibility" survey:

- Women often claim sexual harassment to protect their reputations. Many women claim sexual harassment if they have consented to sexual relations but have changed their minds afterwards.
- Sexually experienced women are not really damaged by sexual harassment. It would do some women good to be sexually harassed.
- Women put themselves in situations in which they are likely to be sexually harassed because they have an unconscious wish to be harassed.
- In most cases when a woman is sexually harassed, she deserved it.

Bernice Lott (this volume) discusses the empirical support she and her colleagues have found for a widely accepted assumption among researchers that sexual harassment is part of a larger and more general dimension of hostility toward women that includes extreme stereotypes of women. Among the mythical images of sexual harassment is that sexual harassment is a form of seduction and that women secretly need/want to be forced into sex.

In some of my new research on why men sexually harass women (Paludi, 1993), I have focused not on men's attitudes toward women but instead on men's attitudes toward other men, competition, and power. Many of the men with whom I have discussed sexual harassment in my research often act out of extreme competitiveness and concern with ego or out of fear of losing their position of power. They don't want to appear weak or less masculine in the eyes of other men so they will engage in scoping of women, pinching women, making implied or overt threats, or spying on women with the goal of impressing other men. When men are being encouraged to be obsessionally competitive and concerned with dominance, it is likely that they will eventually use violent means to achieve dominance. They are also likely to be abusive verbally and intimidating in their body language. Deindividuation is quite common among male office workers, who, during their lunch break, scope women co-workers as they walk by in the cafeteria. These men discontinue self-evaluation and adopt group norms and attitudes. Under these circumstances, group members behave more aggressively than they would as individuals.

The element of aggression that is so deeply embedded in the masculine gender role is present in sexual harassment. For many men, aggression is one of the major ways of proving their masculinity, especially among those who feel some sense of powerlessness in their lives. The male-as-dominant or male-as-aggressor is a theme so central to many men's self-concept that it literally carries over to their interpersonal communications, specially with women co-workers. Sexualizing a professional relationship may be the one area where the average man can still prove his masculinity when there are few other areas in which he can prove himself in control, or be the dominant one in a relationship.

In closing, I believe that rather than changing the level of analysis from the systemic to the individual, as is frequently the case among researchers, it is important to pursue an organizational level of analysis to explain the prevalence of sexual harassment, why men harass women, and to avoid victim blame.

REFERENCES

Adams, J., Kottke, J., and Padgitt, J. (1983). Sexual harassment of university students. *Journal of College Student Personnel, 24*, 484-490.

Bailey, N., & Richards, M. (1985, August). *Tarnishing the ivory tower: Sexual harassment in graduate training programs in psychology.* Paper presented at the Annual Meeting of the American Psychological Association, Los Angeles, CA.

Barickman, R. B., Paludi, M. A., and Rabinowitz, V. C. (1992). Sexual harassment of students: Victims of the college experience. In E. Viano (Ed.) *Victimology: An international perspective.* New York: Springer.

Biagglo, M. K. (1993). Sexual harassment in the workplace: The lesbian experience and the role of homophobia,. In M. A. Paludi (Ed.), *Working 9 to 5: Women, men, sex, and power.* Albany: SUNY Press.

Biaggio, M. K., Watts, D., and Brownell, A. (1990). Addressing sexual harassment: Strategies for prevention and change. In M. A. Paludi (Ed.), *Ivory power: Sexual harassment on campus.* Albany: SUNY Press.

Blackwell, J. E. (1981). *Mainstreaming outsiders: The production of Black professionals.* Bayside: General Hall.

Bond, M. (1988). Division 27 sexual harassment survey: Definition, impact, and environmental context. *The Community Psychologist, 21,* 7-10.

DeFour, D. C. (1990). The interface of racism and sexism on college campuses. In M. A. Paludi (Ed.), *Ivory power: Sexual harassment on campus.* Albany: SUNY Press.

Dziech, B., and Weiner, L. (1984). *The lecherous professor.* Boston: Beacon Press.

Fitzgerald, L. F. (1990). Sexual harassment: The definition and measurement of a construct. In M. A. Paludi (Ed.), *Ivory power: Sexual harassment on campus.* Albany: SUNY Press.

Fuehrer, A., and Schilling, K. M. (1988). Sexual harassment of women graduate students: The impact of institutional factors. *The Community Psychologist, 21,* 13-14.

Mead, M. (1978). A proposal: We need new taboos on sex at work. Reported in B. Dziech & L. Weiner (1984). *The lecherous professor.* Boston: Beacon Press.

Paludi, M. A. (Ed.). (1990). *Ivory power: Sexual harassment on campus.* Albany: SUNY Press.

Paludi, M. A. (Ed.). (1993). *Working 9 to 5: Women, men. sex, and power.* Albany: SUNY Press.

Paludi, M. A., and Barickman, R. B. (1991). *Academic and workplace sexual harassment: A manual of resources.* Albany: SUNY Press.

Paludi, M. A., DeFour, D. C., & Roberts, R. (1992). "Academic sexual harassment of ethnic minority women". Research in progress, Hunter College.

Paludi, M. A., Scott, C. A., Grossman, M., Matula, S., Kindermann, J., & Dovan, J. (1988). *College women's attitudes and attributions about sexual and gender harassment.* Unpublished research, Hunter College.

Project on the Status and Education of Women (1978). *Sexual harassment: A hidden issue.* Washington: Association of American Colleges and Universities.

Rabinowitz, V. C. (1990). Coping with sexual harassment. In M. A. Paludi (Ed.). *Ivory power: Sexual harassment on campus.* Albany: SUNY Press.

Sandler, B. (1988, April). *Sexual harassment: A new issue for institutions, or these are the times that try men's souls.* Paper presented at the Conference on Sexual Harassment on Campus, New York, NY.

Stimpson, C. (1988). Overreaching: Sexual harassment and education. *Initiatives, 52,* 1-5.

Till, F. (1980). *Sexual harassment: A report on the sexual harassment of students.* Washington: National Advisory Council on Women's Education Programs.

Tronto, J. C. (1987). Beyond gender differences to a theory of care. *Signs, 12,* 644-663.

Tong, R. (1984). *Women, sex, and the law.* Totowa: Rowman & Allanheld.

Wilson, K., & Krauss, L. (1983). Sexual harassment in the university. *Journal of College Student Personnel, 24,* 219-224.

Zalk, S. R., Paludi, M. A., & Dederich, J. (1991). Ivory power revisited: Women's consensual relationships with male faculty. In M. A. Paludi & R. B. Barickman, *Academic and workplace sexual harassment: A manual of resources.* Albany: SUNY Press.

18
SEXUAL HARASSMENT: CONSEQUENCES AND REMEDIES

by Bernice Lott

The phenomenon discussed in this chapter and this book did not even have a name until two or three decades ago. The behaviors of men toward women that we only so recently have begun to identify, label, question, and consider serious and problematic realities are strong, well-learned, and accepted in everyday life.

Women have been the targets of men's rudeness, crudeness, insult, and intimidation for a long time in our society, but it was the eye-opening work of people like Lin Farley (1978) and Catherine MacKinnon (1979) that first stirred social scientists, politicians, and lawyers into attention and activity. We have certainly come a long way from then to now, when tenured professors can be fired for sexual harassment—or prodded to retire, censured, or reprimanded. But this long way is not long enough.

Challenges to Stereotypes

The new attention to what we have come to call sexual harassment should not be interpreted to mean that such discussions are welcomed or given high priority in academe. On the contrary, there is enormous resistance to this subject by men and also by women. There is resistance to the recognition of harassment by our colleagues, our students, and by ourselves—and even greater resistance to its reporting.

The subject arouses intense anxiety, discomfort,

An earlier version of this chapter appeared in *Thought and Action,* Winter 1993, *8* (2), 89-104. Portions were read at a symposium on Sexual harassment on campus: Concepts and issues at the NEA Higher Education Conference in San Diego, California on February 29, 1992.

defensiveness, and misunderstanding. Serious discussions of sexual harassment inevitably challenge widely held and, for many, cherished stereotypes and assumptions about heterosexual relationships that support men's privileged position and are, as a result, not easy to change. Men do not want to see themselves as villainous harassers or insensitive louts, and women do not want to see ourselves as victims, or as losing the little power we may have by criticizing or threatening the more powerful. The lesson of Anita Hill demonstrates vividly just how resistant we are to serious discussions about this subject. We have all seen cartoons such as Figure 18.1 and commentaries that focus on how men have been affected by all the "attention" given sexual harassment since the Senate hearings for Judge Clarence Thomas.

Figure 18.1

'The one good thing about the hearings. . .
It made people more sensitive to sexual harassment?"

Reprinted by permission: Tribune Media Services

The resistance to serious discussion about sexual harassment is also illustrated by an essay in the *New York Times Magazine* by an attorney (Mansnerus, 1991) who wrote of her own experiences. Like most women, she did not complain and went on being "nice". She says of herself: "I demonstrated a complete failure of moral resolve," but "I know I did the right thing." She was able to continue her employment and move on in her career. It's difficult to quarrel with her argument—presented not with bravado but with sadness—that "nobody likes a tattletale," and that "to squeal on one's mentor . . . is an idiotic thing to do."

WE ALL IDENTIFY

We resist talking about sexual harassment because the experiences are difficult to talk about, because the subject taps the hidden experiences of so many women and men, because resolutions of the problems seem so out of reach, and because the behaviors we need to examine are so ubiquitous that they are no doubt occurring somewhere close at hand right now.

Anyone who has read a recent novel or autobiography by a serious woman writer cannot fail to be struck by the frequency with which sexual harassment is described as part of women's experience. It is a part of women's experience that we have taken for granted, accepted with little question, and learned to live with, adapt to, circumvent, ignore, or turn to positive advantage. Sexual harassment is part of living in a sexist culture—that is, in a society in which women expect to be the targets of sexual jokes and innuendo as well as the receivers of positive sexual attention. Sexual harassment is deeply enmeshed in the relationships between women and men that we have been taught are natural.

For women, sexual harassment continues to be a source of confusion. How does it differ from flirtation? Did we misinterpret the comments or gestures? Were we at fault by what we wore, or how we looked, or what we said? Should we be flattered by the attention?

Labeling a man's behavior as harassing is as difficult

for many women as for men, for all of the reasons just presented as well as because we do not want to believe that our professors or colleagues or boyfriends want to hurt or demean us. We do not want to see ourselves as victims, and we fear all the negative consequences that may follow from labeling the behavior for what it is—consequences that extend from being perceived as a poor sport or complainer, through loss of a relationship, to serious economic or professional reprisals.

Paralleling the resistance to identifying sexual harassment and to open discussions of remedies are important issues of ambiguity and the clash between one person's rights and those of another. The difficulty of finding answers to our questions may tempt some of us to throw up our hands and retreat to safer and clearer (or cleaner) arenas, while it may serve as a provocative challenge to others. For college administrators, in particular, and gender-sensitive educators in general, there is little choice; the problems are there; they appear to be increasing in urgency; and they must be addressed.

DEFINING THE PROBLEM: A FINE LINE

What Are the Issues?

The first issue, which is related to all the others, and keeps reappearing, is the issue of *definition*. Typically, most women and men would agree that sexual harassment refers to sexual behaviors that are unwanted, unreciprocated, coercive, intimidating, or threatening. Lists of such behaviors usually include objectionable gestures, jokes, as well as more obvious or blatant bribes, threats, and *quid pro quo* offers. Some examples of sexual harassment are clear and would be considered harassment by virtually everyone, but others range over a continuum of increasingly greater ambiguity.

Is speech behavior? Catherine MacKinnon (1993), the noted law professor from Michigan, argues that it is. If we include frequency in our definition of harassment, how do we operationalize it? From whose perspective do we consider whether the behavior in question is unwanted—the perspective of the target of the behavior, the actor, or some neutral and theoretical outside observer, applying the standard of "the average reasonable person" or "the reasonable woman"? Does the definition of sexually harassing behavior take into account the actor's intentions or motives or just the effects?

Definitional problems continue despite the enactment of state laws, the development of institutional guidelines, and decisions in numerous court cases. In 1980, interpretive guidelines were issued by the Equal Employment Opportunity Commission (EEOC). These guidelines reaffirmed that sexual harassment is an instance of sex discrimination and, as such, is an unlawful employment practice under Title VII of the Civil Rights Act of 1964. These guidelines defined sexual harassment as:

> Unwelcome sexual advances, requests for sexual favors, and other verbal or physical conduct of a sexual nature . . . when (1) submission to such conduct is made either explicitly or implicitly a term or condition of an individual's employment (2) . . . is used as the basis for employment conditions, . . . or (3) has the purpose or effect of unreasonably interfering with an individual's work performance or creating an intimidating, hostile, or offensive work environment. (EEOC, 1980)

In the first sexual harassment case to reach the Supreme Court—*Meritor v. Vinson,* (1986)—the Court used these guidelines to rule that workers were protected under the law from discriminatory, sexually harassing workplace environments.

Title IX of the Education Amendments of 1972 also requires discrimination-free environments, specifically prohibits sexual harassment, covers all programs and activities in educational institutions receiving federal funds, and mandates institutional complaint procedures. As pointed out by Hughes and Sandler (1988), "In general, the interpretation of what constitutes sexual harassment under Title IX has followed the concepts developed under . . . Title VII of the Civil Rights Act" (p. 7). On February 2, 1992, a sexual harassment case under Title IX—*Franklin v. Gwinnett County School System* (1992)—was ruled on by the Supreme Court.

Context and Prevalence

How prevalent is sexual harassment in our society? The answer, of course, depends on definition. How often does harassing behavior occur? Are some persons more likely to exhibit harassing behaviors than others? Toward whom is such behavior directed—are some persons more likely targets than others? Where does such behavior take place? Does the situation make a difference—what distinguishes harassment in the workplace from harassment in educational settings or in the offices of doctors, therapists, and lawyers?

To gauge the prevalence of sexual harassment, *Newsweek* asked 704 adults the question: "Has someone you know personally been a victim of sexual harassment at work or school, on the street, in a private club, . . . or in a store or commercial place?" Answering "yes" were 42% of the women and 37% of the men (Kantrowitz, Barrett, Springen, Hager, Wright, Carroll, and Rosenberg, 1991).

Attitudes, Beliefs, and Consequences

How does sexual harassment make people feel? What are the attitudes and beliefs people hold about harassment? What do women think about its frequency, inevitability, or deeper meaning? What do men think?

Psychologists, in particular, are concerned—at least in theory—with the correlates or antecedents of harassing behavior. That is, what variables tend to increase or decrease the probability of harassing behavior? These variables would include: situational and contextual factors; previous experiences and relative status and power of targets and actors; as well as institutional factors such as the existence of well-articulated policies and procedures.

The question of consequences is also particularly important. What are the likely outcomes for targets of sexual harassment who are, of course, primarily women? Experiencing sexual harassment, we have learned:

• reinforces recognition of personal vulnerability.
• teaches women to be ever "on guard," to be alert

for signs of hostility and possible danger.

- increases ambivalence toward heterosexuality, increases the ambiguity of men's sexual behaviors directed toward women, and increases the confusion between sex and power.
- makes it necessary for women to learn ways of avoiding or escaping from sexual harassment, responses that may seriously conflict, compete, or interfere with responses required to achieve important goals such as going to classes, enhancing work status, earning a paycheck, or establishing positive interpersonal relationships.
- increases anxiety and self-doubt.
- encourages the target of harassment to believe that she is not a "good" (i.e, virtuous) woman, or that she is not a competent woman—not skillful enough to avoid harassment (Stanko, 1985).

There are also important likely consequences for those who harass, and here we are speaking primarily of men. Successful sexual harassers, that is, those who get away with it:

- are reinforced for this behavior, increasing the likelihood of its being repeated.
- learn that they are powerful, increasing the likelihood that they will continue to exert this power in sexual and related situations.
- suffer confusion about the distinction between what is a "normal" expression of sexual interest (i.e., what is culturally acceptable) and what is deviant or aberrant (Stanko, 1985).

The above outline can be considered a possible agenda for research in the area of sexual harassment. Some of you may already be engaged in some part of this agenda, in your own work on your campuses or elsewhere. Perhaps others will think of how they, or their students, may contribute to it.

MEASURING TOLERANCE FOR SEXUAL HARASSMENT

My research in this area, in collaboration with Mary Ellen Reilly, has focused mainly on issues of prevalence, attitudes, and correlates. In our work (Lott, Reilly, and Howard, 1982; Reilly, Lott, and Gallogly, 1986), we have used an instrument we developed that we call the "Tolerance for Sexual Harassment Inventory" (TSHI), a scale that consists of 10 statements of belief about sexual advances, teasing, or intimidation in the workplace or campus.

One example of an item is: "Encouraging a professor's or a supervisor's sexual interest is frequently used by women to get better grades or to improve their work situation." Attitudes are inferred from acceptance of such beliefs, and respondents indicate on a 7-point scale how strongly they agree with each statement.

It will probably come as no surprise to learn that in every study in which the TSHI has been utilized, with diverse samples, the average scores of men are found to be significantly higher than the average scores of women, not only in total score, but on every single item of the scale, supporting the general conclusion that men tend to be more accepting and tolerant of sexual harassment than women.

CURRENT RESEARCH AND FINDINGS

Our most recent investigation using the TSHI (Reilly, Lott, Caldwell, and DeLuca, 1992) attempted to find empirical support for a widely accepted assumption among researchers in this area: that sexual harassment is part of a larger and more general dimension of misogyny, or hostility toward women (see for example, Hughes and Sandler, 1988; Pryor, 1987). Such a continuum, if represented linearly, would have behaviors such as put-downs, jokes, leering, and offensive words or gestures on one end, and sexual assault, battering, and the murder of women on the other. Figure 18.2 is a first attempt at a broader model of "sexist responses toward women" that is more complex than a simple straight line.

Figure 18.2

Misogyny Model: Sexist Responses to Women

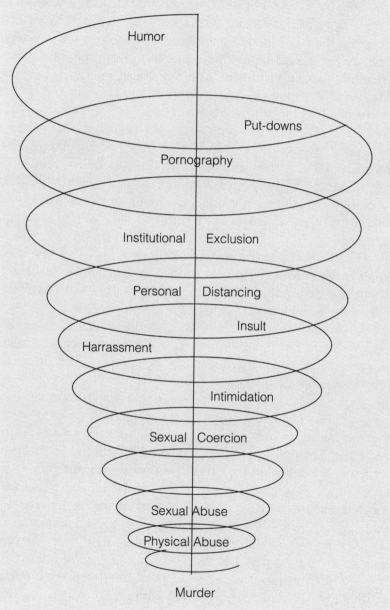

Humor

Put-downs

Pornography

Institutional Exclusion

Personal Distancing

Insult

Harrassment

Intimidation

Sexual Coercion

Sexual Abuse

Physical Abuse

Murder

Whether we are talking about a simple continuum or a more dynamic model, it is typically taken for granted that the various hostile or discriminating behaviors directed against women are related, although these relationships have not yet been fully established empirically. The 1992 study by Reilly et al. was concerned with demonstrating that, in a sample of college men, there are positive relationships among self-reported tolerance for sexual harassment, likelihood to rape, and experience as a sexual victimizer, and that these measures are correlated with the acceptance of rape myths and the belief that heterosexual relationships are adversarial.

For women, the typical targets of sexual harassment and assault, victimization experience was not expected to be related to other variables, but attitude and belief measures were expected to be correlated. The data were collected on my campus in classes attended by heterogeneous groups of students who responded anonymously to paper-and-pencil questions.

Likelihood to rape was measured by a widely used question developed by Malamuth, Haber, and Feshbach (1980); sexual victimizing or victim experiences were assessed by a scale developed by Koss (1981); rape myth acceptance and adversarial sexual beliefs were tapped by scales developed by Burt (1980); and we used our TSHI to measure tolerance for sexual harassment. Figure 18.3 presents the obtained correlations among measures.

For men, as predicted, tolerance for sexual harassment was found to be significantly and substantially related to all other measures. A discriminant function analysis revealed, further, that tolerance for sexual harassment was the single best predictor of likelihood to rape. The two significant predictors of self-reported experience as a sexual victimizer were self-reported likelihood to rape and tolerance for sexual harassment. Among the women, tolerance for sexual harassment was positively correlated with the belief that heterosexual relations are adversarial and with adherence to rape myths.

The findings for men support the proposition that negative behaviors directed toward women are related to one another and to relevant attitudes and beliefs. Links among

Figure 18.3

Correlations Among Measures

	TSHI	ASB	SES	RMA	LR
Women					
TSHI	1.00				
ASB	.46 **	1.00			
SES	.07	.01	1.00		
RMA	.48 **	.46 **	-.09 *	1.00	
LR	.07	.14 **	-.01	.19 **	1.00
Men					
TSHI	1.00				
ASB	.60 **	1.00			
SES	.19	.20 **	1.00		
RMA	.59 **	.59 **	.14 **	1.00	
LR	.32 **	.25 **	.28 **	.31 **	1.00

SOURCE: Reilly, M. E., Lott, B., Caldwell, D., and DeLuca, L. (1992). Tolerance for sexual harassment related to self-reported sexual victimization, *Gender and Society, 6* (1), 122-138.

NOTE: TSHI= Tolerance for Sexual Harassment Inventory; ASB= Adversarial Sexual Beliefs; SES= Sexual Experiences Survey; RMA= Rape Myth Acceptance; LR= Likelihood to Rape; *=p<.05; **=p.<.01.

these negative behaviors, cognitions, and feelings have also been found and reported by others, particularly by Malamuth and his colleagues (Briere and Malamuth, 1983; Check and Malamuth, 1985; Malamuth, 1981, 1986). Pryor (1987), using a likelihood to harass measure, found that men high on this measure were also likely to hold adversarial sexual beliefs, to find it difficult to take the perspective of others, to be more likely to rape and "to behave in [a] sexually exploitive way when their motives can be disguised" (p. 288).

It seems clear, from multiple sources of evidence, that sexually harassing behaviors are not isolated and are not trivial. It should follow, then, that educational efforts directed toward reducing sexual harassment should help reduce the incidence of other hostile behaviors directed toward women by men and to change related attitudes and beliefs held by both genders.

A CASE STUDY: COLLECTIVE EFFORTS

As a case study of one such educational effort, I would like to share with you a summary of the work begun by a group of women faculty and graduate students in the department of psychology at the University of Rhode Island.

Disturbed by the treatment of Professor Anita Hill by the Senate Judiciary Committee and by the evident discounting and discrediting of her testimony, women gathered in hallways and offices to express their frustration—to talk and to share feelings and experiences. Some women were disclosing, behind closed doors, personal incidents of sexual harassment. My colleague Patricia Morokoff and I decided that the best way for us to support one another and to consider strategies and remedies would be for us to get together as a group. We called a first meeting and invited all women faculty, staff, and graduate students. The meeting was attended by a far larger number of women than either of us had expected, and a process was begun that continued for several years.

The first meeting was followed by others on a weekly or biweekly schedule. The decision to hold the "next" meeting was always made by consensus, as a result of having "more to do." In other words, this informal group was fueled and propelled by the recognized necessity for discussion and action.

Important ground rules, set at the first meeting, were maintained. No one may disclose the identity of attendees to persons who were not present at meetings, although we were each free to disclose our own attendance. No one may repeat what was discussed at a meeting outside of that setting, even to persons who attended previous meetings. In other words, the content of group discussions may not be revealed anywhere other than at scheduled meetings. If asked, we said that meetings were "well attended, and that many incidents of sexual harassment were discussed," but we may go no further. At one meeting, the acronym WASH was adopted to identify ourselves publicly as Women Against Sexual Harassment.

If you are surprised by our efforts to protect the identity of WASH members, then you do not understand how much women graduate students fear jeopardizing their careers by antagonizing faculty, or how deeply their self-confidence and self-esteem have been affected by the harassment they have personally experienced or observed. Our coming together to plan joint strategies and to work collectively served to enhance our confidence and increase our feelings of control and effectiveness. We believe that we accomplished a great deal, centering our remedies on efforts to change the social, teaching, mentoring, and supervising environment in our department as well as the behavior of particular individuals.

We directed our social change efforts primarily at the climate or culture in our own department. We planned strategies that would place individuals in the least amount of personal jeopardy. We did not want to increase the vulnerability of students or faculty to retaliation. We did not want martyrs; we wanted success. We believed that acting alone is too difficult and often ineffective, and that only by organizing and working together could we accomplish social change.

WASH INTO ACTION

What did we do? First, our very existence startled, upset, offended, and disturbed some of our colleagues and students. We considered all reactions to be a sign that we were stimulating concern and discussion—even the sneers and such predictable labels as man-haters, man-bashers, lesbian dykes, and whiners.

We publicly invited all interested women faculty, staff, and graduate students to our meetings by posting notices in the department on a few key bulletin boards as well as in the women's restrooms and the department newsletter. We put copies of the university's sexual harassment policy and procedures and related material in all mailboxes and on a table in our department mailroom. We also put copies of the university's Sexual Harassment Incident Report Form in a prominent place.

We developed our own "This is Sexual Harassment!" poster based on actual incidents within our department. This is shown in Figure 18.4. We printed each item of this poster in large black letters on a separate 9 x 11 sheet of paper and posted the entire set on our mailroom bulletin board. The poster sat there undisturbed for approximately one year, in full view of all who entered. (A smaller version of the poster hangs there still.)

Emboldened and empowered, a group of WASH mem-

Figure 18.4
This Is Sexual Harassment!

- Asking questions about a student's, supervisee's, advisee's, or employee's personal sex life.
- Refusing to stop sexual remarks when asked.
- Overusing sexualized content in teaching, such as frequent sexual examples to illustrate more general points in class.
- Making personal sexual comments to students, supervisees, advisees, or employees.
- Unwanted touching of students, supervisees, advisees, or employees.
- Making comments about a student's, supervisee's, advisee's or employee's body or body parts.
- Using patronizing language or making hostile or derogatory comments about women.
- Using primarily women to exemplify negative construfcts, including mental illness.
- Making sexual jokes that contribute to a hostile work/school environment for women.
- Characterizing women who object to sexual harassment as sexually repressed or conservative.

Although men can also be victims of sexual harassment, women are the primary targets.
Prepared and Posted by
Women Against Sexual Harassment (WASH)
Psychology Department, University of Rhode Island

For more information, contact Bernice Lott 401-792-4248   Fall 1991

bers went on to urge the department chair to sponsor sexual harassment workshops for the faculty and graduate students. These workshops were held, led by the university's human relations educator. Other graduate students, supported and encouraged by the group, wrote to and met individually and in small groups with professors in our own and other departments.

Graduate students are vulnerable; their futures lie in the hands of professors who grade them, recommend them for fellowships, and write reference letters for internships, jobs, and postdocs. It is difficult to attempt to educate these powerful persons about sexual harassment.

WASH dealt with issues of academic freedom, and was sensitive to its vital place of in the academic community and how efforts to deal with sexual harassment may be misinterpreted as efforts to curtail this freedom. Its aim was to educate ourselves and others, with the aim of creating and maintaining a positive, enriching workplace for women as well as for men.

POSTSCRIPT

WASH has not met regularly in 1995 partially because of its success in changing the departmental climate for women and partially because the graduate students most actively involved in its work have graduated and moved on. Should circumstances necessitiate it, WASH can be quickly reactivated.

REFERENCES

Briere, J., and Malamuth N. M.. (1983). Self-reported likelihood of sexually aggressive behavior: Attitudinal versus sexual explanations. *Journal of Research in Personality, 17*, 315-323.

Burt, M.R. (1980). Cultural myths and supports for rape. *Journal of Personality and Social Psychology, 38*, 217-230.

Check, J.V.P., and Malamuth N.M.. (1985). An empirical assessment of some feminist hypotheses about rape. *International Journal of Women's Studies, 8* (4), 414-423.

Equal Employment Opportunity Commission Guidelines. (1980, Nov. 10). *Federal Register, 45*, No. 219.

Farley, L. (1978). *Sexual shakedown: The sexual harassment of women on the job.* San Francisco: McGraw-Hill.

Franklin v. Gwinnett County School District. 112 S. Ct. 1028 (1992).

Hughes, J.O., and Sandler B.R., (1988). *Peer harassment: Hassles for women on campus.* Washington, DC: Project on the Status and Education of Women, Association of American Colleges.

Kantrowitz, B., Barrett, T., Springen, K, Hager, M., Wright, L., Carroll, G., and Rosenberg, D. (1991, October 21). Striking a nerve. *Newsweek,* pp. 34-40.

Koss, M. (1981). *Hidden rape on a university campus.* National Institute of Mental Health, Rockville, MD.

Lott, B., Reilly M.E., and Howard D.. (1982). Sexual assault and harassment: A campus community case study. *Signs, 8,* 296-319.

MacKinnon, C.A. (1979). *Sexual harassment of working women.* New Haven: Yale University Press.

MacKinnon, C.A. (1993). *Only words.* Cambridge, MA: Harvard University Press.

Malamuth, N.M. (1981). Rape proclivity among males. *Journal of Social Issues, 37* (4), 138-157.

Malamuth, N.M. (1986). Predictors of naturalistic sexual aggression. *Journal of Personality and Social Psychology, 50,* 953-962.

Malamuth, N.M., Haber S., and Feshbach S.. (1980). Testing hypotheses regarding rape: Exposure to sexual violence, sex differences, and the "normality" of rapists. *Journal of Research on Personality, 14,* 121-137.

Mansnerus, L. (1991, December 1). Don't tell. *New York Times Magazine.*

Meritor Savings Bank FSB v. Vinson. 477 U.S. 57, 106 S. CT. 2399 (1986).

Project on the Status and Education of Women. (1980, August). *Title VII sexual harassment guidelines and educational employment.* Washington, DC: Association of American Colleges.

Pryor, J.B. (1987). Sexual harassment proclivities in men. *Sex Roles, 5/6,* 269-289.

Reilly, M.E., Lott B., and Gallogly S.M.. (1986). Sexual harassment of university students. *Sex Roles,* 15, 333-358.

Reilly, M.E., Lott B., Caldwell D., and DeLuca L.. (1992). Tolerance for sexual harassment related to self-reported sexual victimization. *Gender & Society,* 6, 122-138.

Stanko. E.A. (1985). *Intimate intrusions: Women's experience of male violence.* London: Routledge, & Kegan Paul.

INDEX

245